PENNSYLVANIA QUAKER RECORDS

WARRINGTON, YORK COUNTY;
LITTLE BRITTAIN, LANCASTER COUNTY;
CENTRE, CENTRE COUNTY;
WEST BRANCH, CLEARFIELD COUNTY;
DUNNINGS CREEK, BEDFORD COUNTY (2 PARTS)

PENNSYLVANIA SOCIETY OF FRIENDS

Published by Left of Brain Books

Copyright © 2021 Left of Brain Books

ISBN 978-1-396-32258-7

First Edition

All rights reserved. No part of this publication may be reproduced, distributed, or transmitted in any form or by any means, including photocopying, recording, or other electronic or mechanical methods, without the prior written permission of the publisher, except in the case of brief quotations embodied in critical reviews and certain other noncommercial uses permitted by copyright law. Left of Brain Books is a division of Left of Brain Onboarding Pty Ltd.

Table of Contents

WARRINGTON MM, PA	1
LITTLE BRITTAIN MM OF FRIENDS LANCASTER CO, PA	50
CENTRE MONTHLY MEETING CENTRE COUNTY, PA	203
WEST BRANCH MARRIAGES	239
DUNNINGS CREEK HISTORY	243
DUNNINGS CREEK WOMEN'S MEETING 1803-1887	255

WARRINGTON MM, PA

Warrington - Book 300

Fr of Warrington and Newberry req Sadsbury their MM to request QM to allow MM for discipline
QM of Concord, Chester Co, 2nd of 9th mo, 1747, allowed MM to be established

10-19-1747	-	first mtg, William Underwood, 1st Clerk
2-16-1748	-	Warrington Mtg req Preparative Mtg
2-16-1748	-	Menallen req to have Mtg settled, p 3

Note: Some one has cut out a leaf (pages 116-117) of the B&D Records of Warrington MM, PA

BEALS
Mary   w of Jacob, Sr, d 3-11-1763, age 68y
(Insert: fr Concord MM, PA Marriage Records & M-vl, p 68: Beals, Jacob, s John & Mary (Clayton) of Nottingham, Chester Co, PA, m 20-4mo (June) 1714, OS, at Nottingham MH, Mary Brooks, dt John, dec, of Concord MM, PA, under auspices of Concord MM, PA)

BENNETT
Joseph   d 16- 5-1757
Rebecca Fincher   d 6-11-1757
m 20- 3-1724, at Kennett Mtg, Chester Co, PA
Joseph & Rebekah were rocf Kennett MM, PA, at Sadsbury MM, PA, dtd 4-5-1738)
Ch: William   b 19-12mo   (Feb)   1727/8 OS
     Sarah   b 29- 4mo   (June) 1733   "

Rebecca	b 29-10mo	(Dec)	1734	OS
Mary	b 19- 7mo	(Sept)	1736	"
Phebe	b 30- 1mo	(Mar)	1738	"
Joseph Jr	b 10- 7mo	(Sept)	1739	"
Joshua	b 15- 2mo	(Apr)	1741	"
Elizabeth	b 25-12mo	(Feb)	1742/3	"
Edward	b 7- 5mo	(July)	1744	"
Hannah	b 19-10mo	(Dec)	1745	"
Isaac	b 21- 7mo	(Sept)	1749	"

Joseph   Paper of ack for drinking (very interesting) 1mo-19-1747 p 2-3 (Warrington Book 300)

Joshua
Mary
Ch: Joseph   b 15-8-1781
     James   b 2-5-1783   d 21-8-1784
     Rebecah   b 4-1-1785

William
Liddia
Ch: Enoch   b 23- 1-1754
     Rebeckah   b 6- 4-1756
     William   b 27-11-1757
     Joseph   b 19- 8-1759

BERRY
John
Patience Gregg   Both with 5 ch (1st listed below) rocf Nottingham MM, MD, dtd 29-5-1762
(Note: John Berry, s Samuel, dec, & Margaret, of Little Brittain Twp, Lancaster Co, PA, & Patience Gregg, dt David, dec, & Lydia Gregg, of E Nottingham Twp, Chester Co, PA, were m "in a public Mtg" (place not disclosed) under auspices of Nottingham MM, MD, 20-12-1753. Their 1st ch was

"born too soon" after m; their ack was acc by Nottingham MM, 17-5-1755.)

Ch: (the births of 1st 5 ch are fr Nottingham MM B&D Reg)
    Samuel   b 24- 7-1754
    David   b 14-11-1755
    Margaret   b 16- 8-1757
    John   b   1759
    Lydia   b   7- 2-1761
    Aaron   b 22- 1-1763 (at Warrington)
    Thomas   b 10- 3-1765   "
    Joseph   b 10-11-1766   "
    Patience   b 17- 2-1770 (at Hopewell)
John & Patience & ch (1st 8 named) gct Hopwell MM, VA, 1768 where it was rec 4-7-1768

BLACKBURN

John		b Co Armagh, Ireland d 24-8-1767	
		s John & w & fam, who were rocf Ballyhagen Mtg, Ireland, by New Garden MM, PA, 30-8-1736, dtd 2-4-1736	
Rebecca		d 30- 3-1766	
Ch:	Margaret	b 16-10-1740	m 1763, Solomon Sheppard
	Rachel	b 1- 9-1742	m 1767, Nathan McGrew, s James & Mary
	Thomas	b 19- 8-1744	m 1768, Elizabeth Griffith, dt Thomas & Eve
	Moses	b 16- 9-1746	m 1767, Mary McGrew, dt James & Mary
	Anthony	b 17- 6-1749	m 1770, Mary Griffith, dt Thomas & Eve
	Mary	b 19- 6-1751	
	John	b 21- 6-1753	
	Elizabeth	b 2-10-1755	
	Joseph	b 7-11-1757	
	Rebecah	b 12-12-1760	
	Samuel	b 17- 5-1762	

Abigail	b 9- 5-1764
Eleanor	b 30- 3-1766
	Note: Since all former records prior to 1752 have been carefully written in OS, it seems likely that the first 6 births (above) are also dated in OS. WWH
Joseph	(s of John Blackburn, who emigrated with his w & fam fr Ireland, with cert fr Ballyhagen Mtg, Co Armagh, dtd 2-4-1736 & rec at New Garden MM, PA, 30-8-1736)
Deborah McGrew	b 14- 7-1739, dt James & Mary, of Menallen m 5- 7-1758 at Menallen Mtg, under auspices of Warrington MM
Ch: Mary	b 3- 4-1759
John	b 8- 1-1762
James	b 16-10-1763
Thomas	b 10-11-1765
Anthony	b 12- 6-1767
Joseph Jr	b 11- 2-1769

BONINE
Daniel
1st w Elizabeth
2nd w Sarah
3rd w Mary
Ch: (by 1st w)
    Mary   b 4- 2-1760
    (by 2nd w)
    Sarah   b 13-12-1773
    (by 3rd w)
    Rachel   b 9- 6-1782
    David   b 10- 1-1785
    Rebeccah   b 9- 8-1787
    Isaac   b 22- 3-1790

CADWALLADER
David   d 12- 6-1846

Susanna Penrose	d 11-11-1804, dt William & Ann (Wiley) of Warrington MM		
	m 17- 5-1781		
Ch: William	b 29- 3-1782		
Mary	b 8-10-1783	d	6- 9-1802
James	b 15-10-1785	d	27- 9-1802
Anna	b 10- 9-1787	d	20- 9-1802
Phebe	b 23-10-1789	d	27- 8-1802
Susanna Jr	b 30-10-1791		
Hannah	b 4-12-1793		
Beulah	b 22-10-1795	d	10- 9-1802
Edith	b 14-10-1799	d	29- 8-1802

B&D p 154 (on opposite page of above births, used for deaths, is the following:) Sarah Cadwallader, w of Wm, d 11-11-1839

(Note: Since 6 ch d close together in 8 & 9 mos, 1802, it is inferred it was fr some kind of a plague. WWH)

CARSON
Patrick — accuses Thomas Cox, 1mo-19-1747/8
ack he was wrong

CLARK
Henry & w — prcf East Nottingham 2mo-9-1748
4-18-1748

COOK
Peter — b 4-10mo (Dec) 1700 at Norwich, Cheshire, England
d 28- 4mo (Apr) 1779, age 79y
s Peter & Elinor (Norman)

Sarah Gilpin — b 21- 4mo (June) 1706 at Birmingham, Chester Co, PA
d 7- 6mo (June) 1783, age about 77y
dt Joseph & Hannah (Glover) of Birmingham, Chester Co, PA
m 26- 9mo (Nov) 1730

Ch: Joseph   b 12- 8mo (Oct) 1731 OS, m Elizabeth (Fisher)
                       Wilkinson, wid of Joseph
    Ruth   b 24-12mo (Feb) 1732/3 " d 27- 4mo (June)
                       1733
    Lydia   b 15- 8mo (Oct) 1734   " d 15- 8mo (Oct)
                       1741
    Hannah   b 27- 4mo (June) 1736   " m 10- 5-1753, Wm
                       Nevitt, s Joseph & Mary
    Samuel   b 15-10mo (Dec) 1738   "
    Ann   b 20-10mo (Dec) 1741   "
    George   b 27-10mo (Dec) 1743   " d "when young"
    Jesse   b 15- 9mo (Nov) 1744   " d 18- 8mo (Aug)
                       1818
    Sarah   b 29- 9mo (Nov) 1747   " d 15- 6mo (June)
                                                  1807, m Robert Vale

    Peter Jr   b   "

Jacob
Mary
Ch: Isaac   b 28- 6-1772
    Abraham   b 8- 9-1774   d 20- 4-1778
    Mary   b 12- 5-1777
    Lydia   b 7- 6-1779

Joseph   b 8-12mo-1731   OS, s Peter & Sarah (Gilpin)
1st w Mary   d 15-12-1759
2nd w Elizabeth (Fisher) Wilkinson, wid of Joseph Wilkinson & dt of Thomas
                       & Elizabeth Fisher, of Kennett, Chester Co, PA
                       Elizabeth d at York Co, PA, early in 19th Century &
                       was bur York Frds Grvyd
Ch: (by 1st w)
    John   b 9- 3-1758
    (by 2nd w)
    Sarah   b 7- 7-1767
                       (Historical (quoted fr Bradford MM, PA, as related by
                       A.C. Myers in his bk, p 371) The above named Joseph

6

Wilkinson, s of Frances Wilkinson, of Ballinacree, Ireland, was rocf Ballinacree Mtg by Bradford MM, PA, 16-12mo (Feb) 1737/8 OS, dtd 23-2-1737; he m 31-10-1740 Elizabeth Fisher, dt Thomas & Elizabeth Fisher, of Kennett, PA; they res at East Caln & other places; Joseph Wilkinson d 10-9-1760; the ch of Joseph & Elizabeth (Fisher) Wilkinson were Frances, b 15-12-1741/2; Susanna b 29-12-1743/4; Thomas b 5-12-1745/6; Elizabeth b 30-6-1748; Joseph b 17-4-1750; Mary b 20-3-1752; Ruth b 27-7-1754; Alice b 10-12-1755. The widow, Elizabeth, & ch rem to within the verge of Warrington MM, York Co, PA, soon after Joseph's death; & there she m 2nd the above named Joseph Cook.)

Samuel
Sarah
Ch: Edwin Mode   b 11- 1-1812
     Cornelius Garrettson
                              b   9-12-1813
     Elisha   b 12- 1-1816
     Ruthanna   b 22- 1-1818
     William   b 22- 6-1820
     Hannah Jane   b   8-12-1821
     Joseph   b 22-10-1823

Samuel   d 10- 8-1800
1st w Hannah   d   9- 5-1768
2nd w Ruth   d   5- 4-1789
Ch: (by 1st w)
     Robert   b 30- 6-1765   d   4- 7-1765
     William   b 24- 8-1766   d   20-10-1766
     Hannah Jr   b   3-10-1767
     (by 2nd w)
     Rebekah   b 15- 8-1773
     Israel   b 27- 8-1774   d young

	Sarah	b 7-12-1775	
	Elisha	b 26- 2-1777	
	William (2)	b 27-11-1778	d 27- 5-1854, m Susannah Cutler, 1802 (Nottingham MM)
	Israel (2)	b 16- 2-1780	
	Samuel	b 26- 6-1782	
	Ruth Jr	b 27- 2-1784	d 5- 4-1789

Thomas   practiced drinking strong liquor (fr Newberry) 12 mo-20-1748

COOKSON
Daniel
Sarah

Ch:	Elizabeth	b 30-11-1795	
	Mary	b 6- 4-1797	
	Samuel	b 24-11-1798	d 24-11-1805
	John	b 26-12-1800	
	Sarah	b 11-10-1802	
	Eli	b 18- 8-1806	d 6- 8-1869, m Phebe Vale, dt Wm & Anna
	Ruth	b 12-12-1808	
	Esther	b 22- 3-1812	
	Hannah	b 20- 3-1814	
	Rachel	b 6- 4-1816	
	Daniel Jr	b 16- 9-1818	

Eli		b 18- 8-1806	d 6- 8-1869, s Daniel & Sarah
Phebe Vale		b 7- 1-1801	d 25-12-1887, dt William & Anna
Ch:	Eli Franklin	b 19- 3-1829	
	Hannah Ann F	b 22- 7-1832	d 20- 2-1899 m Joel V Garrettson
	Milton V	b 15- 3-1835	d 15- 6-1898

8

COX
William produced cert ack marrying 1st cousin by a priest
Naomey Cox, his w also   "   "   "   "   "   "   "   "
11-21-1748

DAVIS
Joshua
Jane
Ch: Ruth   b 4- 2-1772
    John   b 9- 4-1773
    Marmaduke b 11- 3-1775
    William   b 30- 7-1777
    Jacob   b 7- 7-1779

DELAP
William & w   pcf Balahagen, Ireland, 5mo-6-1746

DIX
Nathan Jr   req mbrp, 7-17-1748

Peter & w   req mbrp, 7-17-1748

EDMUNDSON
Thomas   b 11- 1-1774, s Thomas & Mary (Penrose) of
                  Warrington Mtg, PA
Elizabeth Morsell dt William & Mary of Pipe Creek, MD
                  m 18- 4mo-1803, Pipe Creek MH, MD
Ch: Mary   b 24- 5-1804
    Rachel   b 7- 1-1806   d 7- 1-1809
    Hannah   b 2-10-1807   m John Griest, s John & Miriam
    Esther   b 11- 5-1810
    William   b 21-11-1812

John
Sarah
Ch: Rachel   b 11-11-1765   d 8- 9-1777
    Joseph   b 11- 4-1769

Easther	b 24- 2-1771	
Thomas	b 8- 3-1773	
Sarah	b 13- 7-1775	
John	b 24-12-1777	
Rachel (2)	b 6- 3-1780	

ELLIOTT
Jacob
Elizabeth
Ch: Jacob Jr   b 11-11-1752
    Elizabeth Jr   b 8- 8-1754
    Hannah   b 24-11-1756
    Israel   b 28- 7-1759

EVERITT
Isaac   d 4- 8-1801
Martha Griest
Ch: Elizabeth   b 8- 6-1761
    Susanna   b 3-10-1763
    Hannah   b 27- 8-1766   d 19- 6-1772
    Mary   b 24-10-1769   d 18- 3-1770
    John   b 3- 2-1771   d 25- 2-1855, age 84y 22d
    Martha   b 27- 8-1773
    Hannah (2)   b 12- 8-1777
    Isaac Jr   b 5-11-1780   m Rebecca March, dt John & Margaret

FISHER
Samuel
Susannah
Ch: William   b 20- 1-1778

FRAZIER
Aaron   d 19- 4-1778
Jane
Ch: (Here much space left open; then the single birth)
    John   b 6- 1-1778

Aaron   prcf Newark MM, 2-2-1748

Alexander   d 6- 3-1758
1st w Sarah Coppock (1715), dt Aaron Coppock
2nd w Phebe Elliott d 9-7-1785 "in her 63rd yr" (bur as widow of John Garretson, whom she m as his 3rd w, & as widow of Alexander Frazier.)

Ch: (by 2nd w)
    Aaron   b 15-11mo   (Jan)   1745/6 OS
    Moses   b 28-11mo   (Jan)   1749/50 "
    Ezekiel   b   3-12mo   (Dec)   1752 NS
    Miriam   b 30- 1mo   (Jan)   1755 "
    Abraham   b 29- 1mo   (Jan)   1757 "

The name is usually written Frazer or Frazier; sometimes Fraser. (It is not known how many ch were b to Alexander Frazier by his 1st w, Sarah Coppock; but their dt Miriam Frazier, m 22-6-1756 Peter Cleaver; & their dt Mary Frazier m William Garretson, 9-9-1742. WWH)

GARRETTSON

Benjamin   b 12-12-1800   d 24-12-1864, age 64y 12d
                            s Samuel & 2nd w Alice (Blackburn)
Orpah   b ca 1803   d 18-10-1841, age 38y 10m 13d
Ch: Ann H   b   1- 7-1824
    Eliza S   b   3- 2-1829
    Sarah S   b   5- 7-1830   d 23- 6-1831
    Asenath   b 24- 3-1832
    Ezra   b 25- 1-1834
    Orpha Jane   b   3- 3-1836   d 6-11-1893, m ----- Evans
    Jesse B   b 17- 4-1838
    Josiah T   b 27- 9-1839
    Alice B   b   8-10-1841   d 11-11-1841

Cornelius   d 29- 4-1829, s John & 2nd w Jane (Carson)
Margaret Atkinson   m ca 1777, dt Cephas & Hannah d 11- 3-1790

2nd w Hannah Johns   b 15- 7-1763   d 9-10-1835   m   ca 1791

Ch: (by 1st w)
    Hannah   b 11-11-1778   m Thomas Leach
    Jane   b 20- 3-1781   m William Leach
    John   b 28- 5-1783
    Samuel   b 7-12-1786   m Ann Pierce; (2) Hannah
                  Cadwallader
    Sarah   b 2- 9-1788   m Samuel Cook (?)
    Cornelius Jr b 9- 3-1790

Ch: (by 2nd w, Hannah)
    Isaac   b 1- 8-1792   m Rachel Ely
    Eli   b 20- 9-1794
    Margaret   b 17- 8-1796
    (Note: tradition lists 3 more ch to his 2nd wife, says Tyson. See below. WWH)
    Joseph   m Elizabeth Kirk
    Jessie
    Rachel

George
Lydia (Wickersham)
Ch: Joseph   b 23- 2-1808
    Jesse   b 23- 3-1810

Israel   b 7- 5-1798, s Jacob & Mary
Ruth   b 25-12-1804   d 6- 2-1880
Ch: Jacob   b 4- 4-1826
    Lydia   b 4- 4-1828
    Israel Jr   b 25- 7-1830
    Ruth Anna   b 28- 1-1833
    Mary   b 6- 1-1836
    Martha   b 8- 7-1839
    Robert N   b 31-10-1842   d 7- 4-1846
    Mariah   b 7- 6-1845

Jacob	d 27- 6-1830	
Mary	d 7-11-1825	
Ch: Lydia	b 11- 6-1796	m Asahel Walker, s Benjamin & 2nd w Ruth
Israel	b 7- 5-1798	
Jacob Jr	b 28- 8-1800	d 3- 5-1801
Daniel	b 6- 2-1802	
James	b 31- 5-1809	d 1- 3-1825

Joel	b 26- 5-1796	d 18- 2-1837, age near 41y
	s Samuel & 2nd w Alice (Blackburn)	
Elizabeth Vale	b 5- 3-1794	d 13- 2-1862, age near 68y
	dt Joshua & Elizabeth	
Ch: Louisa	b 11- 9-1820	d 16- 8-1864
Alice	b 11- 1-1823	d 23- 1-1901 m ----- Wright
Mary	b 20- 9-1825	d 28- 3-1904
Franklin	b 14- 1-1830	d 13-10-1842
Joel V	b 1- 3-1833	d 22- 4-1912 m Hannah Ann F Cookson

Joel V	b 1-3-1833, s Joel & Elizabeth (Vale)	
Hannah Ann F Cookson	b 22-7-1832	d 20- 2-1899, dt Eli & Phebe (Vale)
Ch: Franklin G (Greely)	b 15-11-1857	
Eli P	b 25-10-1859	
Elizabeth Anna	b 28-12-1861	
Willie H	b 26- 3-1864	d 30-10-1864 (Menallen says: Millie H) (b 24-3mo-1864)
Alice Phebe	b 5-11-1865	d 9-12-1866
Annie M	b 5- 9-1867	
Sarah Jane	b 13- 1-1870	
Clara E	b 28- 1-1872 (b at Warrington)	
John J	b 23- 4-1873 (b at Warrington)	
Rebecca F	b 27- 5-1876 (b at Warrington)	

John	b 23-2mo (Apr) 1741 d 12mo-1810	
	s John & Content (Hussey)	
Mary Griest	b 5-8mo (Oct) 1745 OS d 3- 7-1827	
	dt John & Susannah (Pyle) of Warrington MM (form of Bethel, PA) m before 1765	
Ch: Isaac	b 17- 2-1765	
Susanna	b 17- 8-1767 d 2mo-1838	m John Pidgeon
John Jr	b 27- 4-1770 m Rebecca ----	
Content	b 20- 1-1773 d 21-12-1818	m ----- Russell
Hannah	b 17- 6-1775 d 11- 4-1864	
Amos	b 5-11-1777 d 28- 2-1864	
Josiah	b 25- 6-1780 d 5mo-1853	
Joel	b 8-10-1782 d 20- 2-1863	
Mary	b 25- 6-1786 d 30- 4-1881	m Isaac Tudor (s of John Tudor)
Rachel	b 8-12-1788 d 25-12-1824	m ---- Vernon

John	
Tamar Hammond	
Ch: William	b 23- 5-1779 d 12- 8-1840 in OH, m Elizabeth Sleigle
Aaron	b 6- 2-1782
Sarah	b 29-11-1785
John Jr	b 20- 1-1788
Nathan	b 19- 4-1789

John	
Content Hussey	d 30-10 mo (Dec) 1747 OS
	m 5- 9-1736, at Hockessin MH, New Castle Co, Del, under auspices of Kennett MM, PA
2nd w Jane Carson	m ca 1750
Ch: (by 1st w)	
William	b 11-12mo (Feb) 1738/9 OS d 4- 2-1810
John	b 23- 2mo (Apr) 1741 " d 12mo-1810, m Mary Griest
Ann	b 14- 8mo (Oct) 1745 "

(by 2nd w)						
Samuel	b	25- 8mo	(Oct)	1750	"	
Sarah	b	10- 6mo	(June)	1752	NS	
Content	b	26- 4mo	(Apr)	1754		
Cornelius	b	16- 2mo	(Feb)	1756		
Joseph	b	28- 7mo	(July)	1759		

d 22- 6-1814, m Rebeccah McMillan, dt George & Ann (Hinshaw) "

Phebe Garrettson d 9-7-1785 in her 63rd yr (not identified) but she is said to have been the 3rd w of the above John Garrettson, & wid of Alexander Frazier, whom she m as his 2nd w; it is also said that her maiden name was Elliott.

John I   b 6- 7-1784, s Joseph & Rebecca (McMillan)
Ann Pierce   b 24- 6-1784
Ch: Pierce   b 14- 8-1808
       Rebecca   b 10- 7-1810
       Hannah   b 8-10-1811
       Eliza   b 27- 5-1815   d 14- 4-1816
       Eli   b 12- 5-1817
       Maria   b 7- 9-1819
       Sidney   b 22- 5-1823
       Ann   b 12-10-1827

John S   b 5- 5-1782   d 21- 1-1829 in the 47th yr
       s Samuel & 1st w Jane

Rebecca   b   1784   d 16- 3-1861 in her 84th yr
Ch: Barzillai   b 5- 3-1811
       Abel   b 2- 4-1813   d 2- 4-1813 (same day)
       Isaac   b 4- 6-1814   d 4- 6-1837
       Mahlon   b 18- 1-1817
       Samuel   b 18-10-1820

Joseph   b 28- 7-1759   d 22- 6-1814, s John & 2nd w Jane (Carson)

Rebecca McMillan	b 7- 7-1759 d 19-12-1814	
	dt George & Ann (Hinshaw)	
	m 12-10-1779	
Ch: Ann	b 21- 9-1782	
John I	b 6- 7-1784	m Ann Pierce
George	b 23- 1-1787	m 1st Lydia Wickersham;
		m 2nd Ann Griffith
Joseph Jr	b 23- 3-1789	m Mariah McMillan
Rebecca	b 6- 8-1791	d 25-11-1873 m John Wickersham
Jane	b 10-12-1795	
Sarah	b 24- 5-1797	d 25-11-1873 m John Thomas
Elijah	b 11-11-1799	d 26- 7-1873 m 1st Ann Nichol,
	m 2nd Ann Prowell	

Note: The 3 deaths above are all entered in pencil long after listing of births.

Joseph
Mariah McMillan

Ch: Mary Ann	b 11- 9-1817
Ruth	b 13- 1-1820 d 29- 7-1822
Rebecca	b 8- 5-1823
Phebe	b 4-11-1825 d 20- 4-1826

Samuel	b 25-8mo (Oct) 1750 OS d 30-8-1822, age about 72y
	s John & 2nd w Jane (Carson)
1st w Jane	m ca 1773 d 3- 7-1783
2nd w Alice Blackburn	m ca 1784
	b ca 1768 d 15- 7-1823, age about 55y
Ch: (by 1st w)	
Faithfull	b 22- 1-1774 d 18- 6-1808
Jane	b 8-12-1775
James	b 24- 4-1778 d 1- 5-1810
Ann	b 6-12-1780 d 21- 2-1781
John S	b 5- 5-1782 d 21- 1-1829
Ch: (by 2nd w)	

Elizabeth	b 24- 5-1785 d 7- 1-1830, age about 45y 7m 16d m Isaac (?) Cleaver	
Sarah	b 29- 9-1786 d 4-12-1801	
Thomas	b 20- 1-1788 d 25- 1-1862, age 74y, 5d	
Rebeccah	b 12- 9-1789 d 5-10-1823, age 34y 23d, m Joseph McMillan	
Alice Jr	b 14- 5-1791 d 25- 3-1819, age 27y 10m 11d, m Nathan Vale	
Rachel	b 18-12-1792 d 27- 4-1832	
Samuel Jr	b 19-10-1794 d 26- 1-1822, age about 27y	
Joel	b 26- 5-1796 d 18- 2-1837, age 40y 8m 22d, m Elizabeth Vale	
Ann (2)	b 6- 1-1798 d 21- 3-1822, age 24y 2m 15d, m Nathan Vale (2nd w)	
Benjamin	b 12-12-1800 d 24-12-1864, age 64y, m Orpah ----	

Thomas — b 20- 1-1788 d 25- 1-1862, age 74y 5d s Samuel & 2nd w Alice

1st w Susanna — d 4- 5-1816, age 20y 4m 8d

2nd w Jane Warner — widow, having one dt, Mary Warner, by her form husband, William Warner; (sd Mary Warner was b 18-1-1816, d 10-10-1821, age 5y 8m 22d) b 17- 2-1790 d 27- 1-1859, age 68y 11m 10d

Ch: (by 1st w)
  Isaac — b 27- 4-1816 d 7- 5-1816, age 10d
  (by 2nd w)
  Juliann — b 14-10-1818 d 19-10-1823, age 5y 5d
  Sarah — b 21-10-1820
  Warner — b 26- 9-1822 d 7- 3-1823, age 5m 11d
  Susanna — b 12-12-1823 d 23- 2-1853, age 29y 2m 11d
  Eliza Jane — b 23-11-1825 d 11- 4-1848, age 22y 4m 19d
  Rachel — b 18- 9-1827
  Eli B — b 2- 9-1830 d 10- 4-1859, age 28y 7m 8d
  Alfred — b 13- 7-1833 d 14- 8-1847, age 14y 1m 1d

Note: All ch of Thomas Garrettson, excepting Sarah & Rachel, d before his death; & all ch of his 2nd w, Jane, including her ch by 1st husb (Wm Warner) d before her death excepting one (Eli B Garrettson)

William   b   1716   d   15-12-1792, age about 76y
                   s Casparus (d 1726) & Ann, of Christiana Creek, New Castle Co, Del; & gr-s of John Garrettson (van der Hoff) (d 1695/95) fr Gildersland, Holland, to New Castle Co, Del, 1664, & Ann, his w
Mary Frazer   b   1722   d 1782, dt Alexander & Sarah (Coppock) of Kennett Mtg, Chester Co, PA
                   m 9- 9mo   (Nov) 1742 at Kennet Mtg, PA
Ch: Casparus   b 17- 5mo   (July) 1745 OS   d 18-8mo (Oct) 1746
    William   b 11- 3mo   (May) 1748 "
    Ann   b 22- 2mo   (Apr) 1750 "
    Sarah   b 2- 3mo   (Mar) 1753 NS,   m 1773 James Wickersham (s James & Ann)
    Miriam   b 23- 5-1755 NS
    John   b 7- 1-1757
    Aaron   b 16- 1-1759
    Mary   b 6-11-1760
    Naomi   b 25- 8-1762
    Elizabeth   b 16- 8-1764

William   b 11-12 mo (Feb) 1738/9 OS d 4- 2-1810
                   s John & Content (Hussey)
Lydia Beals   m ca 1762   d 21- 9-1803
Ch: Elizabeth   b 25- 8-1763
    John   b 2- 8-1765   d 18- 7-1790
    Jacob   b 29- 8-1767
    Martha   b 21- 7-1769   d 2- 3-1789   m ---- Kirk

William Jr
Mary

18

Ch: Anna		b 18- 7-1775 (Insert: m 10-3-1796 George Walker at Westland MM, PA)
Casparus		b 6- 8-1776
John		b 12-12-1778 (Insert: m 27-11-1800 Henrietta Bright, at Pike Run MH, uc Westland MM, PA)
Mary Jr		b 13- 1-1781
Joseph		b 29-11-1782
Sarah		b 7- 1-1785
Armelle		b 2-10-1788
Patience		b 8- 5-1790

GRIEST

Cyrus
Mary Ann
Ch: Hiram   b 9-12-1826
     George M   b 24- 8-1828
     Jane Cook   b 3- 9-1830
     Ann McMillan   b 20-11-1832
     Cyrus Samuel   b 1- 3-1835
     Jesse Warner   b 20- 6-1837
     Maria Edith   b 7- 3-1840
     Elizabeth Mary b 26-12-1843
     Amos Willing   b 24- 8-1848

John *   b ca   1716   d 4- 5-1780, age about 64y
                     s John & Martha of Bethel, PA, Chester Co, PA
Susannah Pyle   b 3-12-1718   d 15- 5-1776, age about 58y
                     dt Daniel & Mary (Chamberlin) of Bethel
                     m 18- 9-1736 at Chichester Mtg (Concord MM)
Ch: Daniel   b 9-10mo (Dec) 1737   OS
     Martha   b 20-10mo (Mar) 1739/40 OS
     John (1)   b 19- 6mo (Aug) 1742   OS d 6 mo-1743 OS
     John (2)   b 25- 8mo (Oct) 1744   " d 9 mo-1744 "
     Mary   b 5- 8mo (Oct) 1745   " d 3- 7-1827, m John Garrettson

Hannah	b 7-11mo (Jan) 1747/8	"	m Wm Wierman, s Nicholas & Sarah		
John (3)	b 8-10mo (Dec) 1749	"			
Thomas	b 14-20mo (Feb) 1752	NS			
Susannah	b 15- 3mo (Mar) 1754	NS	d 21- 4-1754		
Joseph	b 12- 4mo (Apr) 1755	"			
Ann	b 22-10mo (Oct) 1757	"	d 2-11-1757		
Lydia	b 16-12mo (Dec) 1758	"			

Note: Quote fr Concord MM, PA: "John Griest & w Susannah, gct Sadsbury MM, PA, 7-5-1746"; "John Griest & w Susannah, gct Warrington MM, York Co, PA, 7-6-1749, the cert granted them about 3 yrs ago to Sadsbury MM, PA, was mislaid."

* This name is Griest; but it has frequently been written Grist. WWH

John	s John & Miriam
Hannah Edmundson	b 2-10-1807, dt Thomas Elizabeth (Morsell)
Ch: Miriam	b 12-10-1834
Rebecca	b 14- 1-1836
Lewis	b 6-10-1837
Maria	b 7- 3-1839
Eliza	b 26-12-1840
Emily	b 5- 9-1842
John	b 5- 9-1844
William	b 5- 6-1846
Amanda	b 10-12-1847
Leander	b 14- 8-1849

Note: All above named ch are listed in Menallen B&D, pp 19/48; only the last 4 ch are officially listed in Warrington, b evidently after the fam rem fr Menallen to Warrington. WWH

GRIFFITH
Amos
Mary

Ch:	Susanna	b 24- 7-1810	
	William	b 10- 4-1812	
	Joanna	b 3- 8-1814 26d, res Wash, DC	d 29- 2-1828, age 13y 6m
	Ruth	b 25- 8-1816	
	Amos Jr	b 24- 4-1819 res Wash, DC	d 21- 7-1823, age 4y 2m 27d,
	Mary	b 8- 8-1821 Washington	d 16- 7-1823, age 1y 11m 8d,
	John	b 16- 1-1826	
Benjamin		d 11- 4-1819	
Mary Underwood		d 3- 2-1817	
Ch:	Daniel	b 13- 9-1808	
	David	b 2-11-1810	
	Abraham	b 22- 6-1812	
	Rebecca	b 7- 4-1814	
	Nancy	b 10- 2-1815	
	Mary Jr	b 11- 1-1817	
David			
Rebecca			
Ch:	Abraham	b 24- 2-1808	
	William	b 6-12-1810	
	Daniel	b 9-10-1812	
Jacob		b 27- 2-1757 Esther	d 27- 2-1811, s William &
Lydia		b 27- 3-1757	d 26- 2-1812
Ch:	Isaac	b 5- 2-1779	
	Amos	b 13- 9-1780	d 20-12-1784
	Rebekah	b 23- 8-1782	
	Israel	b 29-12-1784	
	Hannah	b 4- 7-1787	
	Allen	b 19-12-1789	

Amos (2) b after 1791 m 7-12-1820 Edith Price at Gunpowder MM, MD

Note: Amos Griffith, s Jacob & Lydia, of Washington Co, PA, produced a cert of clearness fr Westland MM, PA, dtd 26-10-1820 to Gunpowder MM, MD, to m Edith Price, dt Daniel & Elizabeth (Hussey) of Baltimore Co, MD; they were m 7-12-1820 at Gunpowder MM, MD; Amos & Edith were trans to Redstone MM, PA, 1854 & joined the Orthodox Friends;

Amos was the 2nd of that name, born after 1791 in Washington Co, PA

Jacob & Lydia Griffith & ch, viz: Isaac, Rebekah, Israel, Hannah & Allen were gct Westland MM, Washington Co, PA by Warrington MM, PA, 12-2-1791

Two ch viz: Esther & Amos (2) were born to Jacob & Lydia in Washington Co, PA; see Westland MM PA & Redstone MM PA, H-v4. WWH

Joseph
Rebecca
Ch: Ruth   b 23- 9-1793
    Hannah   b 15- 2-1795
    Maria   b 4- 2-1796
    Levie   b 27-12-1797
    Rebecca Jr b 3-10-1799
    Allen   b 8- 8-1801
    Ethan   b 15- 4-1803
    Edith   b 13- 3-1805
    Mode   b 26- 9-1806
    Phebe   b 5-12-1807
    Gulielma   b 30- 9-1810
    Sarah   b 21-10-1812
    Esther   b 25-10-1814
    Rachel   b 6- 4-1817

William	b 6-11-1764	d 21- 4-1804, s Wm & 2nd w Joanna (Craig) (who after death of her husb, m 2nd John McMillan)
Deborah McMillan	b 6-12-1768, m ca 1791	dt George & Ann (Hinshaw)

(Note: Insert: Deborah m 2nd 13-2-1806 John Vale, s Robert & Sarah, as his 2nd w; she had 4 ch by John Vale, viz: Deborah, John, Jacob & Caroline. They rem to Columbiana Co, OH in 1814)

Ch: George   b 17-12-1792
    Anne   b 28- 9-1794
    William b 1- 2-1796
    Oliver   b 12-10-1797
    Julia   b 28- 8-1799
    Abraham b 9- 3-1804

William   d 21- 9-1778
1st w Esther   b ca 1722   d 18- 4-1762, age 40y
2nd w Joanna Craig d 21- 4-1794, dt Wm & Mary

(Insert: Joanna (Craig) Griffith, wid of William, m 2nd John McMillan, as 2nd w)

Ch: (by 1st w)
    William   b 2-11-1741/2 OS   d 9-10-1746
    Stephen   b 21- 7-1743 "   d 22- 9-1746
    Abraham   b 1-10-1745   "
    Isaac   b 26- 5-1754   d 29-12-1773
    Jacob   b 27- 2-1757   d 27- 2-1811   m Lydia ----
    David   b 2- 6-1759
    (by 2nd w)
    William   b 6-11-1764   d 21- 4-1804, m Deborah McMillan, dt George & Ann
    Esther   b 13- 1-1766   d 7- 6-1818
    John   b 2- 3-1767   d 19- 4-1830
    Joseph   b 5-10-1768
    Ruth   b 22- 1-1770
    Mary   b 16- 3-1771

    Deborah   b 21- 9-1772
    Benjamin   b 22- 3-1774
    Amos   b 27- 4-1776
    Jesse   b 17-12-1778

HAMMEL
James
Mary
Ch: Mary   b 18-11-1756   d 3- 4-1757

HAMMOND
John   (Departed this life - no date)
Deborah
Ch: Sarah   b 11-10mo   (Dec)   1743   OS
     Elizabeth   b 1- 7mo   (Sept) 1745   "
     Nathan   b 1-11mo   (Jan)   1749/50
     John Jr   b 10-10mo   (Oct)   1753   NS   d   (undtd)
     Mary   b 18- 6mo   (June) 1755   "
     Tamar   b 10- 9mo? (Nov)   1759   "

HARRY
Lewis
Maria   b 11-12-1826
Ch: Malinda   b 27- 2-1821
     Naomi   b 23- 3-1822
     Wm Griffith   b 2- 9-1823
     Lewis Hicks   b 20- 9-1825   d 22-12-1826

HINSHAW
Jacob   produced cert, also for wife (no place given) 11-21-1748

HOLLAND
Thomas   d 7- 4-1777, age about 30y
Mary
Ch: Thomas Jr   b 7-10-1777

HOOPES

Job	b 12- 2-1795, s William & Phebe	
Rhoda	b 13- 5-1796	
Ch: Isaac A	b 10- 1-1818	d 11-11-1818, bur Newberry
Lewis	b 18- 8-1819	
Mary A	b 4-10-1821	d 6-11-1886, age 65y 1m 2d,
	m ---- Wright	
Lydia Ann	b 15- 1-1824	d 3- 6-1824, bur Newberry
Joel Garrettson	b 26- 6-1825	
Ann Pearson	b 3- 5-1827	d 25- 1-1835, bur Newberry
Rhoda Ann	b 29- 7-1829	
Phebe Jane	b 18- 9-1831	
Rebecca Wickersham 11-4-1834		
Hannah	b 19- 9-1836	
Elizabeth Selinger b 28-10-1838 (Menallen says Elizabeth Nelinger)		

William	d 17- 9-1843	
Phebe	d 6- 4-1857	
Ch: Job	b 12- 2-1795	
Mary	b 24- 4-1796	
Elizabeth	b 5- 2-1798	
James	b 10-12-1799	
Daniel	b 30-11-1801	
Ruth	b 23- 8-1804	d 3- 6-1828
Jane	b 28- 6-1807	
William	b 10- 4-1809	d 6- 4-1840 (Menallen says d 1846)
Phebe	b 20- 2-1811	
Isaac	b 21- 1-1813	d 1-10-1820
Waln	b 16- 6-1816	
Lydia	b 29- 3-1818	
Sarah	b 7- 2-1824	

HUSSEY

Christopher
Ann Garrettson   m 5- 9-1736 at Hockessin MH, Del, under Kennett MM, PA

Ch:	Elizabeth	b 6- 7mo	(Sept)	1737	OS	
	Stephen	b 10- 7mo	(Sept)	1739	"	
	Naomi	b 29- 2mo	(Apr)	1742	"	
	Ann	b 27- 7mo	(Sept)	1744	"	
	Christopher Jr	b 2- 7mo	(July)	1756	NS	

Jedaiah   s John
Jane Penrose   dt Wm & Ann (Wiley)
                 m 3- 5-1764 at Warrington MH, York Co, PA

Ch: Mary   b 31- 3-1765
     Christopher   b 28- 7-1767
     John   b 28- 4-1769
     Ann   b 31- 5-1771
     Hannah   b 7- 4-1775
     Jedaiah   b 27- 2-1777   d 10- 9-1828 m Ann Vale, dt
                          Wm & Anna
     Nathan   b 12- 8-1778   d 3mo-1808 (Menallen says
                          3mo-1828)
     Jane Jr   b 13- 8-1781
     Lydia   b 21-10-1786

John
Betty
Ch: Margaret   b 7- 1mo   (Mar) 1751
     Nathan   b 16- 7mo (July) 1755 (may be 1753-blurred)
     George   b 9- 3mo   (Mar) 1758 (blurred)
     Betty   b 3-11mo (Nov) 1759 d 26- 3-1847, age 87y
                          4m 23d m Daniel Price (Gunpowder MH)

Reccord (or Richard ?)
Miriam
Ch: Lydia   b 27- 3-1757
     Rebekah   b 4- 5-1758
     Hannah   b 31-10-1759
     Jesse   b 4-12-1761   d in yr 1762
     Amos   b 15- 3-1763

Ruth	b 12- 4-1765		
Jehu	b 12-11-1767	d	in yr 1768
Miriam Jr	b 25-12-1769		
Mary	b 6- 4-1773		
Susanna	b 7- 8- ?	d	young
Edith	b 25- 1-1777	m	14-9-1797 James Marsh, s Jonathan & Rebecca (Morthland)

(Note by Wm Wade Hinshaw-1946: The first named above, is written in Menallen B&D as Richard; but is Reccord in Warrington B&D; also Albert Cook Myers writes it as Record. The correct name may have been Ricard, or Ricardo, forms of Richard; but as Menallen B&D was copied fr Warrington B&D, the copyist must have had reason to write the name Richard.)

HUTTON

Joseph　　　　　b 28- 5-1720, s Joseph, dec, & Mary, of Chester Co, PA
Betty (Elizabeth?) Willis, dt of Henry
　　　　　　　　m 5- 9-1747 at New Garden MH, PA

Ch:	Joshua	b 25- 7mo	(Sept)	1748	OS m 13-5-1772, Rachel Kirk, dt of Timothy
	Rachel	b 21- 8mo	(Oct)	1750	"
	Joseph Jr	b 30-10mo	(Oct)	1755	NS
	Susannah	b 18- 6mo	(June)	1758	d 27- 7-1762
	Betty Jr	b 20- 2mo	(Feb)	1761	
	Simeon	b 17- 2mo	(Feb)	1765	

JENNINGS

Thomas
Susannah

Ch:	Samuel	b 2-10-1764
	Benjamin	b 27- 1-1766
	Sarah	b 10-10-1768

JOHN
Abel
Mary
Ch: Robert   b 26- 3-1763
     Mary Jr   b 27-12-1775

Samuel   d   7- 8-1784, age about 39y

JONES
Edward
1st w Content Garrettson   d   7- 5-1781
2nd w Sarah
Ch: (by 1st w)
     John   b 29-11-1772   d 25- 1-1773
     Jane   b 19- 2-1775   m Thomas McMillan
     Hannah   b 24- 1-1777
     Phebe   b 21- 3-1779
     (by 2nd w)
     Joshua   b 11-11-1788   d 26- 3-1817
     Rachel   b 27- 8-1793   d 13- 1-1844   m ---- Markes

Thomas   b 28- 1-1826
Martha   b 20- 6-1826   d   1- 1-1884
Ch: Hiram Benjamin b   8- 4-1854
     Barzillai Anthony 5- 5-1856
     Edwin Thomas   b 20- 5-1860   d 30-11-1862
     Jane Edna   b 26- 3-1864

KENDALL
Thomas
Sarah
Ch: (by 1st w)
     Mary   b   4-10- ?
     (by 2nd w Margaret)
     William   b 29- 7-1754
     Benjamin   b 31-12-1756

28

    Elizabeth   b 20- 3-1759

KETTLEWELL
John
Margaret
Ch: Sarah   b 6- 3-1784   d 17- 8-1853, age 69y 5m 11d, m Elijah Price

     Thomas   b 17- 2-1792

Note: John & Margaret Kettlewell (often written Kittlewell) were mbrs of Gunpowder MM, Baltimore Co, MD, in 1804 when their dt Sarah m Elijah Price)

KIGHTLEY
James
Elizabeth
Ch: Tamer   b 30-12-1775

     Gulielma   b 8- 1-1780

LEWIS
Samuel
Catharine   Their ch born within the verge of Warrington MM, PA; viz: Elizabeth, b 28-4-1767

McGREW
Finlay   b 13- 1mo (Mar) 1735/6 OS, s James & Mary
Dinah Cox   Finlay & Dinah (Cox) McGrew & ch Jacob & Margaret, gct Westland MM, PA, 15-10-1787 (See Redstone)

Ch: John   b 13-10-1760

     James   b 1-12-1762 m 1795 Rachel Walker (See Redstone MM, PA)

     Mary   b 2-10-1763
     Nathan   b 1- 6-1765
     Finlay   b 27- 3-1767
     Dinah   b 9- 3-1769
     Rebeccah   b 16- 9-1770

Margaret	b 10-8-1777	
Jacob	b ?	(prob b before Margaret)

(Note: Finlay & Dinah lived in Westmoreland Co & belonged to Providence Mtg)

Finlay (A Scotch Irishman, who was assessed in London Grove Twp, Chester Co, PA 1729-1735; mbr Sadsbury Mtg, 1746; settled in Tyrone Twp, now Adams Co, PA & d about 1766)

Elizabeth

Ch: James   b 27-12mo (Feb) 1744/5 OS m Jane ----
    Nathan   b 26- 9mo (Nov) 1746 " m Martha Hendricks
    William   b 24- 1mo (Mar) 1748/9 "
    Finlay Jr   b 23- 2mo (Apr) 1751 " m Mary Hendricks
    Isabel   b 4- 3mo (Mar) 1752 NS d 10- 7-1752
    Peter   b 19- 5mo (May) 1755 " m Patience Hendricks
    Archibald   b 14- 4mo (Apr) 1757 "

James (kinsman & "doubtless a bro of Finlay McGrew" says A.C. Myers)

Mary Both rocf Hopewell MM, VA, dtd 20-2-1750, by Warrington mm, PA, 16-4-1750

Ch: Finlay   b 13- 1mo (Mar) 1735/6 OS m Dinah Cox, rem to Redstone ca 1787
    Deborah   b 14- 7m (Sept) 1739 " m 1758, Joseph Blackburn
    Ann   b 29- 4mo (June) 1741 " m ---- Newlin
    Nathan   b 10- 3mo (May) 1743 " m 1767, Rachel Blackburn
    Simeon   b 5-11mo (Jan) 1745/6 "
    Mary Jr   b 5-11mo (Jan) 1748/9 " m 1767 Moses Blackburn

James Jr	b 25- 6mo (Aug) 1751 " m ca 1774 Elizabeth McFerran, rem to Redstone ca 1794	

(The Marriage Register & Minutes of Fairfax MM, VA show this: McGrew, James, of Menallen Twp, York Co, PA, m 11-12-1760 at Pipe Creek MH, MD, Mary Ridgeway (a widow with ch); Mary (Ridgeway) McGrew, w of James, gct Warrington MM, PA, by Fairfax MM, VA, 28-3-1761. The said James McGrew produced a cert fr Warrington MM, PA, to Fairfax 29-11-1760 "showing his clearness in relation to marriage.")

McMILLAN

Enos	b 9- 9-1799 d 6- 5-1890 Marshalltown, IA
	s Jacob & Ruth (Griffith) of York Co, PA
Sarah Wright	dt John & Alice (Wilson)
Ch: Uriah	b 28- 1-1826
Eliza Ann	b 20- 5-1828 d "sometime"
George	b in Ireland 1732 d 11- 7-1795
	s Thomas & Deborah (Marsh) of York Co, PA
Ann Hinshaw	b 18- 3-1739 in County Armagh, Ireland
	d 29- 1-1815, bur Warrington
	dt Jacob & Rebecca (Mackie) of Warrington MM, PA (form of Ireland)
	m 5-10-1758 at Warrington Mtg, PA
Ch: Rebecah	b 7- 7-1759 d 19-12-1814 m Joseph Garrettson, s John & Jane
George Jr	b 26- 5-1763 d 22- 5-1846 m Rebecca Cutler, dt Benjamin & Susannah (D)
Anne	b 21- 8-1766 d 23- 2-1850 m Willing Griest, s W & Ann (Garretson)
Deborah	b 6-12-1768 m Wm Griffith & John Vale
Mary	b 6- 2-1771 d 8- 8-1827 m Wm Vale, s Robert & Sarah (no issue)

Thomas	b 16-10-1773 d 28- 3-1843 m Jane Taylor, dt Joseph & Jane
Jacob	b 28- 6-1777 d 1- 1-1833 m Ruth Griffith, dt Wm & Joanna (Craig)
Jane	b 29- 9-1780 d 28-11-1782
Joseph	b 10-10-1782 d 26- 3-1826 m Rebecca Garrettson, dt Samuel & Alice (no issue)

Jacob   b 28- 6-1777 d 1 mo-1833, bur Warrington s George & Ann (Hinshaw) of Warrington Mtg, York Co, PA

Ruth Griffith   b 22- 1-1770 d 2- 3-1829, age 59y, bur Warrington dt William & Joanna (Craig) of York Co, PA m 13-12-1798

Ch: Enos   b 9- 9-1799 d 6- 5-1890 m Sarah Wright
     Ann   b 15- 4-1801 d 19- 6-1888 m Joseph Leach (Ann d in OH)
     Cyrus   b 22- 2-1803 d 1872 m Sarah Raney
     Jacob   b 26- 1-1805 d 31- 1-1805
     Edith   b 15- 7-1806 d 20- 7-1812
     Ruth   b 4- 3-1808 d 23- 3-1887 m Jesse Cook, s Henry & Mary (Way)
     George   b 26- 1-1810 d 19- 4 1853 m Sarah Dickinson, of Baltimore, MD
     Rebekah b 21- 4-1813 d 15- 8-1820

John   b 1728 in Ireland d 17-9-1791, bur Warrington s Thomas & Deborah (Marsh) (John being their oldest ch) came to PA with parents, fr Ireland

1st w Jane (Boyd) Green, widow of Joseph Green, dec, of Sadsbury MM, PA & dt John & Jane (Bell) Boyd
b 1728 in Co Antrim, Ireland d 12- 5-1782, bur beside her husband at Warrington Grvyd, York Co, PA
m 4- 5-1756 at Sadsbury MM, PA

	2nd w Joanna (Craig) Griffith, wid of William Griffith, dec, & dt of Wm & Mary Craig d 21- 4-1794 & was bur at Warrington m 15- 7-1784 at Warrington Mtg, (no issue)	
Ch:	(of 1st w)	
	Abigail	b 18- 4-1757 m 1776 Wm Whinery, s Robert & Isabel; 10 ch; rem to Salem, OH
	Sarah	b 3- 3-1760 d 25- 1-1790
	Thomas	b 14- 5-1762 d 12- 4-1831 m 1791 Ruth Moore, dt Joseph & Jane (Marsh); to OH
	John	b 1766 d 16- 3-1838 m 1st Esther Griffith & m 2nd Alice Barnard; to OH
	James	b 4- 9-1768 d 7- 1-1857 m 1798 Mary Griffith, dt Wm & Joanna; 8 ch; to OH

(Historical: (See OH Quaker Records: H vol IV & V) All 4 above families rem to OH; (1) Ch of Wm & Abigail (McMillan) Whinery were: Robert, John, Thomas, Wm, James, George, Zimri, Sarah & Abigail; (3) Ch of Thomas & Ruth (Moore) McMillan were: Joseph, Jacob, Maria & Mahlon; (4) Ch of John & Esther (Griffith) McMillan were: Jane, Ruth, Joanna, Sarah, Amos, John, James, Griffith, Elisha, Jesse & Maria; (5) Ch of James & Mary (Griffith) McMillan were: Uriah, Edith, Asa, Gulielma M, Myra, Ira J, Joanna & Sarah.

Fam (1) rem to near Salem, OH; Fam (3) rem to Short Creek, OH; Families (4) & (5) rem to West Grove, Harrison Co, OH; Esther (Griffith) McMillan was sister to Mary (Griffith) McMillan. All of the above families were well known to my grd-parents. Wm Wade Hinshaw)

John		b 1766 d 16- 3-1838, bur West Grove Mtg, Harrison Co, OH (to which place he rem, via Short Creek MM, OH in 1804, with w & ch, if any at that time.) (Note: W Grove Mtg was a Preparative Mtg belonging to Short Creek MM, Jefferson Co, OH)

1st w Esther Griffith, dt Wm & Joanna (Craig) of Warrington Mtg
                       b   13- 1-1766 in York Co, PA,   d   6- 7-1818, bur
                       W Grove Frds Grvyd, Harrison Co, OH
                       m   1787

2nd w Alice Barnard (doubtless in OH)

Ch   (by 1st w, Esther)
     Jane
     Ruth
     Joanna
     Sarah
     Amos
     John
     James
     Griffith
     Elisha
     Jesse
     Maria
     Mary   b   3- 2-1810
     Jacob   b   9- 6-1812
     Jane   b   17- 8-1814
     Samuel   b   15-11-1816
     Oscar   b   2- 7-1818

                       Warrington p 240 lists: James, Samuel & Oscar; Menallen lists these & also Mary & Jacob; but instead of James (b 17-8-1814) lists the name as Jane. These births "sound" as if given by telephone. Those of Menallen were recorded in the hand of George Hines, of Round Hill, Adams Co, PA, dtd 29-5-1885; telephones were poor at that date; so someone must have written him fr OH. Wm Wade Hinshaw 1946

                       (Note: An error in Menallen Records lists the decease of Esther (Griffith) McMillan as 7-6-1818; and lists the b of her youngest ch Oscar as 2-7-1818. I have corrected the error. WWH)

Thomas		b 14- 5-1762 d 12- 4-1831, bur Warrington
		s John & 1st w Jane (Boyd-Green) (the latter, Jane, being the dt of John & Jane (Bell) Boyd & widow of Joseph Green, dec, of Sadsbury MM, PA)
Ruth Moore		b 30- 1-1763 d 11- 4-1846, bur in Frds burying ground at Short Creek MH, Jefferson Co, OH
		dt Joseph & Jane (Marsh) Moore (See Andrew Moore & his Descendants)
		m 11-10-1791 at W Grove Frds MH, Chester Co, PA
Ch:	Joseph	b 9- 6-1795
	Jacob	b 19-11-1797
	Maria	b 13- 4-1798 (seems wrong; but that is way it is written)
	Mahlon	b 2- 2-1800

William		s Thomas & Deborah (Marsh)
Deborah Holland		m 20- 2-1760 d 4- 9-1797
		dt Henry & Lydia (Fell) of E Nantmeal Twp, York Co, PA res in Warrington Twp, York Co, PA
Ch:	Mary	b 20- 4-1761 m 1st James Miller, 2nd Joseph Baxter, rem to OH 1806
	Thomas	b 22- 4-1763 m Jane Jones, dt Edward & Content (Garrettson)
	Deborah (1)	b 13- 9-1764 d 24-11-1766
	Lydia	b 21- 9-1766 m Wm Jay
	William Jr	b 13-10-1767 rem to Miami, OH, abt 1806
	Samuel	b 26- 2-1770 d 10- 4-1777
	Jonathan	b 2- 3-1772 d 16-11-1797, m Ann Hussey, dt Jediah & Jane (Penrose)
	David	b " m 1797 Hannah Hussey, dt Jediah & Jane; rem to OH
	Henry	b 20-11-1774
	Deborah (2)	b 10- 8-1778
	John	b 18- 7-1785

William
Mary
Ch: David   b 23- 3- ?

MARSH
John
Margaret   (Insert: The afore-sd John Marsh was b 1724 in Ireland; d 10-3-1804; bur Warrington MH, York Co, PA; came to PA with parents 1736; s John & Elizabeth; gr-s Joshua & Elizabeth (Rogers) Marsh; rocf Goshen MM, PA 1752; ack acc for mou to Margaret 1758; Margaret rec on req 12-7-1760)
Ch: Jonathan   b 1- 6-1760   d 21- 3-1850 in OH, m Levinah Naylor (Gunpowder MH, MD)
    Elizabeth   b 27- 7-1762   ct Baltimore 1798
    Margaret   b 28-11-1764   ct   "   1797
    Mary   b 16- 1-1767   ct   "   1801
    Rebeckah   b 16- 3-1769   d 13-11-1770
    Susanna   b 7- 3-1771   m 1793 John Everitt, s Isaac & Martha
    John   b 1- 3-1772   d 1806, m Catharine ----
    William   b 28- 7-1775   ct Baltimore 1797
    Rebekah (2)   b 2- 5-1777   d 14- 4-1858, bur Warrington
    Lydia   b 20-10-1779   m John Walker, s Benjamin, of Warrington
    Hugh   b   disf mou 22-3-1809
    Hannah   b   ack acc for mou 1808
(Note by Wm Wade Hinshaw-1946: Menallen B&D & also Albert Cook Myers, p 418, list the b of John Marsh (above) as 7-3-1771, which would make him a twin with Susannah, altho neither book speaks of their being twins. I believe Warrington correct above.)

MICKLE
John   prcf New Garden   8-31-   rec 2-18-1748

John
Jane
Ch: Sarah   b 29-10mo   (Dec) 1737   OS
    Elijah   b   8- 2mo   (Apr) 1740   "
    Mary   b   4-10mo   (Dec) 1741   "
    Hannah   b 14-10mo   (Dec) 1745   "
    Jane Jr   b 16- 1mo   (Mar) 1747/8 "
    John   b   4-12mo   (Dec) 1753   NS
    Samuel   b 26- 2mo   (Feb) 1756

MILLS
William   d 14-11-1784
Susanna   m   ca 1764
Ch: Mary   b   3- 7-1765
    Rebeccah   b 20-12-1766
    Phebe   b 22- 1-1769
    Susanna   b 11-12-1770
    Robert   b   7-10-1774   d 28- 8-1782

MORTEN
John   9-19-1748, John prcf New Garden, also for w 8-27-1748

MORTHLAND
William
Ruth
Ch: Jane   b 20- 9-1758   d 23- 8-1800   m ----- Squibb
    Robert   b 23- 1-1761   d 15-10-1822, age almost 61y
    Rebekah   b   8-10-1763   d 2 mo-1825   m ----- Davise

NEVITT
Joseph   d 25-11-1761

OLDHAM
William   prcf E Nottingham for w & ch & himself 10-20-1746, cert directed to Sadsbury

37

OZBURN
William   prcf Cold Spring Neck, Sessex Co, to come under care
                                of Friends, 12mo-20-1747/8

PACKER
Moses   d   9-11-1797
Jane   d   3- 9-1788, about 2 in the afternoon
Ch: Lydia   b   11- 9-1777
     James   b   30- 3-1779
     Aaron   b   6-11-1780

PENROSE
Thomas
Abigail   (Insert: (Data fr Albert Cook Myers bk, p 290)
                                Thomas Penrose (above) s of Wm & Ann (Wiley) of
                                Adams Co, PA, m 11-5-1775 at Warrington MH,
                                Abigail Cadwallader, dt of David, late of Loudon Co,
                                VA)
Ch: Amos   b   13- 3-1776
     Hannah   b   29- 4-1779
     Anna   b   22- 6-1781   d 26- 2-1804
     William   b   9- 5-1784
     Thomas   b   3-12-1787
     Josiah   b   28- 3-1790   d 28-11-1860   m Rachel
                                Garretson, dt John & Mary
     Cyrus   b   19- 3-1792

(Insert by Wm Wade Hinshaw, 1946)
William   (prob s of Robert & Mary (Clayton) who came to PA
                                fr Ireland about 1717), was m ca 1738 under care of
                                Exeter MM, Berks Co, PA to
Ann Wiley   About 1762, they rem to Warrington, York Co,
                                bringing a cert fr Exeter MM, dtd 24-6-1762, where
                                both Wm & Ann served as overseers. Late in life they
                                rem to Adams Co, PA, where he d in Autom in 1785;
                                and his widow Ann, d 26-2-1804

Ch: Mary		m 21-10-1762 at Warrington MH, Thomas Edmundson, s Caleb & Mary
Jane		m 3- 5-1764 at Warrington, Jediah Hussey, s of John
Phebe		m 13- 5-1766 at Warrington, Thomas Leach, s Thomas & Sarah (Boyd)
Hannah		m 23- 4-1772 at Warrington, Samuel John, s of Samuel, late of Newberry
Thomas		m 11- 5-1775, at Warrington, Abigail Cadwallader, dt David, late of Loudoun Co, VA
William		
John		
Susanna		m 17- 5-1781 at Warrington, David Cadwallader

POPE
John   1 mo-19-1747/8, req mbrp, granted

TAYLOR
Joseph
Ann

Ch: Betty	b 11-11-1761	
John	b 10-10-1763	
Ann	b 5-11-1765	
Joseph	b 12- 4-1768	
Libni	b 6-10-1770	
Esther	b 7-11-1774	
Mary	b 4- 8-1777	
Rebekah	b 9- 2-1780	

THOMAS
Jehu
Sarah

Ch: Benjamin	b 16- 1-1771	d 19- 8-1777
Martha	b 1- 4-1773	d 11- 8-1777
Rebekah	b 8- 1-1776	d 12- 8-1777
Benjamin (2)	b 14- 8-1778	
Sarah	b 18- 3-1781	

Jehu Jr	b	21- 3-1784		
Susanna	b	27- 5-1786		
Rachel	b	11-10-1788		
Mordecai Williams		18-10-1791		
Isaac	b	11-10-1793		

John
Jane   m ca   1776
Ch: Lydia   b   3-10-1777
    John Jr   b 13- 2-1779
    Edward   b 25- 6-1781
    Hannah   b   8- 4-1783
    Rebekah   b 30- 7-1785
    Elizabeth   b 18-10-1787   d   2-11-1791
    Jonah (Sarah)   b 19-10-1789 (name listed as Sarah in Menallen MM B&D)
    Ann   b 24- 8-1792
    Jane Jr   b   3- 3-1795

B&D p 152 on page of deaths opposite the above list is the following: Rebekah Thomas, wid of John Sr, d 6-8-1791, age near 73y. (It must be interpreted from this that the 1st above named John Thomas was s of John & Rebekah Thomas. Wm Wade Hinshaw-1946)

UNDERWOOD

Alexander   2mo-16-1748, req cert to Fairfax to m Sarah Beales, a Friend belonging to that mtg. Granted.

Benjamin   d   8-12-1803
Susannah   m   ca 1751
Ch: Sarah   b   2- 2-1752
    Nehemiah   b 17-12-1753
    Martha   b   6- 9-1756
    Enoch   b 14-11-1758
    Willing   b 30-11-1761
    Misheal   b   7- 6-1764   dis
    Mary   b 16- 7-1767

Benjamin	b 24-10-1770	d 6- 5-1771	
Aseal	b 14- 4-1773	d 2- 6-1781	

Charles
Hannah
Ch: Mary b 16- 8-1798
    Isaac b 21- 5-1800

Elihu   b 25-12-1745/6, s Wm & Ruth (Beals)
Ann Garretson m 4-10-1770 at Warrington MH, PA
Ch: Mary   b 2-10-1771
    William   b 19- 3-1773   d 1- 4-1773
    Stephen   b 13- 3-1774   d 14-11-1774
    Ruth   b 24-10-1775
    Stephen (2) b 2-11-1777
    Sarah   b   "
    Jacob   b 7- 2-1780
    Susanna   b 28- 1-1782   d 21- 2-1788
    Elihu Jr   b 19- 3-1784
    Elizabeth   b 19- 2-1787
    Benjamin   b 12- 6-1789
    Ann   b 27- 4-1791
    Jesse   b 8- 6-1794

Enoch
Mary   m ca 1793
Ch: James   b 4- 5-1794
    Benjamin   b 15-12-1795
    Mary   b 30- 6-1797   d 9- 8-1798

John   d 4 mo-1776
Mary
Ch: Rebekah   b 6-10-1757
    Alexander b 23-12-1761
    Charles   b 19- 9-1764
    Samuel   b 4-12-1767

William	b ca 1721 d 18- 5-1785, age about 64y	
	s Alexander Underwood of London Grove, PA	
Ruth Beals	b ca 1724 d 14-11-1789, age 65y	
	dt William Beals, dec, of London Grove, PA	
	m 2- 1mo (Mar) 1742/3	
Ch: William Jr	b 26- 3mo (May) 1744 OS	
Elihu	b 25-12mo (Feb) 1745/6 " m 4-10-1770	
	Ann Garretson	
Zephiniah	b 13-12mo (Feb) 1747/8 "	
Lydia	b 29-10mo (Dec) 1749 "	
Jane	b 23- 3mo (Mar) 1752 NS	
Olive	b 27- 3mo (Mar) 1754 " d 22- 3-1777	
Jacob	b 25-10mo (Oct) 1756 " d 28- 9-1784	
Ruth Jr	b 23- 3mo (Mar) 1759	
Hannah	b 4- 7mo (July) 1761	
Obed	b 26-10mo (Oct) 1763	
Jesse	b 6-11mo (Nov) 1766	
Rachel	b 13- 3mo (Mar) 1769	

UPDEGRAF
Harmon
Lydia
Ch: Ann   b 27-12-1760

VALE
John	b 16- 7-1792	d 10- 9-1821, s William & Anna
Lydia Garretson	b 11- 6-1796	d 22- 6-1869, age 73y
	dt Jacob & Mary	
Ch: John	b 6- 2-1817	d 7- 2-1817
Mary	b 9- 2-1818	d 17- 8-1835 m ----- Cook
William	b 21- 4-1819	d 20-10-1846
Jacob Garrettson	b 7- 7-1821	

Joshua
Elizabeth Cleaver   b   1- 4-1757   d 11- 2-1841, dt Peter &
                        Miriam (Frazier)

Ch:	Mary	b 28- 4-1783	d 21- 5-1783		
	Nathan	b 22- 7-1784			
	Mary (2)	b 5-12-1787			
	Peter	b 17- 7-1790			
	Ch no name	b 11-12-1792	d same day		
	Elizabeth Jr	b 5- 3-1794	d 13- 2-1862		
		m Joel Garrettson			
	Joshua Jr	b 27-12-1796			
	Sarah	b 25- 9-1799	d 26- 2-1880	m ----- McMillan	

Nathan
1st w Alice Garrettson, dt Samuel & 2nd w Alice
        b 14- 5-1791   d 25- 3-1919
2nd w Ann Garrettson, dt Samuel & 2nd w Alice
        b 6- 1-1798   d 21- 3-1822

Ch: (by 1st w)
    Elizabeth   b 21- 9-1812
    Rebecca   b   "
    (by 2nd w)
    Eliza Ann   b 10-10-1819

Robert
Sarah Cook   b 29- 9mo   (Nov) 1747   OS   d 15- 6-1807
             Twin with Peter Cook, Jr, dt Peter & Sarah (Gilpin)
             m 1749/50 ?

Ch:	Robert	b 13-12mo	(Feb) 1751/2	OS	
	Ann	b 22- 1mo	(Jan) 1753	NS	
	William	b 22-11mo	(Nov) 1754		
	Joshua	b 18- 2mo	(Feb) 1757		
	John	b 30-12mo	(Dec) 1760		
	Robert	b 7- 7-1786	d 19- 8-1823, age 37y		

             s John & Deborah

Martha
Ch: Eliza   b 15- 1-1809   d 8- 8-1823
    Susanna   b 11- 2-1811
    Isaac   b 1- 2-1813

Deborah	b 16-12-1819	d 13- 3-1820	
John C	b 2- 7-1821	d 15- 8-1823 (Menallen says b 28-7-1821)	

William
Anna   m ca 1778   d 8- 4-1816
Ch: Mary   b 2- 1-1779   d 7- 1-1779
    Sarah   b 17- 5-1780   d 28- 5-1780
    Isaac   b 4- 9-1781   d 10- 9-1781
    Hannah   b 16- 9-1782   d 12- 7-1863   m ----- England
    Joseph   b 30- 7-1784   d 14- 2-1785
    Ann   b 30- 4-1786   d   1819   m Jediah Hussey
    Elisha   b 21- 1-1788   m Martha -----
    Sarah (2)   b 5-12-1789   d 5- 5-1863
    John   b 16- 7-1792   d 10- 9-1821   m Lydia -----
    Mary (2)   b 5-11-1794   d
    Lydia   b 19-11-1797   d   1800
    Phebe   b 7- 1-1801   d 25-12-1887   m Eli Cookson

VORE

Peter
Betty
Ch: Joseph   b 30- 8-1783
    Benjamin   b 5- 5-1785
    Abner   b 27- 4-1787
    Sarah   b 14- 8-1789
    Peter Jr   b 14-10-1791

WALKER

Abel Sr   d 3- 4-1817
Ann   d 4- 3-1824
Ch: Sarah   b 6- 9-1778   d 10- 9-1804
    Rachel   b 24- 3-1781   d 23- 4-1781
    Leah   b 5- 4-1782
    Hannah   b 1- 5-1785
    Joseph   b 20- 8-1787

    Elizabeth*   b 29- 1-1790
    Abel Jr   b 13- 4-1792
    Joel   b 14- 4-1794
    Benjamin   b 13- 1-1797
                            *This name was first written Eliza; then checked & altered.

Asahel   b 6- 9-1786   d 14-10-1877,   age 91y
                               s Benjamin & Ruth
1st w Mary   b   1787   d 18- 4-1827,   age 40y
2nd w Lydia (Garrettson) Vale, dt Jacob & Mary Garrettson & wid of John Vale
                               b 11- 6-1796   d 22- 6-1869,   age 73y
Ch: (by 1st w)
    Isaac   b 13- 7-1808
    Elizabeth   b 1- 9-1810
    Priscilla   b 14-10-1814
    Louisa   b
    Mary Ann   b 16- 3-1816
    Morris E   b 16- 2-1820
    Joshua V   b 3-11-1822
    Sarah   b 4- 1-1827
    (by 2nd w)
    Ruthanna   b 5-11-1831
    Lewis Pierson   b 25- 4-1833
    Garrettson Cook b 5- 6-1835
    Lydia Jane   b 30- 1-1837
    Phebe Angeline   b 3- 5-1838

Asahel
Ann
Ch: Edward   b 21- 1-1772   d 18- 5-1772
      Rebekah   b 23- 3-1774
      Ann Jr   b 7-11-1776
      Isaac   b 22- 7-1779

Benjamin   d 31-12-1821
Ruth   d 5- 8-1817
Ch: Sarah   b 18- 3-1771   m Richard Pilkington,
                s Vincent & Rebecca
    Jerman   b 22- 5 1773   d 31- 8-1782
    John   b 10- 8-1775   m Lydia Marsh, dt John & Margaret
    Phebe   b 18- 8-1777   d 30- 7-1782
    Abner   b 8- 8-1779
    Benjamin Jr b 7- 5-1782
    Hephzibah   b 19-10-1784
    Asahel   b 6- 9-1786   d 14-10-1877 m 1st Mary ----,
                m 2nd Lydia Garrettson
    Isaac   b 8- 2-1792

Joel
Mary
Ch: Lewis Morris   b 11- 2-1822
    Isaac John   b 3-12-1824
    Elias Hicks   b 24-11-1825
    Abel   b 14- 9-1827
    Jeremiah C   b 19-11-1830
    Hannah Anna   b 26- 2-1833
    Rachel M   b 23- 3-1835

WARNER
William
Jane
Ch: Mary   b 18- 1-1816   d 10-10-1821, age 5y 8m 22d
                (Note: Jane Warner, wid of William Warner, m 2nd
                Thomas Garrettson, by whom she had 8 ch. See
                Thomas Garrettson)

WICKERSHAM
Jesse   d 11- 3-1826
Phebe   m   ca 1800
Ch: Thomas   b 27- 4-1801   rem to IA 1851   m Sarah -----

Edward	b 2- 3-1803	
Jesse Jr	b 20- 4-1805	
Sidney	b 22- 3-1807	
Jane	b 19- 3-1809	d 7- 3-1811
John	b 17- 9-1811	d 9- 5-1816
Lydia	b 21- 3-1814	
Joshua	b 22- 5-1816	
Eli	b 23- 5-1818	
Isaac	b 26- 8-1820	
Phebe Jr	b 3- 9-1822	
Thomas	b 27- 4-1801	rem to IA with fam 15-4-1851
	s Jesse & Phebe	
Sarah	b 6- 8-1804, 1851	rem to IA with husb & ch 15-4-1851
Ch: Elias Hicks	b 31- 8-1828	
Eliza Mary	b 3- 9-1830	
Jesse	b 27- 4-1833	
Israel Meredith	b 29- 8-1836	
Adaline	b 23- 2-1839	
Louis Meredith	b 3- 4-1841	
Harriet M	b 18- 7-1844	

WILLIAMS

Jacob
Ruth Cookson
Ch: (the last 4 ch b within the verge of Uwchland MM, PA; & the last 2 ch b within the verge of Warrington MM, PA)

Israel	b 21- 9-1759	
Hannah	b 15- 2-1762	
Sarah	b 13- 9-1764	
Jane	b 12- 5-1767	m Robert Miller (Pipe Creek MM, MD)
Elizabeth	b 16- 9-1769	
Ruth Jr	b 1-12-1772	

WILLIS
William
Betty   d   8- 7-1869 in her 35th yr
Ch: John   b 26- 7-1754
     Susanna   b 19- 8-1756
     Hannah   b   7- 9-1759
     Lydia   b 13- 5-1762
     Joel   b 23- 8-1764

WILLSON
George   prcf Concord, also for wife, 3mo-4-1747

WILSON
Thomas   4-18-1748, prcf Charlemount in Ireland, dtd 4mo-2-1736 recommending except for his marriage, for which he has given satisfaction

WINTER
Daniel   7-17-1748, prcf Balahagen, Ireland, dtd 4mo-5-1737
                     Complained of conduct with sister in law
                     9-19-1748 test against
                     10-17-1748, req delay to clear himself
                     11-21-1748, defense not adequate, test against, dis

WRIGHT
Benjamin   s John & Elizabeth (Emigrants from Castleshane, Co Monaghan, Ireland)
Jane Falkner   dt Jesse of York Co, PA
                     m 20- 5-1766 at York Mtg, PA
Ch: Martha   b 10- 8-1767
     John   b 16- 9-1769
     Alice   b 7-11-1771   d 7 mo-1777
     Jesse   b 30- 3-1774
     Elizabeth   b 12- 7-1776
     Alice (2)   b 16- 2-1779
     Samuel B   b 13- 5-1781

Benjamin	b	21- 7-1783
Thomas	b	20-12-1785
Jane	b	4- 6-1790

YARNALL
Rachel   dt John, m Nehemiah Underwood, s Benjamin of Warrington 10-14-1773 at Warrington Mtg.

LITTLE BRITTAIN MM OF FRIENDS LANCASTER CO, PA

Established 6-10mo-1804

HISTORY

By 1748 a large number of families belonging to East Nottingham Preparative Mtg & West Nottingham Preparative Mtg, as well as to New Garden Preparative Mtg, in lower Chester Co, PA had settled in Little Brittain Twp, Lancaster Co, PA, & were attached to Nottingham Monthly Mtg in Cecil Co, MD when that MM was set off in 1730 from New Garden MM, Chester Co, PA, which had in turn been set off in 1718 from Concord MM, which was also in Chester Co, PA, although located in what later became Delaware Co, PA.

In 1748 the Nottingham MM authorized the Friends living at Little Brittain to establish a meeting for worship amongst themselves & to build a Meeting House, which was done. A Preparative Mtg was also established & called Little Brittain. This meeting grew so rapidly that by 1796, another meeting for worship was established at Eastland, Drumore Twp, Lancaster Co, PA by order of Nottingham MM; the Eastland Meeting House was built and Eastland Preparative Mtg also established.

By 1804 the settlements of Families of Friends in Lancaster Co had grown to such proportions that it was deemed proper to establish a Monthly Mtg amongst them which would set up its own organization & become independent of Nottingham MM; this was approved by Nottingham MM & by the QM, & thus a new Monthly Mtg named Little Brittain Monthly Meeting was established.

On the 6th of the 10th Month, 1804, Little Brittain Monthly Meeting held its first session at Eastland Meeting House, Eastland PM and Little Brittain PM both having been assigned to the control of the new Little Brittain MM. A boundary line was established between Nottingham MM and the new

Little Brittain MM, such boundary lines establishing the verge of the new MM.

To understand the genealogical records of Little Brittain MM, it is needful to bear in mind that ALL GENEALOGICAL RECORDS, such as Marriages, Births, Deaths, Disownments, Certificates of Removal, etc, are kept solely by Monthly Meetings; also that a Monthly Meeting is a business meeting composed of delegates from Preparative Mtgs under control of the MM, who meet once each month to consider such questions as may come up amongst the memberships of said Preparative Mtgs, and to settle them in accordance with the Rules of Discipline as established by the Yearly Meeting. (See full explanation elsewhere.)

The "Verge" of Little Brittain MM embraced within its boundaries all territory embraced by both Little Brittain & Eastland Preparative Mtgs, the members of which had theretofore been attached to Nottingham MM, which had, up to that date, recorded all of their genealogical records. In other words, the entire membership of the two Preparative Mtgs (Little Brittain & Eastland) was transferred in a body from Nottingham MM to the new Little Brittain MM, on the 6th of 10th month 1804. Suddenly the records of these Friends which had been recorded in Nottingham MM came to an end in that Mtg, and in the same act started NEW in the new MM called Little Brittain MM. This means that the "roots" of genealogical records found in the books of Little Brittain MM in its early period will be found in the books of Nottingham MM.

Although Certificates of Removal must generally be issued for the transfer of membership from one MM to another, the rule does not hold when a new MM is set off from an older MM; for in such a case, all families living within the Verge of the new MM are automatically transferred (without certificates) from the older Mtg to the new Mtg. It would be more satisfactory to searchers if certificates had been issued to each person for this transfer, since by such a rule, all members of the new MM would have been clearly identified in the records, and the names of all would have been listed on the opening pages of books.

The Title page of the first book of Minutes of Little Brittain MM reads as follows:

"LITTLE BRITTAIN MONTHLY MEETING BOOK--of the Records & Minutes of Men Friends, from its first establishment into a Monthly

Meeting: first opened the 6th of the 10th mo, 1804 at Eastland Meeting House, and consisting of the Particular & Preparative Meetings of Little Brittain & Eastland, heretofore branches of Nottingham Monthly Meeting; remaining to the Western Quarterly Meeting as one branch thereof."

At this time Little Brittain Preparative Mtg had been in existence since 1748, and as a branch of Nottingham MM had sent representatives to that meeting each month during its entire existence. It had had its Overseers, & other officers and a perfect organization from the beginning, so that when it was established as a Monthly Mtg it was a perfect "working Entity." The opening statement in the Men's Minutes reads as follows:

"At the opening of Little Brittain Monthly Meeting, held at Eastland Mtg House the 6th Day of the 10th Month 1804. The Representatives from the Preparative Meetings are: for Little Brittain, Joshua Brown, Jr & Isaac Webster; for Eastland, Henry Reynolds & Benjamin Mason, who being called were all present." As Preparative Meetings have no regular Clerk, Jeremiah Brown was appointed "Clerk for the Day"; the following members were appointed as a committee to select a regular clerk and submit his name the next meeting, viz: John Webster, Joseph Stubbs, Jeremiah Brown, Samuel Carter, John Kinsey & Reuben Reynolds.

"The following Minute was now produced from our last Quarterly Meeting, and the Friends therein named all attended, except William Mode, (to wit): "Nottingham Monthly Meeting informs they have agreed, that East & West Nottingham Meetings compose Nottingham MM, to be held alternately between them, at East Nottingham in the even months. Little Brittain & Eastland Meetings to compose a new Monthly Meeting to be called Little Brittain MM, to be held alternately on the seventh Day of the week after the first Second Day in each Month, to open at Eastland in the 10th Month next; which report being approbated; James Wilson, John Parker, Enoch Gray, David Wilson, Caleb Swayne & William Mode are appointed to attend the opening meetings and report their care to next Quarterly Meeting." (Later Drumore PM was est & joined to Little Brittain MM.)

"The subject of suitable Friends to fill the Station of Elders for this MM, coming under consideration; the meeting unites in re-appointing the Friends heretofore in that Station, appointed by Nottingham MM who now reside in the compass of this (to wit): Benjamin Mason, John Webster, Isaiah Brown, Sarah Hough, Ruth Webster, Sarah Mason & Elizabeth Harlan."

"The subject respecting the Overseers heretofore appointed (by Nottingham MM) for our Preparative Meetings coming under consideration, and the sentiments of Friends pretty generally expressed in favor of continuing those heretofore in that Station, this Meeting unites in appointing them, with desires they may attend to the weighty trust committed to their care (Viz't): for Little Brittain, Isaac Webster & Isaiah Brown; for Eastland, Samuel Carter & Reuben Reynolds."

"The subject respecting distillation, trading in & unnecessary use of spirituous liquors coming under consideration, the following Friends are appointed to attend to the case agreeable to the directions of our last Yearly Meeting, (Viz't): John Kinsey, John Brown, Joseph Richardson & Joshua Brown, Jr."

"The following Friends are appointed to collect the faithful sufferings of Friends within the compass of this Mtg, for the testimony of a good conscience against Military measures; & to endeavour to strengthen any of our members & young men that may be in danger of giving way therein, (Viz't): Joseph Richardson, Joshua Brown, Jr, Isaiah Brown, Reuben Reynolds & Jesse Pickering."

The first Minutes of the Women's Meeting:

"At the opening of Little Brittain Monthly Meeting, the 6th of 10th mo, 1804; the Representatives were all present, except Ruth Carter (2nd w of Samuel Carter) whom we are informed, was hindered by indisposition in her family."

"Sarah Hough, Dinah Richardson, Miriam Brown, Elizabeth Harlan, Mary Kinsey, Margaret Reynolds, Ann Gray & Hannah Embree are appointed to select suitable persons to ack as Clerk & Assistant Clerk."

"Sarah Hough, Sarah Mason, Elizabeth Harlan & Ruth Webster, who have stood in the station of Elders for Nottingham MM, are reappointed to fill the same station in the Meeting."

At the second Meeting 11 mo-1804, the Women's Mtg appointed the following committees to fill various stations: To attend the next QM: Dinah Richardson, Hannah Webster, Ann Pickering & Ann Gray. To ack as Clerks:

Ruth Webster, clerk & Pamela Harlan, Asst Clerk. To have care of the Poor: Deborah Brown, Hannah Embree & Margaret Reynolds. As Overseers (all of whom had stood as Overseers under Nottingham): Hannah Webster, Deborah Brown, Margaret Reynolds & Ruth Carter are appointed.

At the Second Meeting of the Men's Meeting (11mo-1804) various appointments were made as follows: Joseph Stubbs, James King, Abel Kinsey & John Brown (representatives from the PM); John Kinsey apptd Clerk for the Day, Joseph Stubbs, Thomas Wood, Daniel Kenny & Samuel Richardson are apptd to attend the next QM.

Answer to the 2nd Query: "Love & Unity we believe subsists in a good degree among Friends, although an increase thereof would be profitable, tale-bearing, back-biting & spreading evil reports discouraged to a good degree, & endeavours used to end apparent differences."

At the Second Mtg of both Men & Women, the following minute is shown: "Jonathan Livezey, s of Daniel Livezey, dec, & Margery his wife, and Mary King, dt of Vincent King, dec, & Mary his wife, appeared & declared their intentions of marriage with each other, with consent of parents. Aaron Quinby & Isaiah Brown are appointed to make enquiry respecting his clearness from others in relation to marriage & report to next Meeting; and Lydia Quinby & Dinah Richardson are appointed to make the usual enquiry respecting the young woman & report to the next meeting." (Note: The above combines the minutes of the Men's Mtg & the Women's Mtg; it is quoted here as an example of how marriages are consummated in any Friends' Mtg; the committees appointed visit the parties, and then report to the next meeting whether anything was found to obstruct the marriage; if nothing to obstruct be found, the Mtg then (after a 2nd appearance before it of the parties, who must come "hand-in-hand" before both Men & Women and say that they continue their intentions) "liberates" them to marry, and appoints a committee to attend the marriage and bring the marriage certificate to the Recorder for recording. At the next mtg, this committee reports that the marriage was "orderly accomplished". The actual date of a marriage is not usually given in the minutes, but is found in the Marriage Records, which record the full marriage certificate with signatures of the parties and witnesses.)

In the following compilation of the minutes and records of Little Brittain MM, an endeavor is made to combine marriage certificates & births of children, certificates of removal, etc, of each separate family in a single item, as far as possible. Where definite identifications cannot be made, separate items are entered. Names and items written between parentheses are supplied by the compiler.

9-2mo-1805 (M-vl, p6) "We believe that Friends (our members) are careful to live in the bounds of their circumstances, and not launch into trade or business beyond their ability to manage." At the Mtg on 9-5mo-1807 "the Committee" reported that their MH stands on a lot of 5 acres with a clear patent regularly conveyed to its four Trustees at first and in 1796 to other trustees, viz: Jeremiah Brown, John Webster, James King & Samuel Richardson; John Webster having removed to OH, it is deemed sufficient that the other 3 trustees should hold the trusteeship alone. At the Mtg held 8-8mo-1807 a list of sufferings of properties taken from Friends for exempt fines in lieu of personal military service amounting to $106.03 was rptd & directed to be sent to the QM.

11-1mo-1812 An Indulged Mtg for worship granted to Friends of this Mtg living remote from Little Brittain MH, to be held fortnightly. Mtgs to be held in a school house on David Perry's land; to open on 16th of 2mo-1812. Mtgs were held regularly on First Days; and on 10-8mo-1816 they were allowed to hold Week-Day mtgs on 4th Days. On 12-10mo-1816 this Indulged Mtg was established to be called Drumore Mtg for Worship; to hold mtgs on First & Fourth Days; names of Committee mbrs: Jeremiah Brown, James Hambleton, Aaron Quinby, Thomas Furniss, Manuel Reynolds, Jesse Fell, Mercy Brown, Ruth Webster, Sarah Brown, Mary Thomas, Rebeckah Richardson & Mary Reynolds. A new MH was built at Drumore & a mtg held in it 8-2mo-1817. Nottingham QM was established 9-11mo-1816 to be constituted of: Nottingham MM, Little Brittain MM & Deer Creek MM, the new QM to be a branch of Baltimore YM.

On 6-9mo-1817 it was reported that a large new MH was to be built at London Grove, to fill the space occupied by the 2 old Mtg Houses; the new MH to be 95 ft long & 43 ft in width, to accommodate the QM; the costs were estimated at $5,500.00 of which London Grove MM had subscribed $3,000; the balance to be subscribed by other MMs.

On 9-5mo-1818 Little Brittain MM granted a Preparative Meeting to Drumore MM.

On 19-4mo-1823 it is rptd that: "Whereas Little Brittain MH is to be torn down & rebuilt, the MM will be held at Eastland MH until the other house is finished & comes in course to be held there." On 16-8-1823, it was rptd that "our next MM is to be held at Little Brittain in the new mtg house, which is expected to be finished by that time." Also: this new Mtg House is large enough to accommodate the QM.

Men's Min. vl, p 337: 18-10mo-1823, The New Little Brittain MH is reported completed & ready for use; it is of brick, 50 ft long by 40 ft wide with galleries in front upstairs; cost: $2,053.48. Delivered over to Little Brittain PM as a Mtg for Worship by Joshua Brown, Contractor. Recorded in Little Brittain MM minutes by Gardner Furniss, Clerk.

On 15-8mo-1829 the Little Brittain MM decided that thereafter, members who had been dis and who had made application for re-instatement to the MM within whose compass they might reside, should be rec into mbrp as though they never had a right amongst Friends.

Orthodox Friends ask to held mtgs in Eastland MH; but on consideration, Little Brittain MM decided 18-4-1829 to deny them this privilege, saying that these Friends had been regularly dis, & if they wanted a MH, they should provide for it themselves, since they had willfully separated from this Mtg.

Persons dis for joining the Separatists:

Balance, Joseph Sr, Joseph Jr & Simeon	dis	for	jas	14-3-1839
Kinsey, John	"	"	"	"
Smedley, Joseph	"	"	"	"

56

AILES
Sarah   rec on req 5-5-1821

ALLEN
James
Esther
Ch: Jesse   b   8-10-1803, rpd mcd by Eastland PM 16-12-1826, dis 17-2-1827
    Isaac   b   2- 3-1805
    Ezra   b   19-12-1807, gct Goshen MM, PA 15-7-1826
    John   b   12-12-1809   d 29- 9-1811
John   gct Fallowfield MM, PA, 14-6-1834
Mary   (late Quinby) rptd by Women's Mtg to have been "guilty of fornication which appears by her having a child too soon after marriage"; also "she has been since her misconduct m to a man not a mbr of our Society"; after visiting her, the Women deemed it best to dis her, altho she seemed tender and willing to abide by their judgment. The matter is left to the men, who 12-10-1811.

AMBLER
William   b   9- 8-1789   d 13-11-1861, age 72y, bur Drumore
                        s Edward & Ann of Gwynedd MM, PA
Elizabeth Penrose   b   25-12-1791   d 9- 7-1853, bur Drumore
                        dt Israel Penrose
Ch: Adaline   b   26- 7-1818
    Joseph Penrose   b   18- 1-1820
    Owen   b   8- 3-1822   d 23- 7-1840, age 18y 4m 18d
    Thomas E   b   11-12-1823
    Daira   b   7- 6-1828
    Ann M   b   25- 3-1831
    Edward   b   "
                        Wm, w Elizabeth & 4 minor ch (first 4 listed) rocf Gwynedd MM, PA 15-5-1829, dtd 2-4-1829
                        Date, excepting deaths, taken fr Gwynedd MM, PA

ATKINSON
Ann					(late Hambleton) rptd mcd 17-4-1824 by Little Brittain PM, her ack acc 14-8-1824
Ezekiel				& Ann, his w & 2 minor ch, viz: Ann & Joseph, rocf Byberry MM, PA 12-6-1819, dtd 30-3-1819

BAILEY
William E
Sarah
Ch: Samuel			b
    Ann				b
    Rebecca			b
    Elizabeth		b 14-11-1834
    William			b 23-11-1836
    Tacy			b 26- 1-1839
					Wm E, Sarah, & 3 minor ch (first 3 named) rocf London Grove MM, PA 17-5-1834

BALLANCE
Catherine			dt Joseph & Anna (Pownall) Ballance of this mtg, gct Solesbury MM, Bucks Co, PA, 11-1-1812; left with Joseph Ballance to forward

Elizabeth			a req fr Buckingham MM, PA that this mtg enquire into the present state of mind of Elizabeth Ballance, whom that MM had dis some time ago, & who had asked for reinstatement; our committee visited her & are of the opinion that she should be rst, & so informed Buckingham MM 7-12-1811 (She is not identified); she was rocf Buckingham MM, PA 9-5-1812, dtd 6-1-1812, after having been rst by that MM

Joseph
Anna Pownall		d 9- 7-1830, age 74y
Ch: John
    Rachel

Mary		
Simeon		
Catharine		
Susannah		
Joseph		Joseph, Anna, & 7 minor ch rocf Wrightstown MM, PA 7-5-1800 by Falls MM, Bucks Co, PA
		Joseph, Anna & 4 minor ch (last 4 named) rocf Falls MM, PA by Little Brittain MM, PA 7-7-1810, dtd 7-5-1810, also their adult ch, viz: Rachel & Mary were rocf same mtg same date, all of which are acc by Little Brittain
		(Note: Anna Ballance, w of Joseph, is rec to this mtg as an approved minister.)
		(Note: John Ballance, s Joseph & Anna, was dis for mou 9-7-1806 by Falls MM, PA
Joseph Sr		& Joseph Jr & Simeon Ballance, dis for joining the Separatists (Orth) 14-3-1829
Susan		disunited herself with us, having j Orth Frds 13-6-1829
Joseph Jr		of little Brittain, s Joseph & Anna (Pownall), dec gct Wilmington MM, Del, 16-10-1824 to m
Mary Lacy Betts		b 23- 9-1801, dt Samuel C & Grace (Biles)
		d 14-11-1826 in 26th yr
		m ca 10mo-1824, Wilmington MM, Del
		(Note: her full name was Mary Lacy Betts, evidently named for her gr-m Mary (Lacy) Betts, w of Zachariah B)
Ch: Joseph L		b 14-11-1825
		Mary L (Betts) Ballance, w of Joseph Jr, rocf Wilmington MM, Del, 15-1-1825, dtd 12-12-1824

BARNARD

William	s Richard & Sarah of Sadsbury MM, PA
	prcf Sadsbury MM, PA 15-5-1824 to m

Ruth Stubbs   dt Vincent & Priscilla, the former dec, of Little
                           Brittain Twp, PA
                           rptd m 19-6-1824
                           Ruth (Stubbs) Barnard, w of Wm, gct Sadsbury MM,
                           PA 17-7-1824 "to join husband"

BETTS
Samuel C   s Zachariah & Mary (Lacy)
Grace Biles   dt Wm Biles of Bucks Co, PA
                           m 18-10-1798, Makefield MH, Bucks Co, PA, auspices Falls MM, PA
Ch: Zachariah   b 27-11-1799   d 18-10-1800
     Mary Lacy   b 23- 9-1801
     Hannah Kirkbride   b 23- 5-1804
     Richard Kinsey   b 15- 9-1807
     Alice   b 31-12-1809
     William   b 22- 1-1813
                           Samuel C & Grace & 2 minor ch Mary L & Hannah
                           K rocf Falls MM, PA 8-6-1805, dtd 3-4-1805
                           Samuel C & Grace (Biles) & minor ch Mary L, Hannah
                           K, Richard K, Alice & William gct Wilmington MM,
                           Del, 9-3-1816; to be forwarded

BLACKBURN
Mary   (late Brown) rptd mou 10-10-1812, her ack acc 7-11-1812
                           d 19- 1-1863, age 76y
Rachel   (form Cutler) b 23-4-1794, dt Benjamin & Susannah
                           (Dunn)
                           d   9- 2-1866, bur Little Brittain Grvyd
                           Res Fulton Twp, Lancaster Co, PA
                           Rptd mou to Joseph Blackburn by Little Brittain PM
                           14-5-1825; her ack acc 18-6-1825
Ch: Layman C   b   5-11-1825
     Emily Anna   b   4-11-1827
     Jesse   b 15-10-1829

Mary	b 9- 1-1832	
Joseph R	b 14- 2-1834	

BLAKE
Ann Eliza (beth-?)   (late Job) rptd 15-10-1836 as mou; her ack acc 14-1-1837 ret mbr

BOLTON
Evan   s Isaac & Elizabeth, gct Fallowfield MM, PA 14-3-1835 to m

Mary Ann Floyd   a mbr of that Mtg (a widow with one son)
Mary Ann (Floyd) Bolton, w of Evan & her s by a form m, viz: Henry B Floyd, rocf Fallowfield MM, PA 18-6-1836, dtd 8-8-1835.

Ch: Sarah   b 27- 2-1836
      Rachel Ann   b 24-11-1837 d 11- 8-1838

Isaac   d 7- 3-1853, "in his 82nd yr" bur Drumore MH
Elizabeth   d 9- 5-1854, "in her 75th yr"   "   "   "

Isaac, Elizabeth, & 6 minor ch (listed below) rocf Byberry MM, PA 11-7-1818, dtd 28-4-1818

Ch: Evan   b (See Byberry MM)
      Sarah   b   "
      Abi   b   "
      Margaret   b   "
      Jason   b   "
      Elizabeth T   b   "   d 15-12-1856, age 39y, bur Drumore
      Isaac Jr   b 18- 9-1822 d 1-10-1842, age 20y

BRADLEY
Mary   (w of George) rocf Bradford MM, PA 4-12-1819, dtd 8-9-1819; also a separate cert fr same mtg same date for Lydia Bradley; & the Women's Mtg lists a cert rec fr same mtg same date for Albina Bradley

Mary   rocf New Garden MM, PA 16-6-1827, dtd 5-4-1827
Rachel   rocf Bradford MM, PA 16-11-1822, dtd 3-7-1822

BROOMALL
John   prcf Fallowfield MM, PA 17-4-1830 showing him clear to m
Letitia Parry   b 20- 9-1806, dt David & 1st w Elizabeth E, dec rptd m 19-6-1830 & the mc ret to Recorder Letitia (Parry) Broomall, w of John, gct Fallowfield MM, PA 16-11-1830 "to join husband"

BROSIUS
Abner   & Charles (minors) rocf Fallowfield MM, PA 9-1-1819, dtd 12-10-1818 (Placed with a mbr of this Mtg)
                           Abner gct London Grove MM, PA 19-8-1826
                           Charles gct Fallowfield MM, PA 19-8-1826

Abner
Letitia   Both rocf London Grove MM, PA 13-6-1829, dtd 8-4-1829
Ch: Amanda   b 22-12-1829
    Margaretta W   b 6- 4-1837 d 11- 7-1848, age 11y 3m 5d, bur Drumore
    William H   b 30-11-1839
    Edmund S   b 14- 9-1844
                           Ellen Smith Brosius d 29-11-1837, age 26y 7m 24d, bur Drumore
                           Joseph Addison Brosius d 30-10-1837, age 4y 6m 13d, bur Drumore
Joseph   prcf Fallowfield MM, PA 16-1-1830 to m
Rachel Parry   dt David & 1st w Elizabeth E, dec
                           rptd m 13-2-1830, but the mc not being ret to the Recorder, the comm is continued to that care; the mc ret to the Recorder the next mo
                           Rachel (Parry) Brosius, w of Joseph, gct Fallowfield MM, PA 17-4-1830
                           Rachel (Parry) Brosius rocf Fallowfield MM, PA with s Joseph P Brosius 18-11-1837, dtd 9-9-1837

62

William	rocf Fallowfield MM, PA 12-6-1819, dtd 8-3-1819, gct Fallowfield MM, PA, 4-3-1820

BROWN

Abner	s Samuel & Elizabeth, gct Nottingham MM, MD 14-6-1828
Ann	(late Sidwell) rptd by Eastland PM 19-4-1828 as mou; her ack acc 19-7-1828
Ann	gct Nottingham MM, MD 16-8-1834
Benjamin	of Little Brittain Twp, Lancaster Co, PA
	b 20- 4-1763 d 4- 7-1826 in 64th yr
	s Jacob & Elizabeth (called "Betty") (Way), dec, of Nottingham MM, MD
Rebeckah Sidwell	b 7- 3-1766 d 10-10-1824, age 58y 7m, bur Little Brittain Graveyard
	dt Isaac & Ann (Brown), form dec, of same place
	m 6-10mo (Oct) 1796 at Little Brittain MH, PA
Ch: Azariah	b 16- 8-1798, gct Center MM, OH 16-5-1835
Son unnamed	b 24- 2-1800 d 26- 2-1800
Anne	b 26- 3-1801 gct Center MM, OH 18-4-1835
Benjamin Jr	b 1-10-1802 rptd mcd 18-6-1825 to Eliza Webster
Elizabeth	b 27- 6-1804 gct Center MM, OH, 18-4-1835
Rebeccah	b 30- 4-1806
Rachel	b 1- 4-1808 gct Center MM, OH 18-4-1835
Mary	b 11- 7-1811 d 15-10-1811
Benjamin Jr	s Benjamin & Rebeckah (Sidwell), dec
Eliza Webster	dt Joshua & Mary (Richardson), dec
	rptd mcd before a Justice of the Peace by Little Brittain PM, 18-6-1825
	Both mbrs of Little Brittain MM
	On 17-9-1825 the comm visiting them both rptd that "it appears by his wife having a ch too soon after their marriage that they have been guilty of fornication"
	Dis jointly 17-12-1825

David	rocf London Grove MM, PA 6-7-1805, dtd 5-6-1805
David	s John & Mary of Little Brittain MM
Martha Furniss	b 31- 1-1784, dt Thomas & Mary, form of Concord MM, PA, now of Little Brittain MM, PA m 11- 6-1808
David	s John & Mary, dec, of Little Brittain MM d 1853, bur Eastland
Sarah Reynolds	dt Henry, dec, & Mary, of Little Brittain MM, PA m 11- 4-1812 d 9 mo-1836

Ch: (listed as ch of David & Sarah Brown; but the 1st dt (Sarah) is thought to have been dt of David & Martha, tho not proved by these records.)

Mary Brown   b 15- 9-1813   d 6 mo-1852 "age 38y & 9m, bur Eastland m ----- Kirk

Sarah Brown   b 25- 8-1808   d 1846 "in 38th yr, bur Eastland m ------ Kirk

(Note: The above is the exact manner in which these 2 births are written; but the birth of Sarah Brown was evidently written some time after the birth of Mary was written, and is in a different hand & different ink. Also, it is not proved that the David Brown (above) is identical with the David Brown, first above written, tho he appears to have been the same man; nor is it proved that either of the David Browns, is the David Brown to whom the two ch viz: Mary & Sarah, are accredited, tho they seem identical. WWH)

Elwood	rec on req 18-3-1826, gct Sadsbury MM, PA 19-2-1831, to m (s of Joseph)
Hannah Webster	Elwood gct Nottingham MM 13-8-1831 Elwood & w Hannah & dt Emina W rocf Nottingham MM, MD 17-5-1834 (undated)
Ch: Emma W	b 8- 4-1832
Albert	b 3- 7-1834
Howard	b 9- 7-1836

George	b 27- 3-1838
Wilmer	b 8- 4-1840
Webster	b 3-12-1841
Francis F	b 25- 3-1843
Channing	b 28- 1-1854

Hannah   rocf Nottingham MM, MD 19-3-1836, dtd 15-6-1835

Jacob Jr   rocf Nottingham MM, MD 16-11-1822, dtd 18-10-1822

Jeremiah   b 15- 2mo (Apr) 1750 (OS)   d 7- 7-1831 "in 86th yr"
        s Joshua & Hannah (Gatchell), dec, of Little Brittain Twp, Lancaster Co, PA
        Jeremiah was an Elder in Eastland PM & mbr Little Brittain MM

1st w Hannah England, dt Samuel & Sarah (Slater) of East Nottingham Twp, Cecil Co, MD
        b 3- 3mo (May) 1748 OS   d 25- 9-1801
        m 15-11-1770, East Nottingham MH (Issue 7 ch)

2nd w Ann (Shipley) Jones, widow of John Jones
        b ca 1758   d 10-12-1803 "in her 46th yr) bur Little Brittain Grvyd
        An Elder in Nottingham Mtg
        m 9-12-1802 (No issue by this m)

3rd w Mercy Shreeve   Jeremiah was gct Upper Springfield MM, NJ 6-10-1804 to m Mercy Shreeve; but he changed his mind & did not m her then; the matter was fixed up satisfactorily; on 10-9-1808 he was again gct Upper Springfield MM, NJ to m Mercy Shreeve; this time the m was orderly accomplished.
        Mercy (Shreeve) Brown was rocf Upper Springfield MM, NJ 8-4-1809, dtd 4-1-1809; it rec her as a Minister; she d 25-10-1823 "in her 60th yr"; a Memorial was sent for her. (Her death is listed in Little Brittain MM as of 24-10-1823.)

4th w Sarah Lukens   Jeremiah was gct Baltimore MM, MD, 17-9-1825 to m Sarah Lukens; Sarah (Lukens) Brown, w of Jeremiah, rocf Baltimore MM, MD 17-12-1825, dtd 9-12-1825 (No issue)

Ch: (by 1st w)
    Sarah   b 15- 3-1772   m Timothy Haines
    Joanna   b 11- 3-1774   d 4- 7-1775
    Levi   b 24- 2-1776   d 11- 9-1846   m Harriett -----
    Hannah   b 15-10-1778   m Isaac Stubbs
    Deborah   b 25- 5-1782   d 21- 5-1845   m John Kirk
    Jeremiah Jr b 14- 4-1785   m Ann Kirk
    Slater   b 27- 3-1787   d 5- 6-1855   m Mary -----

Jeremiah   appt Clerk for opening mtg 6-10-1804; John Kinsey appt Clerk for the day 10-11-1804; at next mtg appt regular Clerk

CLERKS:

MEN:	WOMEN:
1806 John Kinsey	Ruth Webster
1807 Jeremiah Brown	" "
1808 " "	" "
1809 Daniel Kenney	Eleanor Kenney
1810 Samuel Richardson	" " (rem)
1811 " "	Sarah Haines (sub)
1812 " "	Mary Smedley
1813 Abel Kinsey	Joanna Furniss
1814 " "	" "
1815 " "	" "
1816 " "	" "
1817 " "	" "
1818 " "	" "
1819 " "	" "
1820 Timothy Haines	Agness King
1821 " "	" "
1822 John Kirk	" "

1823	John Kirk	Agness King
1824	" "	" "
1825	" "	" "
1826	Jesse Wood	" "
1827	" "	" "
1828	" "	" "
1829	Abel Kinsey	" "
1830	" "	" "
1831	" "	Mary Coale
1832	" "	Sarah Pennock
1833	David Parry	" "
1834	" "	" "
1835	William E Bailey	" "
1836	" "	" "
1837	" "	" "

Jeremiah Jr   of Little Brittain MM, s Jeremiah & Hannah (England) b 14- 4-1785
gct Nottingham MM, MD to m

Ann Kirk   b 20- 5-1788   d   8- 9-1816, bur Little Brittain Grvyd
dt Roger & Rachel (Hughes) of Little Brittain Twp, Lancaster Co, PA
m 14- 5-1807
Ann (Kirk) Brown, w of Jeremiah Jr, rocf Nottingham MM, MD, 12-9-1807, dtd 8-8-1807 "to join husband"

Ch: Hannah   b 14- 7-1808
      Rachel K   b 5- 4-1810
      Kirk   b 5- 1-1812
      Levi K   b 27- 6-1814
      Lewis H   b 6- 9-1816   d 31-10-1851, m Elizabeth H Bradway (Philadelphia) she d 18-4-1880; both bur Philadelphia

Jeremiah Jr   voluntarily ack himself mou at the Mtg held 7-11-1818 & req that he be dis; he also ack striking a man

    & also using profane language; the comm tried to persuade him to ack his errors, which he did, but insisted upon being dis; his req was granted; dis 6-3-1819

John   of Little Brittain Twp, Lancaster Co, PA
     b   ca 1794   d   8-10-1842, age 48y
Sarah   rptd mcd 8-4-1815
     Sarah Brown, w of John, rocf Nottingham MM, MD 8-2-1817 his ack acc 8-7-1815

Ch: Joshua R   b   4- 5-1816   d   3- 2-1849, bur Baltimore
    David   b   10- 3-1818
    Isaiah   b   30- 1-1820   d   27- 8-1837
    Milton   b   30-12-1821
    Stephen   b   8- 3-1824   d   24- 7-1840
    Amos   b   19- 8-1826   d   8-10-1842
    John Jr   b   3-11-1828   d   19- 4-1850, bur Baltimore
    Elisha   b   17- 1-1831   d   24- 9-1854, bur Little Brittain
    Benjamin   b   4- 5-1834   d   16- 6-1858, bur   "   "
    Edwin   b   30- 1-1836   d   2- 9-1837
    Alben   b   26- 5-1838   d   12- 1-1857, bur   "   "

John
Mary   d 24-11-1810, age 55y, bur Eastland, late res West Nottingham, Cecil Co, MD
Ch: Catharine   d 19- 1-1807, age 23y
    Sarah   d 23- 4-1839, bur Little Brittain

Joshua   s John, dec, rptd 14-2-1829 as mou, dis 18-4-1829

Joshua   of Fulton Twp, Lancaster Co, PA & Little Brittain MM
     b   1- 2-1862   d   24- 2-1831 in 70th yr, bur Little Brittain
     s Elisha & Rachel (Littler); grson Joshua & Hannah (Gatchell) Brown

Deborah		d 2- 8-1848 in 84th yr, bur Little Brittain
Ch: Mary		b 27- 9-1785
Rachel		b 18-11-1787 m Thomas King
Samuel		b 30- 4-1790 d 15- 4-1877 in 87th yr, bur Little Brittain m Esther -----
Esther		b 23- 9-1792 d 5- 5-1812 in 20th yr, bur Little Brittain
Josiah		b 6-10-1795 d 12- 9-1868 in 73rd yr, bur Little Brittain

Joshua — a minor, gct New Garden MM, PA 6-4-1816; to be forwarded; rocf New Garden MM, PA 18-1-1823, dtd 6-6-1822

Kirk — rptd 15-6-1833 by Little Brittain PM to have "for some time past been in the practice of taking strong drink to excess & using profane language & has also been guilty of fornication which appears by his having a child too soon after marriage, which he acknowledges." On 17-8-1833 it was rptd that "he denies that he has taken strong drink to excess but ack that he has taken too much; dis 15-2-1834

Levi — b 24- 2-1776 d 11- 9-1846, age 70y
Res Fulton Twp, Lancaster Co, PA
s Jeremiah & 1st w Hannah (England) of Little Brittain Twp, Lancaster Co, PA

Harriet — b   1779 d 14- 3-1835, age 56y, bur Little Brittain
Harriet, w of Levi, & their 3 young ch Hannah, Mary Ann Mercy rec on req of Levi, 9-3-1811

Ch: Hannah B		b 23- 2-1806 d
Mary Ann		b 14- 7-1808 d 4- 6-1840, age 31y, bur Little Brittain
Mercy		b 10- 1-1811 d 5- 2-1837, age 26y, bur Little Brittain

       Deborah   b   4- 3-1814
       Levi Jr   b 19-10-1816   d 13- 5-1838, age 21y, bur Little Brittain

Levi K   b 27- 6-1814, s Jeremiah Jr & Ann (Kirk) Voluntarily offered an ack for mcd 15-8-1835 which was acc & he ret a mbr

Hannah C (?)
Ch: William Henry   b 29- 2-1836
      Mercy Ann   b 16-12-1837   d   8- 9-1842, age 4y 8m, bur Little Brittain
      Joseph M   b   4-10-1840   d 20-10-1840, age 2 wks, bur Little Brittain
      Jacob K   b   5- 9-1842
      Charles E   b 23-12-1843
      Theodore F   b 29- 8-1845
      Levi K   b 29-12-1846   d 28- 4-1864, age 17y 3m 29d, bur Little Brittain
      Mary L   b 29- 4-1856
      Anna S   b   9-10-1857

Margaret   (late Reynolds) rptd by Eastland PM 12-6-1819 as mou by the assistance of a Justice of the Peace; dis for same 4-12-1819

Martha   dt Thomas & Mary (Jessop) d 21- 4-1810, bur Eastland

Mary   (now Blackburn) rptd mou 10-10-1812, her ack acc 7-11-1812

Mercy   (late Hambleton) rptd by Women's Mtg 6-6-1818 mou "to man not in mbrp with Friends" (dt James & Elizabeth Lupton (Paxon) Hambleton, b 14-4-1783) disf same 7-11-1818

Nathan		s Jacob (the carpenter) & Elizabeth (Cook)
		d 14-3-1864 in his 74th yr, bur Little Brittain
		rocf Nottingham MM, MD 7-12-1816, dtd 6-12-1816
Rachel		w of Nathan, who was dis some time past by Baltimore MM for Eastern Dist, is rein by Little Brittain MM with consent of that MM, 18-6-1825
		d 3- 4-1878, bur Little Brittain
Ch:	Mary	b 26- 8-1825
	Alice Ann	b 5- 7-1828
	Lewis	b 12- 2-1831
	Margaret	b 14-12-1832
	Mercy	b 8- 2-1835
Rachel		rptd by Little Brittain PM 17-4-1830 to have been mcd to Jabes Hutton, both mbrs of this Mtg; both disf same 14-8-1830
Rachel		rec on req 16-5-1820 on rec of Women's Mtg; gct Nottingham MM, MD 14-1-1832
Samuel		
Elizabeth		rocf Nottingham MM, MD 8-6-1805, dtd 8-3-1805
		their eldest 5 ch rec on req of Elizabeth 6-7-1811
Ch:	Deborah	b 12- 1-1801 mcd 1823 to John W Passmore, ack acc
	Sarah	b 27- 1-1803
	Elizabeth	b 3- 4-1805
	Abner	b 13- 7-1806 gct Nottingham MM, MD 1828
	Mira	b 11- 5-1809
	Phebe	b 18- 7-1811
	Samuel	b 1813 d 19- 9-1846 in 34th yr
	Elwood	b 1819 d 17- 8-1847 age 28y, m Rachel Kirk
		Elizabeth, w of Samuel, & their minor dts: Phebe, Sarah Mira, gct Nottingham MM, MD 19-4-1828

Samuel	b 30- 4-1790, s Joshua & Deborah, Little Brittain Twp, Lancaster Co, PA, gr-s Elisha & Rachel (Littler) of same place; res Fulton TWP, PA d 15- 4-1877 in his 87th yr, bur Little Brittain Grvyd
Esther	b 9-10-1815
Ch: Adeline	b 9-10-1850
Sarah	an Elder mbr of Eastland PM & Little Brittain MM d 29- 9-1836 in 62nd yr of her age
Slater	of Little Brittain Twp, Lancaster Co, PA b 27- 3-1787 d 5- 6-1855, bur Little Brittain s Jeremiah & Hannah (England) & gr-s Samuel & Sarah (Slater) England of East Nottingham Twp, Chester Co, PA
Mary	rptd mcd 9-6-1810 d 6-11-1857 rocf Nottingham MM, MD 9-3-1811, dtd 8-3-1811 Slater Brown disf mcd 7-7-1810; on 6-10 he informed he would appeal to QM; the QM reversed the Little Brittain MM disownment, rptd 8-6-1811; he is rst in mbrp
Ch: Sarah	b 5- 9-1811 d (no date)
Jeremiah	b 23-11-1812 d 9- 4-1817, age 4y 4m 16d
Elisha	b 12-12-1814
Jeremiah (2)	b 14- 2-1818
Rachel Anne	b
Mary	b
William	of this mtg, s Jeremiah, dec, & Anna (Wilson) of Lancaster Co, PA b 1-11-1784 d 28- 5-1837 gct Nottingham MM, MD to m 6-2-1808
Esther Kirk	b 7- 2-1786 d 27- 2-1855, age 69y dt Eli & Susannah (Brown) of West Nottingham Hundred, Cecil Co, MD m 24- 3-1808 at East Nottingham MH

Esther (Kirk) Brown, w of Wm, rocf Nottingham MM, MD 11- 6-1808

Ch: Jeremiah b 2- 9-1809 d 18-11-1842, age 33y 2m 16d
Susannah b 8- 2-1811 d 15- 9-1830 in 20th yr
(Fam rem to Nottingham; following ch listed in that MM)
Rachel b 5-12-1812 d 11- 2-1813, age 2m 6d
Abner b 3-12-1813 d 6-10-1821, age 7y 10m
Anna b 14- 4-1816 d 2-12-1849, age 33y 7m 16d, m ------ Sutton
Elizabeth b 4-12-1818
Wm Kirk b 24- 7-1821 d "age abt 4 yrs"
Timothy K b 4- 4-1824 d 17-12-18?? in his 40th yr
William P W b 1- 3-1827
Kirk b 17- 3-1831 d 7- 4-1832

William & w Esther (Kirk) & their 3 minor ch, viz: Jeremiah, Susannah & Abner, gct Nottingham MM, MD 9-4-1814; to be forwarded

William   s Isaiah & Miriam (Churchman)
Rachel Milner dt Nathan & Mary
              rptd m 6-4-1805
              This fam rem to IL

Ch: Miriam b 23-12-1805 mcd (ct White Water MM, IN 1837)
Isaiah b 14- 3-1808 mcd ("   "   "   "   "   ")
Joshua b 11- 8-1809   ("   "   "   "   "   ")
Milner b 20- 3-1812   ("   "   "   "   "   ")
Mary b 23-11-1814 d 5- 2-1816, age 1y 2m 12d
Eliza b 24-11-1816 d 15- 7-1835, age abt 18y, (d in IL)
Hester b   (see below)
Rachel b   "   "
Daniel b   "   "

William & Rachel (Milner) & ch: viz Miriam & Isaiah (both m but not according to Friends' rules), Joshua, Milner, Eliza, dec, Hester, Rachel & Daniel, "rem some time since to Tazewell Co, IL without a cert", gct White water MM, IN 15-4-1837 "it being found that this MM is nearest to their new res."

CARTER

Amos	b 12- 3-1799, s Samuel & 2nd w Ruth (Taylor), dec, of West Nottingham Twp, Chester Co, PA gct Nottingham MM, MD 19-11-1825 to m
Sophia Haines	b 26- 4-1805 d 7- 8-1853, age 48y dt Joseph & Rebeccah (Reynolds), both dec m 21-12-1825, West Nottingham MH Sophia (Haines), w of Amos, rocf Nottingham MM, MD 15-7-1826, dtd "yesterday"

Ch:
Caroline	b 28- 1-1827	
Jacob	b 6- 6-1828	d 10- 4-1860, age 31y 10m, bur Eastland
Jeremiah	b 21- 1-1830	d 21- 8-1831
Amanda	b 13- 8-1831	
Hannah	b 4- 6-1834	
George	b 26- 3-1838	
Mary Rebecca	b 8- 9-1839	d 7- 1-1865, age 25y 3m 29d, bur Eastland
Ruth Ann	b 15- 8-1847	
Samuel	b 18- 6-1849	

Enos P	b 24-10-1810, s Joel & 1st w Margaret (Reynolds), dec, of Little Brittain Twp, Lancaster Co, PA
Philena Griest	b 23-12-1813, dt William & 1st w Lydia, dec, of Eastland Twp, Lancaster Co, PA rptd m 14-11-1834 Enos P & Philena (Griest) gct Little Falls MM, MD 17-1-1835
Henry	a minor, rocf Green St., Philadelphia MM, PA, 16-8-1823, dtd 22-5-1823
Henry	rptd mcd by Eastland PM 19-8-1826; dis 18-11-1826

(Note: He m Mary Ann Jackson, dt Joel & Alice of Fulton Twp, Lancaster Co, PA, form of Wilmington MM, Del.)

Mary Ann (Jackson) Carter, w of Henry, disf mcd 18-11-1826

Mary Ann (Jackson) Carter's ack acc

Jeremiah   b 30- 7-1791   d 11- 7-1825
s Samuel & 2nd w Ruth (Taylor), of Little Brittain MM, PA gct Nottingham MM, MD 7-12-1816 to m

Susan Moore   b 24- 7-1797, dt Joseph & Mercy (Cutler), of West Nottingham Hundred, Cecil Co, MD

m 22- 1-1817, West Nottingham MH

Susan (Moore) Carter, w of Jeremiah, rocf Nottingham MM, MD 12-7-1817, dtd 9-5-1817

Ch: Abner   b 11-12-1818
     Samuel   b 17-10-1820
     Mercy Moore   b 29-11-1822   m Lewis Wood
     Ruth   b 29- 1-1825

Joel   b 15- 9-1774, s Samuel & 1st w Sarah (Sidwell), dec, of West Nottingham Twp, Chester Co, PA

Margaret Reynolds   b 17- 1-1780   d 22-11-1820, dt Samuel & Isabella (King), dec, of Colerain Twp, Lancaster Co, PA

m 26- 7-1798

Joel & Margaret (Reynolds) lived in Lancaster Co & were trans to Little Brittain MM fr Nottingham MM, on its organization 1804

Joel & Margaret (Reynolds) & their five ch, viz: Hannah, Isabella, Sarah, John & Samuel gct Deer Creek MM, Harford Co, MD 9-8-1806

(Note: the above Joel Carter m 2nd 16-1-1823 at Little Falls MH, MD, Hannah Hollingsworth, dt Nathaniel & Abigail (Green))

(Enos P Carter, s Joel & Margaret (Reynolds), dec, rptd m 14-11-1834 at Little Brittain Mtg, Philena Griest, dt Wm & 1st w Lydia, dec.)

Samuel	of East Bradford Twp, Chester Co, PA
	b 16- 2-1750 d 28- 2-1836, age 86y
	s John, dec, & Hannah
1st w Sarah Sidwell	b 29- 9-1755, dt Henry & Ellen (Huff), dec, of West Nottingham Twp, Chester Co, PA
	m 1-12mo (Dec) 1773, West Nottingham MH, auspices Nottingham MM, MD
2nd w Ruth Taylor	b 12- 3-1756 d 22- 6-1825 "in her 69th yr"
	dt Enoch Taylor; she was an Elder
	m 6- 9-1781

Ch: (by 1st w)

Joel	b 15- 9-1774 m Margaret Reynolds, 1798 & Hannah Hollingsworth
John	b 30- 5-1776 d 30- 8-1799, age 23y

(by 2nd w)

Abner	b 13- 7-1782 d 19-11-1802, age 20y
Hannah	b 20- 3-1784 d 31- 7-1850, m David Wood
Sarah	b 10-10-1785 d m Cyrus Milner, 1806
Samuel	b 16- 7-1787 d 2- 8-1806, age 19y
Rachel	b 12- 5-1789 d 18-12-1817, m Jesse Wood
Jeremiah	b 30- 7-1791 d 11- 7-1825, m Susan Moore, 1817
Anna	b 28- 8-1793
Cyrus	b 12-12-1795 d 5- 5-1815, age 23y
Amos	b 12- 3-1799 m Sophia Haines, 1825

CHANDLEE

Edward	rocf Green St MM, Philadelphia PA 15-5-1830, dtd 19-11-1829
	d 1-11-1853 in his 55th yr, bur Little Brittain Grvyd
Edward	rptd 18-11-1837 by Eastland PM to have been mou ack acc & he ret a mbr 13-1-1838
Lydia	(late Reynolds) rptd mou (to Evan Chandlee) by Eastland PM 9-5-1818; her ack acc 8-7-1818
	gct Nottingham MM, MD 7-11-1818

rocf Nottingham MM, MD 14-6-1823, dtd 16-5-1823
gct Deer Creek MM, MD 19-9-1829

CHANDLER
William G   rptd 16-5-1829 by Little Brittain PM to have been mcd; also that he "keeps a public house & sells spirituous liquors" & "that he acknowledges himself to be a mbr of Green St MM, Philadelphia, PA;" our comm is directed to give said Mtg this information.
On 19-6-1830 he told our comm that he had resigned fr mbrp in Green St MM, Philadelphia, & had so notified them.
(The case discontinued)

CHANNELL
John   & his 3 minor ch gct Deer Creek MM, MD 12-4-1806
(Note: names of ch not listed.)

CHANTRY
Thomas
Hannah   Both with 3 minor ch, viz: Sarah, Eliza & Wm Alfred, rocf London Grove MM, PA 13-9-1828, dtd 4-6-1828

CHURCHMAN
Margaret   & Hannah rocf Nottingham MM, MD 16-12-1837, dtd 13-10-1837
(the former dec since the date)

CLENDENNIN (or Clendennon or Clendennen)
Ann   rocf Kennett MM, PA 7-3-1818, dtd 6-1-1818
d 26- 5-1819, age 28y 5m 11d

Benjamin Clendennon
Martha   Both rocf Fallowfield MM, PA 19-4-1834, dtd 7-3-1834
gct Fallowfield MM, PA 14-3-1835

Isaac Clendennon	
Mercy	Both with their 2 minor ch viz: Ann & Elizabeth, rocf Fallowfield MM, PA 14-3-1835, dtd 7-3-1835 gct Deer Creek MM, MD 14-5-1836
Joshua Clendennon	rocf Fallowfield MM, PA 19-4-1834, dtd 7-3-1834 gct Deer Creek MM, MD 14-5-1836
Lydia	rocf Kennett MM, PA 10-1-1818, dtd 2-10-1817 gct Muncy MM, PA, 13-5-1826
Mira Clendennen	rocf Kennett MM, PA 7-11-1818, dtd 6-10-1818 gct Philadelphia MM, PA 16-10-1824
Phebe Clendennen	gct Kennett MM, PA 12-10-1805
Robert	
Elizabeth	both rocf Kennett MM, PA 6-12-1817, dtd 2-12-1817 gct Muncy MM, PA 13-5-1826
Ch: Ann	d 26- 5-1819, age 28y 5m 11d

COALE

Ellis P	b 1- 5-1802, s Samuel & Lydia (Pusey) of Deer Creek MM, Harford Co, MD
Ruthanna Moore	b 2- 9-1804 d Richmond, IN, dt Joseph & Mercy (Cutler) of West Nottingham, Cecil Co, MD m 2- 3mo (Mar) 1825 West Nottingham MH, MD Ellis P & w Ruthanna (Moore) & minor s Joseph M rocf Nottingham MM, MD 13-10-1827, dtd 14-9-1827 They came fr Sadsbury MM, PA to White Water MM, IN, dtd 3-12-1833, rec at White Water MM 22-1-1834, with ch: viz: Joseph, William, Mary J & Emma E; a dt Lydia T was b 20-7-1834 at Richmond, IN
Ellis P	gct Baltimore MM, MD by White Water MM, IN 23-11-1836 to m

2nd w Eliza Smith	rocf Baltimore MM, MD by White Water MM, IN 26-7-1838, dtd 5-5-1837,(Hicksite records)
Lydia T	dt Ellis P, rocf White Water MM, IN 15-2-1840, dtd 23-10-1839
Lydia T	b 20- 7-1834 in Richmond, IN, her res Fulton Twp, Lancaster Co, PA (Note: Here she is listed as dt of Ellis P & Ruthanna (Moore) Coale)
Ellis P	& w Ruthanna (Moore) & 2 minor ch, viz: Joseph M & Mary Jane gct Sadsbury MM, PA 17-10-1829 (See previous historical note.)
Samuel Mary	Both with infant s Benjamin, rocf Kennett MM, PA 1-6-1822, dtd 7-5-1822. Samuel & Mary Coale & their 6 minor ch, viz: Benjamin, Joshua, George, Samuel Jr, Lewis & Edward, and Jane M Reynolds, a minor in their care, gct White Water MM, IN 13-9-1834
Ch: Benjamin	b 17- 8-1821
Joshua	b 24- 2-1823
George	b 20- 6-1825
Samuel Jr	b 14-10-1827
Lewis	b 20-10-1830
Edward	b
	Sufferings: Coale, Samuel, "had taken fr him in 1824 by Samuel Porter, Collector, leather valued at $2.00 for a demand of $2.00;" and in 1826 "had taken fr him by Joseph Price, leather valued at $2.00 for a demand of $2.00"

COATES

Hartt G (Grandom)	rocf Fallowfield MM, PA 13-7-1833, dtd 7-6-1833 gct Birmingham MM, PA, 19-10-1833 to m Eliza Darlington

Hartt G		b 10- 1-1808 d 20-11-1873, s Warwick & Eleanor (Pusey) of Londonberry
		prcf Little Brittain MM, PA dtd 19-10-1833 to m
Eliza Darlington		b 9- 8-1814 d 5- 1-1889, dt George & Lydia (Barnard) of Birmingham MM, both dec
		m 7-11-1833, Birmingham MH, PA
		Eliza (Darlington) rocf Birmingham MM, PA 17-5-1834, dtd 3-5-1834
Ch:	Lydia	b 14- 2-1835 d 26- 9-1869, age 34y 7m 12d, bur Eastland
	Warwick	b 8- 8-1837 d 1-11-1837
	Edith	b 13- 7-1839 m A David Keech (nm) (1875 bef Phila Mayor)
	George D	b 31-11-1840 m Philena Reynolds (no ch)
	Granville	b 3- 7-1843
	Howard	b 30-10-1845 m Alice M Sutton (1872 Fairfax CtH, VA) 6 ch
	Stephen	b 20- 5-1848 m Lydia A Pugh (1876 E Nottingham MH, MD) 4 ch

Levi	of Fallowfield MM, PA
	Prcf that Mtg 8-8-1818, dtd 13-7-1818, showing him clear to m
Ann Smith	dt Joseph & Eleanor of Little Brittain MM, PA & form of London Grove MM, PA
	m 12- 9-1818
	Ann (Smith) gct Buckingham MM, PA 10-10-1818 "to join husband"

COBOURN

Benjamin		of Little Brittain Twp, Lancaster Co, PA
Abigail		Both with 7 ch (1st 7 named) rec on req 12-1-1811
Ch:	David	b 23- 3-1792 rptd mou 8-11-1817
	John	b 18- 7-1795
	Abigail Jr	b 30- 7-1797
	Benjamin	b 9- 7-1800

Sarah	b	9- 5-1804
Hannah	b	4-12-1807
Jacob	b	3- 1-1810
Elizabeth	b	13- 4-1812

Benjamin & Abigail & 5 minor ch, viz: Benjamin, Sarah, Hannah, Jacob & Elizabeth gct New Garden MM, OH 11-4-1818; to be forwarded

Likewise, John Cobourn & Abigail Cobourn Jr (adult ch of Benjamin & Abigail) gct same mtg same date

COBURN
David — req cert New Garden MM, OH 8-11-1817; an obstruction was found; and on 10-1-1818 the committee rptd he had been mou; the comm was instructed to write to that MM in OH asking their aid; his ack acc 12-12-1818 on recommendation of New Garden MM, OH; and he was gct that Mtg 9-1-1819

CONARD
Joseph
Rebecca — Both with 2 minor ch Lewis & Charles, rocf New Garden MM, PA, 18-6-1836, dtd 9-6-1836

Ch:	Lewis	b 27- 7-1829		
	Esther	b 27-11-1831	d	17-10-1832
	Charles	b 19- 7-1834		
	Evans	b 14- 1-1837	d	11- 4-1839
	Franklin	b 19- 8-1839		

COOK
Allen — b 31- 3-1808   d 24- 5-1847, age 39y, bur Little Brittain Res Fulton Twp, Lancaster Co, PA
s William & Susannah (Cutler) of same place, form of Warrington MM, PA

Rachel K Brown — b 5- 4-1810, dt Jeremiah Jr & Ann (Kirk) of Little Brittain Twp, Lancaster Co, PA
rptd mcd 19-2-1831 by Little Brittain PM

		Both Allen Cook & Rachel K Brown are mbrs of Little Brittain MM; their ack's acc & they retained in mbrp 16-4-1831
Ch:	Edward	b 15- 9-1831 d 16-12-1854 in San Francisco, CA age 23y 1m
	Jeremiah	b 22- 6-1834
	Anna Mary	b 29- 4-1836
	William	b 15-12-1837
	Charles	b 7- 9-1840
	Henry	b 22- 4-1843
	Julia Ann	b 22- 4-1846 d 23- 4-1855, age 9y
William		b 27-11-1778 d 27- 5-1854 in 77th yr, s Samuel & 1st w Ruth, of Warrington MM, PA
Susannah Cutler		of Little Brittain Twp, Lancaster Co, PA b 24- 3-1779 d 14- 2-1863 in 84th yr, bur Little Brittain Grvyd Res Fulton Town dt Benjamin, dec, & Susannah (Dunn) of Little Brittain m 29-11-1802, Little Brittain MH, under auspices of Nottingham MM, MD Wm & Susannah (Cutler) & 2 ch, viz: Allen & Mercy, rocf Warrington MM, PA 10-8-1811, dtd 23-5-1811
Ch:	Ann	b 28- 4-1804 d 10- 9-1808
	Kersey	b 24-10-1806 d 18- 9-1808
	Allen	b 31- 3-1808
	Mercy	b 21- 1-1810
	Franklin	b 10- 7-1812
	Clarkson	b 22- 3-1814
	Ruth	b 12- 1-1816
	Reuben	b 8- 5-1818 d 12- 1-1879, age 60y 8m 4d, bur Little Brittain
	Julia Ann	b 6-10-1822
	John	b 5- 6-1824 d 18- 6-1825

COPE
Samuel   rptd by Eastland PM to hav j the M.E.Ch 8-9-1810
                        dis 10-11-1810

COPPOCK
Jehu   rptd by Little Brittain PM to have rem to OH without
                        a cert; gct Salem MM, OH 6-2-1813

Rachel   cof fornication & bearing an illigitimate ch 11-2-
                        1809; dis 8-4-1809
                        (Note: For clarification & probable name of the
                        father of her illigitimate ch, see Joseph Webster) The
                        Womens Mtg rpts 8-1-1814 they had rec a letter fr
                        Salem MM, OH, saying that Rachel Coppock now
                        res within their compass that she has asked to be rein
                        in mbrp; permission granted Salem MM to rein her if
                        they so desire, 12-2-1814
                        (The reason for including the circumstances rather
                        fully is that the ch and its descendants may know the
                        father, as there seems to be no reason to doubt his
                        identity. WWH)

Samuel   s John & Margaret (Coulson)
Ellen Sidwell   dt Isaac & Ann (Brown) of Little Brittain MM
                        b   2- 7-1756   d   3 mo-1806
                        m 7-12-1775, Little Brittain MH, under auspices of
                        Nottingham MM, MD
                        Samuel rocf Nottingham MM 11-4-1812
                        with his 2 minor ch, viz: Aaron & Ruth, gct Short
                        Creek MM, OH 9-5-1812
                        Samuel & Ellen (Sidwell) Coppock had 15 ch (See
                        Nottingham MM, MD, B&D, p 186)
                        Rebecca Coppock & Ellen Coppock, adult dts of
                        Samuel & Ellen (Sidwell) Coppock, each gct same
                        Mtg same date

COX

Ann — w of William & their 3 minor ch (listed below) rocf Gwynedd MM, PA 11-7-1818, dtd 30-4-1818 "who is settled within the limits of Little Brittain MM with her husband"

Ch:
- Martha Whelan b 6-8-1810
- Joseph b 22-3-1812
- Charles J b 8-10-1816
- William b — rec on req ?
- Mark James b — rec on req 13-2-1830

Ann Cox & 5 minor ch, viz: Martha Whelan, Joseph, Charles J, William & Mark James gct Robeson MM, PA 15-3-1830

Sarah — (form Wilson) produced an ack of mou 18-11-1826; acc 14-12-1826; removed, she was gct Flushing MM, OH, 15-3-1828, cert to be forwarded

CULBERSON

Isabella — (late Reynolds) rptd 7-6-1833 by Women's Mtg as "guilty of fornication, and is married to a man not in mbrp with Friends"; dis for same 18-1-1834

CURL

John — & his minor s, Benjamin, rocf New Garden MM, PA 1-12-1821, dtd 4-10-1821, gct Sadsbury MM, PA 17-8-1822

CUTLER

Alben — of Drumore, Lancaster Co, PA, s Jesse & Mary (Stubbs) of same place
b 20-4-1817

Mary
Ch:
- Theodore P b 10-10-1847 d 8-6-1850, age 2y 7m 28d, bur Drumore
- Horace b 25-5-1853

Cassandra S	b 20- 8-1855	
Mary Ella	b 30-10-1859	

Anna   gct Warrington MM, PA 8-5-1813

Benjamin Sr   of Lancaster Co, PA   d 6- 9-1794
Susannah Dunn
Ch: Rebecca   b   d 14- 4-1816, m George
                  McMillan 6-11-1792 (1st w)

     Mercy   b   d 7-11-1822, m Joseph
                  Moore 27-10-1791 (1st w)

     Jonathan   b 6- 6-1777
     Susannah   b 24- 3-1779   d 14- 2-1863, m Wm Cook
     Jesse   b 17- 1-1782   d 5- 8-1867, m Mary Stubbs
     Anne   b 24-12-1783
     Benjamin Jr b 20-12-1785   m Miriam Quinby, 1811
     Jacob   b 12-11-1787   d 5- 7-1805
     Hannah   b 2- 2-1790   m John Fulton, 1817
     Ruth   b 25-12-1791
     Rachel   b 23- 4-1794   d 9- 2-1866, mou 1825
                  Joseph Blackburn

Benjamin Jr   b 20-12-1785   d 3-10-1821
                 of Little Brittain, Lancaster Co, PA
                 s Benjamin Sr, dec, & Susannah (Dunn) of same place
Miriam Quinby   b 22-12-1790, dt Aaron & Lydia of Little Brittain
                 MM, PA
                 m 7-12-1811
Ch: Chalkley B b 20- 3-1817   m 1st Ann ------,
                 M 2nd Elizabeth ------

Chalkley B   of Cecil Co, MD, s Benjamin Jr, dec, & Miriam of
                 Little Brittain, Lancaster Co, PA
                 b 8- 4-1819   d 17- 4-1881
1st w Ann H   b   1820   d 4- 2-1850, age 29y 10m
2nd w Elizabeth

Ch: (by 1st w)
 Rebecca Ann   b   2- 8-1844
 Benjamin C   b   5- 5-1846   d   5- 8-1864, age 18y 3m
 Joseph P   b   16- 1-1848
 (by 2nd w)
 Charles F   b   11- 2-1857
 Anne M   b   23- 2-1860
 Edith H   b   9- 7-1864

Jesse   of Drumore Twp, Lancaster Co, PA
  s Benjamin (dec 6-9-1794) & Susannah (Dunn) (dec 18-10-1823) of Little Brittain
  b 17- 1-1782   d   5- 8-1867, age 86y, bur Little Brittain Grvyd

Mary Stubbs   b   7- 6-1788   d   8- 2-1839   res Drumore
  dt Joseph & Ruth (Pyle) of Little Brittain MM, PA
  rptd m 8-12-1810

Ch: Joseph Stubbs   b   8-11-1811   d   8- 8-1869, age 58y, bur Little Brittain Grvyd
 Adaline   b   14- 3-1815
 Alben   b   20- 4-1817
 Philena   b   14- 4-1819
 Benjamin   b   19-12-1822   d   10-11-1824
 Benjamin (2)   b   13- 2-1825

Rachel   (now Blackburn), dt Benjamin & Susannah (Dunn) rptd mou to Joseph Blackburn by Little Brittain PM, 14-5-1825; her ack acc 18-6-1825 (See Blackburn)

EASTBURN
Benjamin   of Little Brittain Twp, Lancaster Co, PA
  d 30- 9-1806, age 50y 2m 26d, bur Elk Ridge
  His w Keziah & dt Sarah, gct Philadelphia MM, PA, by New Garden MM, PA 7-11-1811, which was end by Philadelphia MM to Gwynedd MM, PA (They had previously rem to New Garden, Chester Co, PA)

Ch: (of Benjamin & Keziah)
    Hannah   b 31- 3-1796
    Francis   b 26- 4-1798
    Joseph R   b 26- 1-1802
    Sarah   b
    Elizabeth   b

On 12-4-1806 Eastland PM informed that Benjamin Eastburn req a cert to Baltimore MM for himself, Keziah, his w, & 5 minor ch, viz: Sarah, Eliza, Hannah, Francis & Joseph Ross Eastburn. An obstruction was found & before the matter could be fully settled, Friends in Baltimore wrote that Benjamin had deceased 30-9-1806; consequently, this Mtg issued a cert to Baltimore MM, MD for Keziah (his widow) & the 5 ch listed above. The B&D records show the births of only 3 ch (above), with a marginal note stating: "Now of Chester Co; late of Little Brittain." On 12-7-1806 the Women's Min states: "There is no cert prepared for Benjamin & Keziah Eastburn & their minor ch; but one being prepared for their dt Rachel Eastburn to Baltimore MM is approved & signed

Mary   gct New Garden MM, PA 10-5-1806 (not identified, but thought to be a dt of Benjamin & Keziah Eastburn)

Rachel   dt Benjamin & Keziah Eastburn, gct Baltimore MM, MD, 12- 7-1806

EMBREE
Samuel
Hannah   Both with their 5 ch (listed below) gct Baltimore MM, MD 8-2-1806
Ch: Lydia   b 28- 2-1797
    Joseph   b 25-11-1798
    Phebe   b 1- 5-1801

John	b	2- 8-1803
James	b	1- 9-1805

FELL

Benjamin   d 20- 5-1847 in 74th yr, bur Eastland
Jane   d 15-10-1834, age 61y   "   "

Benjamin, Jane & 4 minor ch, viz: Mary, Leah, Rachel & Jacob gct Sadsbury MM, PA 6-6-1807

Ch: Mary   b   d 23-10-1862, age 65y, bur Eastland
     Leah   b
     Rachel   b
     Jacob   b 12-10-1806

Benjamin rocf Kennett MM, PA 17-4-1830, dtd 6-4-1830; gct Kennett MM, PA 16-4-1831; rocf Kennett MM, PA 16-6-1832, dtd 3-4-1832
Mary Fell rocf same Mtg, same date

Jesse
Rebecca   Both with their 6 minor ch (1st 6 listed below) rocf New Garden MM, PA 11-5-1816, dtd 7-3-1816
Jesse resigned fr mbrp 18-10-1828; acc 13-12-1828
Rebecca, w of Jesse, made a minister 13-6-1829 & approved by QM

Ch: Joshua   b 21- 1-1804 (at New Garden);   gct Uwchland MM, PA 19-10-1822
    Thomas b 11- 6-1806 " " " gct Nottingham MM, MD 19-6-1824
    Jesse Jr   b 10-11-1808 " " " gct White Water MM, IN 15-7-1837
    Mary   b 23- 3-1811 " " " gct Bradford MM, PA 13-2-1830
    Robert   b 8- 5-1813   " " " gct Uwchland MM, PA 13-2-1830
    Kersey   b 1- 5-1815   " " " gct Bradford MM, PA 13-2-1830
    Rebecca b 11- 8-1817 Little Brittain "   "   "   "
    Vickers b 26- 9-1819   "   " " " " "

Rebecca, w of Jesse & r ch, viz: Kersey, Rebecca, Vickers & Phineas gct Bradford MM, PA 13-2-1830; her s Robert gct Uwchland MM, PA, same date

	(Note: Her son Phineas is not listed in B & D records of Little Brittain MM) Hannah Fell gct Bradford MM, PA, 13-2-1830 (She is not listed in Little Brittain B & D, but is assumed to be an adult dt of Jesse & Rebecca Fell, though she may have been the w of Robert Fell)
Jesse Jr	s Jesse & Rebecca, gct White Water MM, IN 15-7-1837
Leah	rocf Green St MM, Philadelphia, PA 13-2-1836, dtd 15-6-1835
Robert Hannah	Both rocf New Garden MM, PA 3-6-1820, dtd 4-5-1820
Thomas	a minor, gct Nottingham MM, MD, 19-6-1824 on req of his father Jesse Fell
FIELD Anna	gct Short Creek MM, OH 11-5-1816, to be forwarded
FLOYD Henry B	minor s of Mary Ann (Floyd) Bolton (by a form m but now w of Evan Bolton) rocf Fallowfield MM, PA 18-6-1836, dtd 8-8-1835 (Note: he came with his mother after her m to Evan Bolton)
FRAZIER Susannah	(late Lamborn, dt George & 2nd w Mary (Smedley) Lamborn) rptd 16-5-1829 by Drumore PM to have been mou to David Frazier (nm); dis for same 15-8-1829
FULTON John	s Thomas & Hannah, dec, prcf Sadsbury MM, PA, clear to m

Hannah Cutler	b 2- 2-1790, dt Benjamin, dec, & Susannah (Dunn) of Little Brittain MM rptd m 6-12-1817 Hannah (Culter) Fulton, w of John, gct Sadsbury MM, PA 7-2-1818 "to join husband"

FURNISS

Gardner	b 19- 3-1782 d 5-11-1854 "in 77th yr", bur Little Brittain Res York Co, PA, s Thomas & Mary rocf Concord MM, PA 8-3-1806, dtd 5-3-1806 gct Kennett MM, PA 12-11-1808 to m
Joanna Lambourn	m 1808 d 27- 7-1827, bur Little Brittain Joanna rocf Kennett MM 11-3-1809, dtd 7-2-1809
2nd w Anna Landis	b ca 1788 d 27- 5-1841, age 53y, bur Little Brittain m 1829 On 11-12-1813 Gardner Furniss ack he had furnished a gun & ammunition to a man for military purposes; acc same date
Ch: (by 1st w)	
Martha	b 16-10-1811 Gardner Furniss (of this record) gct Middletown MM, PA 16-5-1829 to m Anna Landis, a mbr of that Mtg; Anna (Landis) Furniss, 2nd w of Gardner Furniss, rocf Middletown MM, PA 15-8-1829, dtd 7-8-1829
Oliver	b 11- 1-1794 d 19-11-1859, bur Eastland s Thomas & Mary of Little Brittain Twp, Lancaster Co, PA form of Concord MM, PA & m at Buckingham MM, PA gct Bradford MM, PA 3-11-1821 to m Tamsen Windle, a mbr of that Mtg
1st w Tamsen Windle	rocf Bradford MM, PA 30-3-1822, dtd 6-2-1822 d 14-11-1822

2nd w Ann Kent	Oliver gct Fallowfield MM, PA to m Ann Kent, mbr of that mtg 18-2-1826
	rocf Fallowfield MM, PA 17-6-1826, dtd 5-5-1826
	d 2- 1-1872, age 72y 6m 10d, bur Eastland

Ch: (Oliver & Ann)
- Benjamin   b 24- 2-1827
- Thomas   b 18- 5-1829
- Gardner   b 3- 7-1832
- Mary   b 24-11-1837
- Joseph   b 27- 9-1840
- Esther   b 29- 1-1843

Thomas	& w Mary rocf Concord MM, PA with ch listed below 6mo-1806, dtd 7-5-1806, the adult ch rec by separate certs, except those previously dec
	d 12- 2-1831 in his 76th yr; an Elder in Eastland PM
Mary (1st w)	d 25- 3-1826, age 72y
	Thomas gct Buckingham MM, PA 18-8-1827 to m
2nd w Mary Holcomb	

Ch: (Thomas & 1st w)
- Ann   b 26- 7-1780
- Gardner   b 19- 3-1782   d 5-11-1854 in 77th yr, m Joanna; m (2) Anna
- Martha   b 31- 1-1784
- Newbury   b 8-12-1785   d 8- 5-1786
- Sidney   b 1- 5-1787   m Jacob Haines, s Wm & Rebeckah, 1807
- Hannah   b 23- 7-1789
- Thomas   b 19-11-1791   d 21- 7-1794
- Oliver   b 11- 1-1794   d 19-11-1859, in 66th yr, m 1st Tamsen Windle, 1821; m 2nd Ann -----
- Phebe   b 31- 7-1798   d 9- 6-1849, age 50y 10m 9d

Thomas Furniss, gct Buckingham MM, PA, 18-8-1827 to m Mary Holcomb, a mbr of that mtg; Mary (Holcomb) Furniss, w of Thomas, rocf Buckingham MM, PA 17-11-1827

Mary Furniss gct Buckingham MM, PA 19-3-1831 (Note: her ct Buckingham MM was issued the next mo after the d of her husband, Thomas Furniss, who d 19-2-1831 in his 76th yr. Mary (Holcomb) Furniss was his 2nd w, by whom he had no issue.)

GARRETTSON

John   a minor, gct Middletown MM, Bucks Co, PA 17-9-1831

John   d 31- 1-1815 in 32nd yr, bur Little Brittain
s of Garrett Garrettson

Sarah Webster   m ca 1807
b 14-10-1785   d 22- 3-1818, bur Little Brittain
dt Isaac & Ruth (Milhouse) of Little Brittain Twp, Lancaster Co, PA, mbrs of Nottingham MM, MD

Ch: Lydia   b 15- 2-1808
    Isaac W   b 26- 1-1810   d 6 mo-1839, age 29y, bur Little Brittain Res Oxford, PA
    Eliakim   b 23-10-1812
    John   b 9- 2-1815

Isaac   a minor, gct Kennett MM, PA 18-9-1824, rocf Kennett MM, PA, 13-10-1832

GATCHELL

Hannah   (not identified but thought to have been 2nd w of Samuel Gatchell) rocf Nottingham MM, MD 9-9-1809, dtd 11-8-1809; gct New Garden MM, PA 11-9-1819

Matilda Jane   & Sarah rocf Goshen MM, PA, 13-2-1830, dtd 30-12-1829

Rachel   prcf Nottingham MM, MD 19-9-1829, dtd 14-8-1829; but it not being satisfactory, it is directed to be returned

Samuel	& w Hannah & their 3 minor ch, viz: Joseph, Abraham & Thomas rocf Fallowfield MM, PA 14-9-1833, dtd 5-7-1833 Mary Gatchell rocf same mtg, same date
	Hannah Gatchell, 2nd w of Samuel, d 1-8-1839, age 59y 6m 18 d, bur Little Brittain
	Samuel Gatchell d 18-3-1845, age 80y 4m 20d, bur Little Brittain Grvyd
	Mary Gatchell d 27-4-1871, age 61y 11m, but Little Brittain
GAUSE	
Lea W	rocf Spruce Street MM, Philadelphia 13-1-1838, dtd 25-10-1827
GOOD	
Charley	gct New Garden MM, PA 17-2-1838 to m
Betsy Moore	rocf New Garden MM, PA 14-7-1838 "to join husband"
GRAY	
Ann Jr	rptd "guilty of fornication" 20-10-1806
	Disf same 10-1-1807
Elizabeth (Grey ?)	rptd 19-3-1831 as having been "guilty of unchastity as evidenced by her having a child in an unmarried state", dis 14-5-1831
Hannah	(now Wickersham) rptd 16-10-1837 as "guilty of unchastity with a man whom she has since married", disf same 16-12-1837
Henry	rptd 14-7-1832 by Eastland as ack having trained in the Militia; disf same 15-9-1832
Jacob	s Joseph, dec, & Ann of Little Brittain Twp, Lancaster Co, PA

Elizabeth Reynolds	b 6-10-1790 d 18- 8-1876, in her 86th yr dt Henry & Elizabeth (Sidwell); gr-dt Henry & Mary (Haines) Reynolds; also gr-dt Hugh & Anne (Haines) Sidwell of East Nottingham Twp, Chester Co, PA (Note: Their 1st ch being b about 5 mos after their m, they were cof fornication; Jacob was dis; Elizabeth's ack acc 2 mo-1809
Ch: Sophia	b 15- 8-1808 d 15- 5-1820
Henry	b 9- 3-1810
Joseph	b 5- 1-1813
Elizabeth	b 24- 2-1815
Hannah	b 25- 7-1818
Sophia Jane	b 26- 5-1821
Joseph	(a minor), s of Ann Gray, gct New Garden MM, PA 10-1-1807 on his mother's req; Joseph Gray, a minor, rocf New Garden MM, PA 10-6-1809, dtd 6-4-1809
Joseph	Rptd by Eastland PM 11-5-1816 to be charged by a young woman with being the father of her illegitimate child; & that being treated with he denies it, but refuses to face the young woman or to take any other method in order to establish his innocence; disf same 10-8-1816

GRIEST

Elizabeth	rocf Nottingham MM, MD, 7-12-1816, dtd 11-10-1816
John	rocf Nottingham MM, MD, 16-7-1825, dtd "Yesterday"; gct Nottingham MM, MD 15-5-1830
William	a widower & his 2 minor ch, Philena & Milton, (by his 1st w Lydia, dec) rec on req 15-3-1823 s Thomas & Priscilla
2nd w Margaret Wiley,	dt Thomas & Catharine, dec rptd m 19-7-1823 d 6- 4-1861, age 67y, bur Eastland

Ch:	Philena	b 23-12-1813
	Milton	b 30- 6-1815
	(by 2nd w)	
	Elwood	b 17- 6-1824
	Thomas	b 29- 3-1831
	William Jr	b 19- 2-1834
	Henry	b 10- 2-1837 d 1- 1-1841, bur Eastland

GRIFFITH

John   (a minor) rocf Abington MM, PA 9-3-1811, dtd 26-11-1810 gct Kennett MM, PA 9-5-1812 on req of Benjamin Mason, in whose company he travelled, his c being included with that of Benjamin Mason, w Sarah & s Benjamin Jr

Thomas
Christiana   Both with their 2 ch, viz: Hannah Gibson Griffith & Charlotte Griffith, rocf Wilmington MM, Del, 6-5-1809, dtd 6-4-1809
This fam (intact) gct Sadsbury MM, PA 12-5-1810

HAINES

Jacob   of Nottingham MM, MD
b 14- 4-1784, s Wm & 2nd w Rebekah (Barrett), dec, prcf Nottingham MM, MD to m

Sidney Furniss   b 1- 5-1787 d 1- 9-1817
dt Thomas & Mary of Little Brittain MM, PA (form of Concord MM, PA)
rptd m 10-10-1807
Jacob Haines rocf Nottingham MM, MD 9-7-1808, he having moved into the compass of this Mtg; Jacob & 2 minor sons, Thomas & William, gct Nottingham MM, MD, 18-3-1826; same rocf Nottingham MM, MD 14-6-1834, dtd 16-5-1834

Ch:	Mary	b 20- 5-1808 d 5- 6-1808
	Thomas	b 16- 8-1809

	William	b 3- 7-1811
	Rebecca	b 28- 6-1813 gct Nottingham MM, MD, 15-11-1828
	Phebe	b 18- 9-1815 d 26-11-1817

Jeremiah
Mabel Hutton   (both mbrs of this Mtg) rptd Little Brittain PM 30-9-1820 as mcd by a Justice of the Peace. Also rptd that Jeremiah had att Military Exercise. Dis 3-3-1828, both

Lewis   rptd 19-6-1830 by Little Brittain PM as in the "practice of selling spirituous liquors as an agent for others"; disf same 14-7-1832 "after long care"

Margaret   (late Hutton) rptd 30-6-1821 by Little Brittain PM to have been "guilty of fornication with a man to whom she is since married"; dis 1-9-1821; also her husband, Edwin Haines, was dis at same time.
Edwin Haines rptd 30-6-1821 by Little Brittain PM to have been guilty of fornication with a woman whom he has since married; dis, with his wife, Margaret (Hutton) Haines, 1-9-1821

Mark   b 11- 9-1805 d 16- 9-1870, age 65y 5d, bur Little Brittain MM, s Timothy & Sarah (Brown) of Little Brittain MM

Mercy Cook   b 21- 1-1810 d 27- 4-1859, bur Little Brittain Grvyd
dt William & Susannah (Cutler) of Little Brittain MM
rptd 13-8-1836 as mcd
Both produced ack's which were acc 17-12-1836
(Note: They were m "by the assistance of the Mayor of Lancaster, PA")

Ch: William C   b 21- 1-1837
     Levi   b 14- 9-1838

	Howard	b 10- 7-1840 d 31- 3-1863, age 22y 8m 21d, bur VA
	Mary Susan	b 16- 1-1842
	Sarah Ann	b 25- 5-1843 d 18- 2-1844, age 8m 23d, bur Little Brittain Grvyd
	Emeline	b 27- 2-1845
	Priscilla	b 30-12-1846
	James Leander	b 27- 1-1852
Nathan		b 24-11-1803 d 9-7-1876 "by a hurt", bur Eastland
		s Joseph & Rebeckah (Reynolds), both dec, of West Nottingham Hundred, Cecil Co, MD
		rocf Nottingham MM, MD 17-9-1831, dtd 12-8-1831
Elizabeth Wood		b 27- 3-1804 d 31- 7-1831, bur Eastland
		dt David & Hannah (Carter) Wood of Little Brittain MM rptd m 16-6-1827
Ch:	Isaac	b 18-10-1828 d 22- 7-1830, age 1y 9m, bur Eastland
	Isaac (2)	b 26- 6-1831 d 14- 4-1870, age 38y 9m 13d, bur Eastland
Rebecca		a minor, dt Jacob & Sidney (Furniss), dec, gct Nottingham MM, MD, 15-11-1828 on req of her father, Jacob
Sarah		(late Hutton) rptd 16-4-1831 by Little Brittain PM as mcd; her ack acc 13-8-1831, ret in mbrp
Thomas		rptd 16-4-1836 by Eastland PM as mou; disf same 16-7-1836

HAMBLETON

Ann		(now Atkinson) rptd mcd 17-4-1824 by Little Brittain PM, her ack acc 14-8-1824

Ann (form Neal), w of Joseph, rptd guilty of fornication & since then of being m before a magistrate 10-10-1812; disf same 6-3-1813

Benjamin Jr & William, minor sons of Benjamin, gct Short Creek MM, OH (on req of their father, who informs he has rem them to within the compass of that Mtg) 8-3-1806

Isaac gct Kennett MM, PA 17-8-1822

James of Little Brittain, Lancaster Co, PA
    d 27- 1-1833 "in 80th yr", bur Little Brittain Grvyd
Elizabeth Lupton Paxon m ca 1780
    d 14- 3-1832, in 81st yr, bur Little Brittain Grvyd

Ch: Hannah   b 8- 5-1781
    Mercy   b 14- 4-1783   mou 1818 to ----- Brown (nm)
    Alice   b 10- 1-1785   m Jehu Kinsey (1816)
    Elizabeth   b 14- 5-1786   d 24- 3-1858; m Eli Smedley
    Rachel   b 23- 5-1787
    Mary   b 2-10-1788
    John   b 2- 2-1790
    Joseph   b 10- 5-1791
    Stephen   b 30- 7-1793   d 16- 5-1806
    Sarah   b 17- 5-1795
    Anne   b 10- 6-1797

John rptd by Little Brittain PM 6-2-1819 to be "guilty of fornication with a young woman whom he has since married." He does not deny the charge; disf same 12-6-1819. (He m Rachel Kinsey)

Rachel (late Kinsey) rptd by Drumore PM 8-5-1819 "hath been guilty of unchastity with her 1st cousin which is evident by her bearing an illigitimate child"; disf same 7-8-1819 (She m John Hambleton) (The disownment paper states: "Whom she has since m."); her ack acc

	13-5-1826 & she rst in mbrp; gct Stillwater MM, OH, 17-2-1827
Joseph	& Ann, his w (late Neal) rptd 10-10-1812 to have been guilty of fornication & have since been m before a Magistrate. Disf same 6-3-1813
Martha	rocf Deerfield MM, OH, 18-9-1830, dtd 19-6-1830
Mary	rptd 3-3-1821 by Women's Mtg as "hath been guilty of fornication which is manifest by her bearing a child in an unmarried state; and that on being treated with "she did not appear qualified to make satisfaction, & thinks best to issue a testimony against her." Dis 31-3-1821
Mercy	(now Brown) rptd 6-6-1818 mou "to a man not in mbrp"; Disf same 7-11-1818 She was dt James & Elizabeth Lupton (Paxon) Hambleton; b 14-4-1783
Sarah	(now Pickering) rptd mcd to Anthony Pickering 16-1-1836; her ack acc 16-4-1836, ret a mbr (See Pickering)

HAMILTON

Rachel	a minor, rem some time, gct New Garden MM, PA 6-4-1805 (Note: In other records this name is written Hambleton)

HAMPTON

James	rocf Pipe Creek MM, MD 30-11-1819, dtd 16-11-1819
Emily Walton	b 24-10-1798, dt Amos & Elizabeth, Little Brittain MM, PA rptd m 4-11-1820 James & Elizabeth (Walton) Hampton gct Pipe Creek MM, MH, 2-12-1820

HANNUMS
Ann   (late Bronw) rptd mcd by Women's Mtg 7-4-1810; disf same 8-9-1810; her ack acc & she rst 10-6-1815

HARLAN
Benjamin   (s James & Elizabeth (Swayne) Harlan) charged with being guilty of fornication by Eastland PM 9-6-1810; as he "left these parts without waiting to be visited by the MM" & was not available, he was disf same 8-9-1810. The comm visited the young woman who is his accuser who charges that he is the father of her bastard child (7-7-1810); on 11-10-1817 he presented an ack & asked to be rst; his ack acc 8-11-1817 (a widower now)
On req of Benjamin Harlan, his minor ch, viz: Elwood & Minerva are rec on req 8-8-1818
(Note: Harlan Fam, p 145/348 states that the above named Benjamin Harlan, m 1st 1812 Ann Gray, who d at Eastland, Lancaster Co, PA, 8 mo-1815; & m 2nd Mary (Ballance) Miller, wid of Thomas Miller & dt Joseph & Anna (Pownall) Ballance of Little Brittain MM, PA)
The records of Little Brittain MM show that the above note is true; the identity of Mary (Ballance-Miller) is supplied from Little Brittain MM records.
mc: fr Little Brittain MM, pp 4-9/411/414 Men's Min; W-vl, pp 272/3/4; Benjamin Harlan, s James & Elizabeth (Swayne), the form dec, & Mary Miller (wid of Thomas Miller & dt Joseph & Anna (Pownall) Ballance) having consent of surviving parents, ami 14-4-1827; ltm 19-5-1827; rptd m 16-6-1827

Ch: (by 1st w Ann)
    Elwood   b 11- 4-1813   d 1832, bur Eastland MH (unm)
    Minerva   b 13- 2-1815   m Joseph Lewis
    (by 2nd w Mary)
    Anna   b 24- 4-1828   m Charles Reed

Mary	b 18- 1-1834 m William K Brown
	Benjamin Harlan (above) b 12-9-1788; d 31-10-1840, bur Eastland MH
	James Harlan, father of Benjamin, above, d 31-8-1819, bur Eastland MH
Elwood	Merchant & Friend, of Eastland, Chester Co, PA
	b 9-11-1780, s James & Elizabeth (Swayne), Lancaster Co, PA d 11-10-1810 at Oak Run, near Eastland MH, bur there gct New Garden MM, PA 25-2-1807 to m
Rachel Paxon	dt Henry (shoemaker) & Matilda (Kimble) of Chester Co, PA
	m 12- 3-1807, New Garden Mtg, PA
	Rachel (Paxon) Harlan rocf New Garden MM, PA 6-6-1807, dtd 7-5-1807 "to join husband"
Ch: Hannah	b 23-11-1807; dis mou 1829 to Levi Springer (nm) (by NGMM)
John Paxon	b 13- 3-1809 d 12- 4-1860, m Mary Ann Hoopes, 1836
Matilda	b 24- 9-1810; dis mou 1829 to Lewis Springer (nm) (by NGMM)
	Elwood Harlan req cert Deer Creek MM, MD for himself, wife & ch 10-12-1808; but objection was found in that he had paid a fine for Military service & training; for this he was dis 12-8-1809; his w & 2 ch, viz: Hannah & John Paxon were gct Deer Creek MM, MD, 9-9-1809
Ezekiel	of Little Brittain Twp, Lancaster Co, PA
	b 15-10-1775 d 19-10-1839
	s Joseph & Hannah (Webster) of same place
Hannah Heston	b 31- 1-1776 in Chester Co, PA
	d 17- 4-1867 in Farmington, Oakland Co, MI; bur there
	dt John & Hannah (Jarrett)

		m 23-10-1806 at Little Brittain MH, PA

(Note: Hannah (Heston) Harlan, for many yrs familiarly known as "Blind Grandmother" rem to MI with fam 1845)

Ch: Mary W   b 14- 8-1807   d 17- 5-1884, m Patrick Gallaher, 1849

Pamela   b 17-12-1808   d 24- 8-1883, m 1st Wm Pusey; 2nd Martin Spaulding

David H   b 28- 4-1810   d 29- 7-1819, in Bucks Co, PA, bur there

Sarah   b 26- 5-1812   d 6- 5-1871, m Wm P Roberts, 1829

John H   b 11- 4-1814   d 29- 5-1873, m Mary Bailey, 1834

Joseph   b 6- 7-1816   m 1st Sarah Jane Cowan, 1840, 2nd Charlotte Knight, 1847

Hannah   b 22- 1-1819   m Benjamin Moore, 1839

Ezekiel & Hannah (Heston) Harlan & minor ch, viz: Mary W, Pamela, David Heston, Sarah & John, gct Middletown MM, PA, 6-5-1815

Hannah   & dt Phebe, each gct Fallowfield MM, PA 10-6-1815

James   b 2- 1-1750 in Kennett Twp, Chester Co, PA
d 31- 8-1819 in Lancaster Co, PA, bur Eastland MH, same Co
s Isaac & Hannah (Few) of Chester Co, PA

Elizabeth Swayne   b 16- 4-1758 in Kennett Twp, Chester Co, PA
d 22- 2-1832 near Eastland, Lancaster Co, PA, bur Eastland
dt Jonathan & Mary (White) of Kennett Mtg
(mc fr Kennett MM, PA)
m 25-10-1779 at Kennett MH, PA

Ch: Elwood   b 9-11-1780   d 11-10-1810, m Rachel Paxon, 1807

Hannah   b 24-11-1782   d 24- 6-1806, m Joseph Paxon, 1803

	Mary	b 5-4-1785 d 25-9-1825, m Richard Reynolds, 1807 (1st w)
	Benjamin	b 12-9-1788 d 31-10-1840, m 1st Ann Gray, 1812, m 2nd Mary B Miller
	Milton	b 7-1-1790 d ca 1828 at Cadiz, OH, unm dis by Little Brittain MM 17-1-1824
	Jonathan	b 16-8-1794 d 13-9-1835, m Elizabeth Thompson 24-8-1820
	Sarah	b 12-6-1798 d 12-8-1835, m Isaac Paxon
John P		rocf New Garden MM, PA 15-4-1826, dtd 9-2-1826
John Paxon		b 13-3-1809 d 12-4-1860, s Elwood & Rachel (Paxon) of Little Brittain MM, PA rptd by Eastland PM 14-5-1835 as mou his ack acc 16-7-1836
Mary Ann Hoopes		b 20-7-1815, Chester Co, PA, dt Abraham & Mary (Lynn) d 23-8-1851, in Lancaster Co, PA, bur Eastland Mtg Grvyd
Ch:	Elwood	b 25-1-1837 d 6-3-1838
	Francis	b 15-12-1838 d in infancy
	Alice	b 5-3-1841 d " "
	Janella	b 18-12-1842 d " "
	John Paxon	b 27-10-1844 m Elizabeth Fredd, dt Amos & Lanina
	Mary Amelia	b 29-12-1846 m Wm C Dickey (iron master, West Chester)
Jonathan		who had been uc for "taking too much strong drink" ack 6-9-1817 that he had att military training & had answered to his name on several occasions; his ack acc 10-1-1818
Jonathan		s James & Elizabeth (Swayne) of Little Brittain Twp b 16-8-1794 in Chester Co, PA

                d 13- 9-1835 in Wayne Co, IN to which place he had rem in 1835; bur in Friends Grvyd in Richmond, IN (Note: this record is taken from the Harlan Genealogy, pp 145/349; but there is an error here, since his youngest ch, Wm T, is listed as b 12-12-1737)

Elizabeth Thompson (a Presbyterian) of East Nottingham Twp, Chester Co, PA

        m 24- 8-1820 in Chester Co, PA (This was mou)

        b 7- 7-1796 d 9- 9-1872 in Lancaster Co, PA to which place she had returned with her ch soon after Jonathan's death in IN; she was dt Wm Thompson (physician) & w Elizabeth. (The foregoing & the ch listed below, taken from Harlan Gen)

Ch: (Harlan Gen states: "All ch b in Lancaster Co, PA", impossible, however.)

John Milton	b 4- 5-1821	living unm 1890 in Kirksville, PA
George W	b 10- 2-1822	d 23- 6-1888, m Emma W Brown, 1849
Lucetta M	b 21- 5-1827	m Isaac Richards Taylor 1846
Mary E	b 10- 4-1828	m James Barnes 1851
Margaret	b 6- 2-1832	m William T Leonard, 1862
Sidney W	b 2- 1-1835	m James Wright
William T	b 12-12-1837	m Emily M Wright, 1860

        Eastland PM, Lancaster Co, PA prtd to Little Brittain MM, 10 mo-1820 that "Jonathan Harlan was guilty of fornication with a young woman, which he does not deny, & has since m another young woman with assistance of a hireling minister"; dis 3-2-1821

Joseph   req cert London Grove MM, PA 6-10-1804, cg 10-11-1804

Mary   gct London Grove MM, PA 6-6-1807
        rocf London Grove MM, PA 9-1-1808, dtd 6-1-1808
        dis for j Orth Friends 13-6-1829

Mary	w of George Harlan rocf Kennett MM, PA 7-7-1810, dtd 10-5-1810 d 24-1-1813, bur Little Brittain MM Grvyd
Milton	s James & Elizabeth (Swayne) of Little Brittain MM dis for drinking to excess of alcoholic liquors, 17-1-1824 after long care
Sarah	dt Ezekiel & Hannah (Heston), gct Uwchlan MM, PA 7-12-1811 Ezekiel appt to forward it rocf Uwchlan MM, PA 11-6-1813, dtd 4-3-1813; gct Middletown MM, PA 10-6-1815

HARTLEY

Ann	rptd by Eastland PM 8-5-1819 "hath been guilty of unchastity which is evident by her bearing an illigitimate child." dis for same 7-8-1819 Her ack acc & she rein 14-10-1826; gct Wilmington MM, Del, 13-8-1831
Benjamin	s Joseph & Phebe, dec, gct Wilmington MM, Del, 16-4-1825
David	a minor, s Joseph & Phebe, gct Nottingham MM, MD 14-8-1824
Joseph Phebe	Their 17 ch are recorded in Nottingham MM B&D, p 198; the deaths of 3 of them are recorded here & must be listed here.
Ch: Samuel (5th ch)	d 31-1-1822, age 23y 5m 22d
Sarah (6th ch)	d 5-12-1820, age 20y 1m 19d
Amos (8th ch)	d 8-3-1822, age 18y 5m 11d
	Joseph & Phebe Hartley & 13 minor ch rocf Nottingham MM, MD, 8-6-1816, dtd 7-6-1816; names of ch: Benjamin, Samuel, Sarah, Martha, Amos, Josiah, David, Phebe, Joseph, William-Bunting,

	Margaret, Jeremiah & Milton (the last named was a twin with Elwood, who d in infancy)
	(Note: their 3 eldest ch were: Elizabeth, James & Ann)
	Ann Hartley, dt & 3rd ch of Joseph & Phebe, rocf same Mtg same date
	Phebe Hartley, w of Joseph (of this record) prtd dec "lately" 18-9-1824
	Joseph Hartley & 4 minor ch gct Wilmington MM, Del, 15-1-1825
	(Note: His son David & dt Martha had separate certs to same mtg.)
Josiah	"res for some time within the verge of Sadsbury MM, PA" gct that Mtg, 13-12-1828
Martha	gct Wilmington MM, Del, 18-12-1824
William	a minor, gct Wilmington MM, Del, 16-6-1827

HARVEY

Benjamin	rocf Wilmington MM, Del, 10-1-1807, dtd 10 mo-1806; cof visiting a "resort of diversion & there quarrelling & fighting" by Eastland PM, 10-10-1807 His ack acc 12-12-1807; gct Nottingham MM, MD 8-10-1814
Ellis	rocf Kennett MM, PA 6-7-1816, dtd 7-5-1816 gct Kennett MM, PA, 7-6-1817

HATTON
William
Sarah Ann   Both with 6 minor ch (1st listed below) rocf Concord MM, PA 14-5-1831, dtd 31-3-1831
(Note: Concord MM, PA shows the following entries: Hatton, Wm, mcd 28-11-1816; ack acc 30-1-1817)
Ch: Joseph   b 6- 4-1817   d 27- 9-1839, bur Little Brittain
    Eliza P   b 12- 7-1818

106

Rebecca Ann	b 29- 2-1820
Alice F	b 6- 5-1822
William	b 12- 5-1824
Priscilla	b 29- 5-1830
Susanna	b 19- 1-1833 d 12- 1-1839, bur Little Brittain
Samuel	b 8-12-1835 d 3- 2-1839, bur Little Brittain
	Sarah Ann, w of Wm, d 19-3-1863, age 67y 2m 3d, bur Little Brittain
	William Sr, d 27-9-1871, age 79y 10m 3d, bur Little Brittain

HESTON

Charles	rptd 14-4-1827 by Little Brittain PM as mou; dis 19-5-1827
Mary Jr	rptd 8-2-1817 by Little Brittain PM to be "guilty of fornication"; dis for same 8-3-1817 (She is rptd to have "had a child born in an unmarried state")

HEWES

Aaron	gct Wilmington MM, Del, 9-9-1815
Edward	s Joseph & Ann, dec
Mary Stubbs	b 19-11mo (Jan) 1751/2 OS; dt Daniel & Ruth, of Little Brittain Twp, Lancaster Co, PA
	m 11-10-1770, Little Brittain MH, PA
Ch: Joseph	b 5- 9-1771, Little Brittain Twp, Lancaster Co, PA
	d 28- 9-1841, age 70y 23d
	(m 3 times: 1st Lydia Harrison; 2nd Hannah Brown; 3rd Ann King (See Joseph Hewes))
George Harrison	b 18-11-1802, s Joseph & Lydia (Harrison)
	rocf Nottingham MM, MD, 11-3-1809, dtd 10-3-1809
	rptd 17-9-1836 by Little Brittain PM as mou "by the assistance of an Alderman"; disf same 17-12-1836

Joseph	b 5- 9-1771 in Little Brittain Twp, Lancaster Co, PA
	d 28- 9-1841, age 70y 23d
	s Edward & Mary (Stubbs) of same place
1st w Lydia Harrison,	b 4- 3-1772 d 8-12-1807, age 35y 9m 4d
	dt George & Lydia m 2- 6-1800, at Nottingham
	Joseph rocf Nottingham MM 12-6-1813, dtd 9-4-1813
2nd w Hannah Brown rptd m 8-8-1818; no issue listed; Hannah's dec unlisted	
3rd w Ann King	b 3-12-1782 d 24- 2-1850, age 67y 2m 21d
	dt James & Phebe (Pyle)
	m 13- 1-1827, Little Brittain MM
Ch: (by 1st w)	
Mary	b 27- 4-1801
George Harrison	b 18-11-1802
(by 3rd w)	
Ann	d 21- 3-1877, m Isaac Webster
Mary	a minor, dt Joseph, rocf Wilmington MM, Del, 11-1-1812, dtd 7-11-1811

HICKS

Mercy (late Pickering) rptd 11-2-1815 as mou to Charles Hicks, nm; she having rem fr the neighborhood with her husb, was dis for her mou 12-8-1815; altho she appeared desirous of retaining her mbrp, she did not make an ack; but on 10-10-1818 she sent her ack & req rst; she living within the compass of Goshen MM, PA, this mtg asked that mtg to visit her & report their opinion as to her sincerity; a reply came in her favor & she was rst 9-1-1819. She was gct Goshen MM, PA 6-3-1819, directed to be forwarded.

HOLCOMB

Hannah (late Pickering) rptd 18-8-1837 as mcd; inquiry shows that she res within the verge of Buckingham MM, PA

	which mtg was req to treat with her; their report rec 17-2-1838 said that she had produced an ack which they deemed satisfactory; this mtg acc it & ret her a mbr
Mary	wife of John, gct Buckingham MM, PA 10-10-1818

HOLLINGSWORTH

Joshua Hannah	(Historical) Concord MM, PA; 3-6-1801 Joshua & w Hannah (Hollingsworth) & s Harvey rocf Kennett MM, PA, dtd 16-4-1801; 5-9-1804 Joshua Hollingsworth, w Hannah & ch, viz: Harvey, Wm & Caleb gct Kennett MM, PA (end Historical)
Joshua Hannah	Both with 3 ch, viz: Harvey, William & Caleb, rocf Kennett MM, PA 9-8-1806, dtd 4-7-1806. With his w Hannah & 5 minor ch, viz: Harvey, William, Caleb, Thomas & Mary, gct Nottingham MM, MD 12-3-1814; to be forwarded

HOOPES

Thomas Mary	Both & 4 minor ch, viz: Phebe W, Sidney, Thomas Smedley & Jane rocf Nottingham MM, MD, 16-6-1827, dtd 18-5-1827
Thomas	rocf London Grove MM, PA 6-8-1808, dtd 6-7-1808; gct London Grove MM, PA 10-6-1809

HOUGH

Sarah	gct Deer Creek MM, MD, 7-11-1807

HOWELL

Caleb	rptd by Little Brittain PM 19-3-1831 to have "gone off & enlisted in the Army of the United States for five years"; dis this date

John	gct London Grove MM, PA 16-6-1827
John	rocf Nottingham MM, MD, 10-1-1807, dtd 11 mo-1806 d 22-3-1812, s John & Ann, West Hottingham Hundred, Cecil Co, MD
Sarah	Both with 2 minor ch Joseph & John, req mbrp 6-6-1807 Sarah, w of John, rec on req 6-8-1808, ch rec on req 7-9-1811
Ch: Joseph John Jr Elizabeth Caleb Sarah Ann	b 22- 5-1804 b 13- 9-1805 b 30- 3-1807 b 15- 4-1809 b 6- 4-1812
Joseph	a minor, rptd 14-9-1822 by Little Brittain PM to have absconded fr his Master about 4 months ago & nothing heard fr him; the comm found him the next month & brought him home, whereupon he promised to "stay his time out with his master & try to behave hereafter." Little Brittain PM rptd 14-6-1823 that Joseph Howell had absconded fr his Master three months ago & nothing had since been heard fr him; dis 16-8-1823
Sarah	rptd 31-3-1821 by Eastland PM "guilty of fornication which is manifest by her bearing a child in an unmarried state;" dis 30-6-1821 On 3-11-1821 "an account of the attendance & burial of Sarah Howell's child amounting to $8.92½ was directed to be paid in equal shares by each of the Preparative Mtgs."

HUTTON

Benjamin	rptd mou 10-8-1816 by Little Brittain PM; his ack acc 11-1-1817; gct New Garden MM, PA 16-8-1823

Isaac J	rocf New Garden MM, PA 11-5-1816, dtd 4-4-1816
Jabes	rptd by Little Brittain PM 17-4-1830 to have been mcd to Rebecca Brown (both mbrs of this Mtg); both disf same 14-8-1830
Jacob	a minor, gct Nottingham MM, MD, 17-9-1823, rocf Nottingham MM, MD 15-12-1827, dtd 14-12-1827
Joseph Sarah	Both & their 6 minor ch, viz: Margaret, William, Jabez, Jacob, Sarah & Kersey, rocf New Garden MM, PA, 11-5-1816, dtd 4-4-1816
Mabel	& Jeremiah Haines (both mbrs of this Mtg) rptd by Little Brittain PM 30-9-1820 as mcd before a Justice of the Peace. Both dis 3-3-1828
Mabell	rocf New Garden MM, PA, 11-5-1816, dtd 4-4-1816 (cert produced by Women's Mtg)
Margaret	(now Haines) rptd 30-6-1821 by Little Brittain PM to have "been guilty of fornication with a man to whom she is since married;" dis 1-9-1821; her husband, Edwin Haines, also dis at same time.
William	rocf New Garden MM, PA, 11-5-1815, dtd 4-4-1816
William	rptd 16-11-1822 by Little Brittain PM as mou by assistance of a hireling minister; dis 15-2-1823

IDOL

Mary	(late Streeper, dt William & Martha) rptd 17-1-1835 as mou; she res within the verge of Abington MM, PA, our comm is directed to write to that Mtg & req them to treat with her; on 15-8-1835 Abington MM rptd she had made a satisfactory ack which is acc by this mtg; she

was gct Abington MM, PA, 17-10-1835. On 14-5-1836 Mary Idol ret the cert granted her (above) to Abington MM, with the explanation that she had come (with her husband) to live within the verge of this mtg, which was read & acc. d 4 mo-1860, age 50y

IRWIN
Hannah   (late Kirk) rptd 16-6-1832 as mou; her ack acc 14-7-1832; gct Sadsbury MM, PA, 16-11-1838 (Note: Name written both Irwin & Erwin) cert to be forwarded.

IVES
John   of Philadelphia, PA, prcf Philadelphia MM for N.D. 9-11-1805 to m Pamelia Harlan & req being allowed to m her at the close of the Mtg, which was agreed to;
Pamelia Harlan b 22- 3-1774 d 15- 9-1842 m 9-11-1805 dt Joseph, dec, & Hannah (Webster) (who gave consent as the sole surviving parent)
Pamelia (Harlan) Ives, w of John, gct Philadelphia MM, N.D, PA, 11-1-1806 "to join husband"
Note: Pamelia (Harlan) Ives, m 2nd 7-8-1818 Daniel Kent

JACKSON
Alice   w of Joel & 4 minor ch, viz: Mary Ann, Alice Anna, Catharine & Jonathan Morris, rocf Wilmington MM, Del, 10-10-1812, dtd 6-8-1812
Alice, w of Joel, d 10-3-1854, bur Family Burying Ground, Fulton Twp

Ch: (of Joel & Alice Jackson)
    Mary Ann   b 18- 9-1803; mcd 1826 to Henry Carter, both dis
    Alice Anna   b 29-12-1805 d 9- 9-1842, bur Family Burying Ground
    Catharine (Kitty) S 8- 4-1808
    Jonathan Morris b 30- 9-1810; dis mou 16-6-1835

Eliza	b 13- 3-1813
John	b 3-12-1815 d 13- 3-1835
Hannah	b 2- 6-1818
Amelia	b 11- 1-1822

Hannah   w of Mordecai M Jackson, rocf Goshen MM, PA 6-2-1813, dtd 8-1-1813
She d 4- 5-1872, age 89y; bur near Millsboro, PA

Jonathan Morris   s Joel & Alice Jackson, rptd 14-2-1835 by Little Brittain PM as mou; disf same 13-6-1835

Mary Ann   dt Joel & Alice, rptd by Little Brittain PM, 16-9-1826 as mcd to Henry Carter (also a mbr); dis 18-11-1826 (See Carter)

JOB

Ann Eliza(beth-?)   (now Blake) rptd mou 15-10-1836; her ack acc 14-1-1837

Hannah   rocf Nottingham MM, MD, 11-7-1818, dtd 8-5-1818; gct Nottingham MM, MD, 19-4-1823

Jacob   rocf Nottingham MM, MD, 8-11-1806, dtd 8 mo-1806; rptd mcd 7-1-1809; disf same 8-4-1809

Lettitia   & 4 minor dts, viz: Rachel Brown, Mary, Ann Elizabeth & Sophia M, rec on req of mother, Lettitia, 18-9-1824

JONES

Abigail   rocf Nottingham MM, MD, 17-7-1824, dtd 16-7-1824; gct New Garden MM, PA 13-12-1828

John   d 12-12-1819
rocf London Grove MM, PA, 10-10-1812, dtd 7-10-1812; on 6-1-1816 London Grove MM, PA rptd that

John Jones (who had req cert London Grove MM on 9-12-1815) had become so deprived of his reason that a group of his relatives had advised placing him in the Poor House of Chester Co, PA, which has been done. He, being a mbr of Little Brittain MM, a comm is appt to look into his case & do what may be found needful for him. On 7-2-1818, Little Brittain MM directed that $200 be provided for his additional care & that Gardner Furniss & Jesse Wood be appointed guardians for said John Jones & have care also to preserve his property. On 1-1-1820, Jesse Wood & Gardner Furniss rptd they "had found John Jones in the public alms house in Philadelphia, in a bad state of health & died while they were preparing to move him. The expense of boarding & clothing while there exclusive of their expenses amounted to $205., which Jeremiah Brown & Thomas Furniss are directed to procure & pay the demand." On 14-4-1827 Gardner Furniss produced a claim of this mtg against the estate of John Jones for the money that had been spent upon his living & care amounting to about $615., all of which was returned from his estate.

KENNEDY
Mary   (late Mullen) rptd mou 7-7-1810; dis for same 12-1-1811

KENNY
Daniel
Elinor   (late of Chester Co, PA; now of Little Brittain, Lancaster Co, PA)
Ch: Daniel   b 14- 8-1799
   Maxwell   b   4- 2-1802
   James   b 22- 7-1805
   Eleanor   b 16-11-1808

Both & 4 minor ch, viz: Daniel, Maxwell, James & Eleanor, gct Baltimore MM for W Dist, MD, 7-4-1810. On 6-4-1816 Eleanor Kenny req cert Baltimore MM, for W Dist, for her s Daniel, a minor; grtd 11-5-1816.

(Note: his name was clearly included in the cert grtd 7-4-1810 for his parents & ch; but on 10-6-1815, Daniel & James were rocf Baltimore MM for W.D.) James, s Daniel & Elinor, gct Baltimore MM for W Dist, on req of his mother, Elinor, 2-3-1822

KENT

Elizabeth — rocf Fallowfield MM, PA, 18-9-1830, dtd 10-9-1830; gct New Garden MM, PA, 17-10-1835

Joseph — rocf Fallowfield MM, PA, 12-9-1818, dtd 8-6-1818; gct Deer Creek MM, MD, 30-9-1820

KILLOUGH

Mary — (late Job) rptd 15-8-1835 as mou; her ack acc 14-11-1835

KING

Amos — b 26- 7-1791 d 30- 3-1870, age 78y 8m 4d, bur Little Brittain Grvyd
s James & Phebe (Pyle) & gr-s James & Isabell (Pennell) King

Agnes Thomas — dt Thomas (d 27-2-1828, bur Little Brittain) & Mary (d 31-5-1837, bur Little Brittain Grvyd)
rptd m 11-2-1815
Sufferings: Amos King, "had taken fr him in 1824 by Wm Ralston, Collector, six sheep valued at $9. for a demand of $2."

Hiram — s Joshua & Elizabeth (Rogers) of Little Brittain PM, gct Stillwater MM, OH, 17-9-1825

On 17-12-1825 Hiram ret his cert which he had not presented to Stillwater MM & is again a mbr of Little Brittain MM; on 16-6-1827 he was rptd by Little Brittain PM to have been mcd before a Justice of the Peace; a comm is appt to write Friends of Deerfield MM, OH, where he is said to res, to treat with him. His ack was rec 15-3-1828 & acc; gct Deerfield MM, OH, 19-4-1828; rocf Deerfield MM, OH, 19-9-1835, dtd 15-7-1835; rem, he was gct Nottingham MM, MD, 16-7-1836; this cert was ret 13-8-1836; investigation showed that Hiram King had become a "charge" upon his neighbors for aid; this Mtg decided to retain him in mbrp, as its own "charge."

James Jr	of Little Brittain PM, rptd mcd to a woman not a mbr, 11-6-1808, disf same 8-10-1808
James	b 16-10-1756, s Thomas & Ann (Coppock) of Little Brittain MM, Lancaster Co, PA, & gr-s James & Isabell (Pennell) King, dec, of same place
Phebe Pyle	m 3-1mo (Jan) 1782, dt Moses & 2nd w Mary (Cook), dec, of same place
Ch: Ann	b 3-12-1782 d 24- 2-1850, age 67y 2m 21d, m Joseph Hewes, as 3rd w
Thomas	b 2-12-1783 m Rachel Brown
Mary	b 26- 2-1785 d 11- 8-1792, age 7y 5m
Phebe	b 26- 5-1786
James	b 3- 9-1787 d 3-12-1875, m Rebecca Smedley & Deborah Doane
Moses	b 11- 5-1789 d 28- 8-1799, age 10y 9m
Amos	b 26- 7-1791 d 30- 3-1870, age 78y 8m 4d, bur Little Brittain, m Agnes -----
Pyle	b 10- 2-1793 d 26- 6-1794, age 1y 4m 14d
Lewis	b 26- 8-1794
John	b 15- 4-1799 d 17- 9-1853; m Mary Reynolds, dt Joshua & Rachel

James Jr 2nd		of Little Brittain, Lancaster Co, PA, later of Bartlett, Washington Co, OH
		b 6- 7-1817, Lancaster Co, PA; s James Jr & Rebeckah (Smedley); gr-s James & Phebe (Pyle) King, of Little Brittain
Deborah Stephens		b 11- 1-1819 d 4-11-1893, dt Wm & Phebe
		m 15- 4-1841
Ch:	Malon	b 4- 2-1842 d 10- 4-1842
	William	b 5- 2-1843 d 28- 2-1844
	Rebecca Smedley	b 19- 7-1844 m Addison Naylor
	Phebe	b 9- 9-1845 m David R Moore
	James Lewis	b 21-10-1846 m Emily Romans
	Anna Melissa	b 24- 9-1848
	Ida Ann	b 8- 2-1850
	Josiah S	b 25- 8-1852
	Sarah Lydia	b 14- 4-1856
	Mary Virginia	b 18- 1-1858
	Helena Adelaide	b 2mo-1861
	Chase	b 1- 8-1863

James Jr		b 3- 9-1787 d 3-12-1875, s James & Phebe (Pyle) of Little Brittain, Lancaster Co, PA
		gct NY MM 11-4-1812, rocf NY MM dtd 7-7-1813; clear; recd & acc 9-10-1813
Rebekah Smedley (1st wife)		b 6- 9-1794 d 8- 4-1850, dt Joseph & Rebeckah (Lewis) of Little Brittain, PA
		m 23- 3-1815, Little Brittain MH
2nd w Deborah Doane		b 30- 9-1796 still living in 1900, her mind clear & body erect, at Stillwater, Morgan Co, OH
		m 3- 9-1862
		James & Rebekah (Smedley) & their 6 eldest ch were gct Stillwater MM, OH, 1-5-1825, where James was a farmer & prominent mbr of the Mtg
Ch:	Joseph	b 27- 4-1816 d 1- 8-1825
	James	b 6- 7-1817 m Deborah Stephens

117

Sarah	b 28- 6-1819	d 7-11-1885 m Joshua King
Rebekah	b 13-11-1820 Livezey	d 13- 3-1895 m Samuel M
Phebe	b 20- 9-1822 C Hill	m Benjamin Morris & 2nd David
Mercy (Ch b in OH)	b 21- 4-1824	m Isaac Hoopes
Lewis	b 6-12-1825 (Winner) Bingman	m Alice Bingman & 2nd Isabella
Joel	b 13- 1-1828 Graham	m Elizabeth Bingman & Elizabeth
Joseph (2)	b 30- 3-1830	m Phebe Harris & Martha Harris
Ann	b 24- 1-1832 (She jM.E.Ch)	d 29- 4-1881 m Wm Manley
Perley J	b 4-12-1835 tharine Ady, dt Joshua & Hannah (Sp.)	d 2- 5-1863 m Sarah Ca-
Infant	b 4-10-1837	d without name

(Note: Slight differences in birth dates between Little Brittain & Smedley Fam. WWH)

Jeremiah   "rem & settled in Philadelphia" gct Philadelphia MM, PA & forwarded
rocf Philadelphia for S. D. 10-6-1809, dtd 26-4-1809; "and Joseph Richardson & Aaron Quinby are appt to visit him & encourage him in a more diligent performance of his religious duties."
Disf non-attendance 12-12-1812

Joel   gct Wilmington MM, Del, 18-9-1824 "to be forwarded"

John   of Little Brittain Twp, Lancaster Co, PA
b 15- 4-1799   d 17- 9-1853 "in his 54th yr"
s James & Phebe (Pyle), form dec, of same place
gct Nottingham MM, MD 16-4-1825 to m

Mary Reynolds		m 25- 5-1825, W Nottingham MH, auspices Nottingham MM, MD
		dt Joshua, dec, & Rachel of W Nottingham Hundred, Cecil Co, MD
		Mary (Reynolds) King rocf Nottingham MM, MD 17-9-1825, dtd 15-7-1825
Ch:	Ann	b 7- 9-1829
	Amos L	b 25- 8-1833 d 21- 9-1862, age 29y 26d

Joshua		b 3- 5-1817 d 27-10-1877, age 60y 5m 24d, bur Little Brittain Res Fulton Twp, Lancaster Co, PA
		s Thomas & Rachel, gr-s James & Phebe (Pyle) King
Mary M		b 11- 9-1816 d 18- 9-1879, age 63y 7d, bur Little Brittain
Ch:	Rebecca P	b 24- 9-1844
	Thomas	b 4-12-1845 d 5- 6-1857, age 11y 6m 1d, bur Little Brittain
	Philena	b 24-11-1847
	Rachel	b 9- 7-1849
	Mary Ann	b 13- 3-1851 d 31-12-1853, age 2y 9m 18d, bur Little Brittain

Joshua		of Little Brittain Twp, Lancaster Co, PA
		b 6- 9-1776, s Vincent & Mary (Brown), form dec, of same place
Elizabeth Rogers		b 25- 3-1781, dt Thomas & Katharine (Brown) of Cecil Co, MD
		m 13- 5-1802, at East Nottingham MH, MD, auspices Nottingham MM, MD
Ch:	Hiram	b 17- 9-1803
	Mary	b 26- 2-1805
	Hannah	b 7-10-1806
	Katharine	b 9- 7-1808
	Rebecca	b " d 28- 8-1808
	Thomas	b 17- 6-1810

Joshua	b 6- 9-1812 d 6-12-1872, m Sarah King, dt James & Rebekah, 1838
Jeremiah	b 14- 8-1814
Elizabeth	b 5-10-1816
Deborah	b 26- 5-1818
Miriam	b 16- 5-1821

Joshua	b 6- 9-1812 d 6-12-1872
	s Joshua & Elizabeth (Rogers) of Little Brittain, Lancaster Co, PA
Sarah King	b 28- 6-1819 d 7-11-1885
	dt James & Rebeckah (Smedley) of same place
	m 24- 2-1838
	Joshua Jr & Sarah & eldest ch rem to Morgan Co, OH; Res Pennsville
Ch: Rebecca	b 6- 5-1839 d 6- 6-1884, m Abner G Lewis, s Wm & Hannah
Mary	b 31- 3-1841 OH m Montillion Brown, s Wm & Deborah (King)
Elizabeth	b 13-12-1842 d 6 mo-1886, m Amos Pierpont, s Benj & Rachel
James	b 10- 3-1844 d 13-10-1846
Sarah	b 27- 7-1845 m Daniel Marion McInturf, s Daniel & Catharine (Smith)
Ann	b 27- 7-1848 d 24- 7-1849
Lewis	b 22- 4-1850 m Rebecca Pierpont, dt Benjamin & Rachel
Isaiah	b 22- 2-1852 d Neb m Ada Vestilla Rosa
Lydia	b 21- 8-1854 m Charles w Parsons, s Joseph & Martha (Harris)
Louisa	b 7- 3-1861 m Joseph Lowe, Muscatine, IA, s Stephen & Martha (Durf)

Lewis	b 26- 8-1794 d 10- 3-1851 in 57th yr, bur Little Brittain Graveyard; Res Fulton Twp, Lancaster Co, PA

Sarah Thomas   s James & Phebe (Pyle); gr-s Thomas & Ann (Coppock) King
rptd m 30-3-1822
d 10- 1-1847, age 52y 2m 4d, bur Little Brittain
dt Thomas & Mary Thomas, Little Brittain MM, form of Goshen MM, PA

Ch: Thomas P   b 19- 7-1824   d 10- 6-1889 m Phebe Moore Preston (25-11-1847)
     William   b 9- 8-1826
     Alfred   b 15- 2-1829
     Edith   b 15- 1-1832
     Phebe Ann   b 18- 2-1835

Rachel   rocf Concord MM, PA 11-1-1812, dtd 9-10-1811

Samuel   b 28- 2-1826   d 15- 9-1872, age 46y 6m 17d, bur Little Brittain Grvyd
Res Fulton Twp, Lancaster Co, PA
s Thomas & Rachel, gr-s James Phebe (Pyle) King

Grace Ann   m

Ch: Rachel Elizabeth b 8- 9-1857   d 26-10-1857, bur Little Brittain
     Mary Ann   b 18- 8-1858
     Phebe   b 3-10-1860
     Joel H   b 1- 4-1864
     Emma   b "

Thomas   & Joshua (s of Joshua) gct Deerfield MM, OH 13-5-1837

Thomas P   of Fulton Twp, Lancaster Co, PA
b 19- 7-1824   d 10- 6-1889
s Lewis & Sarah, dec

Phebe Moore Preston of Octoraro Hundred, Cecil Co, MD
b 2- 4-1827   d 5- 2-1889, age 61y 10m 3d, bur Little Brittain
dt Joseph & Rebeckah (Reynolds) of same place

	m 25-11-1847, Octoraro MH, MD	
Ch: Elmira	b 26- 8-1849	m Alfred Wood, 31-1-1878
Lauretta Ann	b 20-11-1852	
Luella	b 22- 7-1857	m Lewis Wood, 25-1-1893
William P	b 1- 9-1861	

Thomas b 2-12-1873 d 27- 1-1863, age 79y 1m 25d
s James & Phebe (Pyle); gr-s Thomas & Ann (Coppock) King
Res Fulton Twp, Lancaster Co, PA
(James, father of Thomas, d 8-5-1825, age 68y 6m 22d; Phebe, mother of Thomas, d 5-12-1831, age 72y 7m 22d, both bur Little Brittain)

Rachel Brown b 18-11-1787 d 26- 9-1852, age 64y
dt Joshua & Deborah of Little Brittain MM, PA
rptd m 9-5-1812

Ch: Esther b 17- 1-1813 d 5- 4-1872, age 59y 2m 19d, bur Little Brittain
 Phebe b 28-12-1814
 Joshua b 3- 5-1817 d 27-10-1877, m Mary M
 Amos b 7- 7-1819 d 28- 3-1871, age 51y 8m 21d, bur Little Brittain
 James b 17-12-1823 d 3- 8-1825, in 2nd yr, bur Little Brittain
 Samuel b 28- 2-1826 d 15- 9-1872, age 46y 6m 17d, m Grace Ann
 Deborah b 24- 9-1828
 Lindley b 28- 6-1834

Vincent Jr (M.D.) of Little Brittain & Philadelphia
b 12-11-1781 d 1825 "a sudden death at his res"
s Vincent & Mary (Brown) & gr-s Thomas & Ann (Coppock) King

1st w Phebe Trimble b 4- 7-1786 d 12 mo-1816, Columbia, PA
d William (b 19-9-1737 OS, Concord, PA; d 26-2-1821, W. Whiteland; s Wm & Ann (Palmer) Trimble)

	& w Ann (EdgeParke-Taylor) Trimble, dt John & Ann (PIM) Edge & widow of (1) Thomas A Parke & (2) Benjamin Taylor, when she m William Trimble) mcd 6-6-1807
2nd w Patience Wright m 1821	
Ch: Mary Ann	b 6mo-1807 d 1820
Lydia Trimble	b 2- 6-1809; a minister; unm; res Media, PA
Jane P	b 30- 6-1812 d 14- 1-1892, m John G Edge
William T	b 1814 d 1816
Jeremiah	b d "in infancy"
	Vincent King Jr (M.D.) was disf mcd by Little Brittain MM, PA 12-12-1807 after receiving a rpt fr Philadelphia MM that he "does not condemn his outgoing in marriage."
Vincent	(miller) rptd mcd (before a Magistrate) by Little Brittain PM, 12-4-1806 (wife's name not listed)
	(Note: Altho not so stated, this is assumed to have been his 2nd m, his 1st w, Rachel Reynolds, having d 7-1-1804. See Nottingham MM)
	He offered a paper of ack 12-7-1806, which was not immediately acc; after months of care he was disf same 10-1-1807
	On 7-3-1807, Vincent King informed the Mtg in writing that he intended to appeal his disownment to the QM; on 11-7-1807, he informed he had decided not to appeal; the Mtg then re-approved his disownment.
Vincent	b 5- 5mo (July) 1720 OS d 13 (or 14)-10-1801, bur Little Brittain (left w, Mary & 5 ch)
	s James & Isabel (Pennell), both dec, of Little Brittain, Chester Co, PA
Mary Brown	b 6-10 mo (Dec) 1747 OS
	dt Joshua & Hannah (Gatchell), dec, of Little Brittain Twp, Chester Co, PA

		m 12-12-1771, Little Brittain MH, PA, auspices Nottingham MM, MD
Ch:	Hannah	b 19-10-1772 d 20- 6-1782, age nr 10 yrs
	James	b 13- 5-1774
	Joshua	b 6- 9-1776 m Elizabeth Rogers, 1802
	Mary	b 24- 7-1779 m Jonathan Livezey, 1804
	Vincent Jr	b 12-11-1781 d 2-12-1825 m (1) Phebe Trimble (2) Patience Wright
	Jeremiah	b 13- 6-1784

William — of Kirk's Mills, Lancaster Co, PA
Rebecca Daye Reynolds

Ch:	Sarah Lucretia	b 19- 8-1852
	Hannah Ida	b 1- 6-1857 m 28-11-1878 John Evans, s Thomas Passmore & Phebe (Smedley) Evans

KINSEY

Abel — s John & Mary (Rice) gct Bradford MM, PA 18-11-1825 to m

Edith Whitacker — a mbr of that Mtg
(Folio 7 says: Edith Kinsey, w of Abel Kinsey, d 10-2-1828 in 42nd yr, bur East Caln, Eastland)
Edith (Whitacker) Kinsey, w of Abel, rocf Bradford MM, PA 17-3-1827, dtd 7-3-1827

Benjamin
Margaret — Both with their 6 minor ch, & one adult (who came with a separate cert) all 7 listed below, rocf New Garden MM, PA 9-5-1818, dtd 7-5-1818
Benjamin Kinsey & his 2 minor ch, viz: Aaron & Abi, gct Stillwater MM, OH 17-3-1827
(Note: Nothing is said about his w, Margaret; so we must assume she has dec)

Ch:	Rachel (adult)	b 24- 8-1796
	Elias	b 8- 3-1800 gct Goshen MM, PA 14-5-1825
	Hannah	b 16- 6-1802

Martha	b 12- 5-1805 gct Goshen MM, PA 17-6-1826
Tacy	b 17-11-1807 gct Goshen MM, PA 17-6-1826
Aaron	b 27- 8-1810
Abi	b 6- 4-1813

Elizabeth M — dt Isaac by his 2nd w Rachel (Matthews) gct Gunpowder MM, MD, 1-7-1820
(Note: She m 7-12-1820 at Gunpowder MH, Samuel Scott)

Hannah — rocf Indian Spring MM, MD, 8-3-1806, dtd 15-11-1805

Isaac — (dec) his 3 minor ch, viz: Oliver, Thomas & Elizabeth M
rocf Baltimore MM, MD 12-1-1805, dtd 13-12-1804

Jehu — rocf Buckingham MM, Bucks Co, PA 12-8-1809, dtd 7 mo-1809

Jehu
Alice Hambleton — s Joseph & Ann, both dec
b 10- 1-1785, dt James & Elizabeth Lupton (Paxon) of Little Brittain MM (who came consent)
rptd m 9-11-1816
On 12- 4-1817 Little Brittain PM rptd that Jehu Kinsey had been "guilty of fornication with two women, one of them (Alice Hambleton) he has since m & to the other he has given his obligation; on being treated with he does not deny the charge." On the same date the Women's Mtg rptd that Alice Kinsey (late Hambleton) "had been guilty of fornication, made evident by her having a ch too soon after marriage"; both Jehu Kinsey & Alice (Hambleton) Kinsey, his w, were dis 12-7-1817; Alice Kinsey made ack 1-9-1821 which was accepted & she was rein in

	mbrp; Alice Kinsey, w of Jehu, gct Deerfield MM, OH, 19-9-1829
John	of Little Brittain, Lancaster Co, PA; form of Buckingham MM, Bucks Co, PA
	rocf Buckingham MM with w & ch (listed below) dtd 1801
Mary Rice	dt Edward & Elizabeth; their res Little Brittain
	(A note says: "Recorded heretofore in Buckingham MM, PA)
	d 22- 5-1816, age 63y 1m 24d
Ch: Alice	b 27- 1-1775 d 20- 9-1863, bur Salem, OH, m John Matthews (3rd w)
Elizabeth	b 7- 3-1777
Hannah	b " d 14- 2-1837, age 61y, bur Eastland
Abel	b 13- 6-1779 m Edith Whitacker, who d 10-2-1828 in 42nd yr
Phebe	b 18- 6-1782, m Job White
Seth	b 23- 1-1785 m Rachel Pickering
Elam	b 9- 4-1787 d 15-10-1787 (not listed in cert)
Ashur	b " d 24-10-1787 (" " " ")
	John, with others, disf jas (Separatists: Orth) 14-3-1829
Joseph	(form Philadelphia; rocf Philadelphia MM, PA by New Garden MM, 708-1790, dtd 28-5-1790; disf mou by New Garden MM, PA, 2-4-1796, rein by his req 7-7-1814; gct Little Brittain MM, PA, by New Garden MM, 4-8-1814)
Elizabeth	m ca 1796 (mou)
	Joseph Kinsey rocf New Garden MM, PA 6-8-1814, dtd 4-8-1814; Elizabeth, his w & their 5 minor ch rec on req 18-9-1814
Ch: William	b 1- 3-1798
Robert C	b 9-12-1801
Eliza Ann	b 15- 7-1804

Maria	b 18-12-1806	
Thomas	b 8- 8-1809	
	Joseph & Elizabeth Kinsey & their 5 minor ch listed above, gct Westland MM, PA 12-11-1814	
Oliver	gct Baltimore MM for W Dist 9-2-1811	
Seth	b 23- 1-1785, s John & Mary (Rice) of Little Brittain Twp, Lancaster Co, PA (form of Buckingham MM, Bucks Co, PA	
Rachel Pickering	b 31- 1-1786, dt Jesse & Ann, of Little Brittain Twp, Lancaster Co, PA	
	rptd m 8-6-1811	
	Seth & Rachel (Pickering) & 2 minor ch Mary R & Charles Clark, gct Deer Creek MM, MD 13-6-1835 (Other ch granted separate cert same mtg.)	
Ch: Ann	b 18- 7-1812, gct Deer Creek MM, MD 18-7-1835	
Elam	b 12- 3-1814, " " " " 13-6-1835	
Mary R	b 5- 2-1818, " " " " "	
Charles Clark	b 24- 9-1820, " " " " "	
Thomas	gct Baltimore MM for Western Dist, MD 3-2-1820	

KIRK

Deborah	(now Webster, w of Samuel) rptd 16-1-1830 by Little Brittain PM to have been mcd to Samuel Webster, both mbrs; her ack acc 13-3-1830
Hannah B	gct Nottingham MM, MD 16-11-1833, to be forwarded
Hannah	(late Stubbs) rptd by Little Brittain PM 19-5-1832 as mcd; her ack acc 16-6-1832, ret mbr
Jacob	rptd by Eastland PM to have ack his mcd to his form wife's sister before a Justice of the Peace; disf same 8-6-1816

1st w Sarah England m 3- 3-1803 d 28- 4-1812
2nd w Hannah Haines England, sister of Sarah & dt John & Elizabeth (Gatchell) mcd d 16-11-1873
Hannah Haines (England) Kirk was dis 1816 by Nottingham for her m to Jacob Kirk; she was rein by Little Brittain MM 18-12-1824 by consent of Nottingham MM

Ch: (by 1st w Sarah)
 John   b 9- 1-1804
 Mary   b 8- 4-1805   d 21- 6-1826, age 21y 2m 13d, bur Eastland
 Roger   b 3- 3-1807   d 4- 6-1807
 Hannah   b 22- 1-1809
 (by 2nd w Hannah H)
 Sarah   b 1- 2-1817   rec on req 19- 2-1825
 Rachel England b 26- 3-1820   " " " "
 Elizabeth   b 12- 9-1822   " " " "
 Levi   b 14- 3-1825   " " " 15-10-1831
 Mary (2)   b 16- 5-1827   " " " "
 Lewis Jacob   b 9-11-1829   " " " "

Jane   (late Milner) rptd by Women's Mtg 16-4-1836 as mou; her ack acc 13-8-1836, ret a mbr

Jeremiah   of Little Brittain, Lancaster Co, PA
        b 24- 5-1815, s John & Deborah (Brown) of same place

Eliza P
Ch: Hannah I   b 20- 3-1841
 Sarah Ann   b 7- 2-1843
 Deborah Brown b 21- 1-1848
 Anna Rebecca b 26- 5-1851

John   of Little Brittain, Lancaster Co, PA
        b 23- 3-1781 d 9- 9-1853, age 73y, bur Little Brittain Grvyd s Roger & Rachel (Hughes)

Deborah Brown		b 25- 5-1782 d 21- 5-1845, age 63y, bur Little Brittain Grvyd dt Jeremiah & Hannah (England) (Hannah being his 1st w, d 1801) rptd m 11-7-1807
Ch:	Rachel	b 2- 5-1808 d 21- 5-1814, bur Little Brittain Grvyd
	Deborah	b 15- 9-1810
	Hannah	b 4- 1-1813
	Jeremiah	b 24- 5-1815
	Rachel (2)	b 9- 8-1818 d 14- 4-1854, age 35y 8m 1d, Philadelphia m ------ Irwin
	Mercy	b 9-12-1820
	John	b 12- 9-1823 d 10- 8-1824
	Slater B	b 18- 7-1825 d 17- 3-1848, age 22y, bur Little Brittain Note: John Kirk (above) was a twin with Timothy Kirk.
Mary		(late Brown) rptd herself 17-9-1836 as mou; her ack acc 19-11-1836
Sarah		(late Brown) rptd 16-7-1836 as mou; her ack acc 15-10-1836, ret mbr
Timothy		rocf Nottingham MM 17-9-1831, dtd 12-8-1831
Mary		w of Timothy, rocf Nottingham MM, MD 12-10-1811, dtd 6-9-1811 Jacob & Rachel Kirk, minor ch of Timothy & Mary rec on req of the mother, Mary Kirk, with approval of the father, Timothy Kirk, 6-5-1815 Mary & her 2 minor ch, Jacob & Rachel, gct Nottingham MM, MD, 10-6-1815

LAMBORN

Ann	gct London Grove MM, PA 6-12-1817

Benjamin	rocf London Grove MM, PA 17-8-1822, dtd 8-5-1822
Benjamin Rachel Bradley	rptd m 14-2-1824, surviving parents giving consent Benjamin & Rachel (Bradley) gct New Garden MM, PA, 19-6-1824
George	b 23-12-1768 d 19- 9-1856 in Knox Co, OH, bur Millwood s Robert & Ann (Bourne) of Kennet & London Grove, Chester Co, PA
1st w Martha Marshall	d 6- 5-1804, age 33y, bur Kennett, PA m 2-12-1790
2nd w Mary Smedley	b 7-11-1783 d 10- 1-1857, dt John & Susannah (Dawson-Cowgill) Smedley, of Willistown m 14- 3-1806 George & Mary (Smedley) & 5 ch, viz: Lewis, Thomas, Ann, Marshall & Smedley, rocf Kennett MM, 8-8-1807, dtd 6 mo-1807

Ch: (by 1st w)

Lewis	b 7- 9-1791	m Phebe West
Thomas	b 13- 5-1793	m Lydia Bradley
Ann	b 24- 3-1795	m Joseph Fell
Benjamin	b 25- 9-1797	m Rachel Bradley
Marshall	b 21- 4-1800	m Esther Michener
Lydia	b 6- 4-1802	m Jacob Baker
David	b 19- 4-1804	d 20- 4-1804

(by 2nd w)

Smedley	b 6- 1-1807	d 26- 9-1851	m Margaret Bolton
Susanna	b 8-10-1808	d 28- 1-1871	m David Frazier
John	b 9-10-1810	d 24- 3-1891	m Harriet Cummings & Helen Michel

Esther	b 10-10-1812	m Joseph Kinney		
Robert	b 1- 5-1816	d 30- 6-1818		
Mary	b 25- 7-1818	d 3- 8-1818		
Philena	b 11-10-1819	d 1mo-1821		
Jacob	b 11- 4-1822	d 8- 5-1856	m Polly S Hollister	
Lindley	b 28-12-1824	d 12- 3-1881	m Margaretta Jane Benninghuff	
Martha	b 13-12-1828	d 14- 1-1862	m Orange J Hollister & Philip Yarnal	

George & Mary (Smedley) & their minor ch, viz: John, Esther, Jacob, Lindley & Martha gct Smithfield MM, Jefferson Co, OH, 14-7-1832; to be forwarded

Jesse
Letitia   Both & s Joseph Cox Lamborn, rocf Kennett MM, PA, 6-7-1811, dtd 4-6-1811

Ch: Joseph Cox   b 7-12-1810   d 9 mo-1815, age 5y, bur Kennet Sq
     Joannah   b 13- 9-1812
     Mary Ann   b 1- 8-1814
     Martha   b 17- 5-1816
     Elizabeth   b 9-10-1818
     Clarkson   b 16- 2-1821
     Alexander   b 2- 2-1823

Jesse Lamborn of this record was dis 4-5-1822 for bringing a suit at law against a Friend & refusing to withdraw it, pay the costs & settle the matter among Friends. He appealed to the QM & to the YM; both decided against him.

Lewis   rem some time past, gct Sadsbury MM, PA, 18-11-1826; to be forwarded

Marshall   gct New Garden MM, PA 17-9-1823
Richard
Alice   (who was dt George & Mary Owens)

Smedley		Both with dt Mary, gct Nottingham MM, MD, 12-4-1806 (Note: They were mbrs of Eastland PM) of Drumore Twp, Lancaster Co, PA b 6- 1-1807 d 26- 9-1851 in 44th yr, bur Drumore MH Grvyd, Lancaster Co, PA s George & 2nd w Mary (Smedley) of Drumore Twp, Lancaster Co, PA, later of OH
Margaret Bolton		b 26- 8-1810 d 21-11-1855, age 45y, bur Drumore Grvyd dt Isaac & Elizabeth of Liberty Square, Lancaster Co, PA m 22-12-1830 Smedley Lamborn was a blacksmith & farmer & a dealer in horses which he brought fr OH to sell.
Ch:	George S	b 24-11-1831 m Sarah W Coates
	Acquila B	b 23- 2-1833 m Ann M Ambler
	Emeline	b 30- 9-1834 d 11 mo-1880 m Joseph L Shoemaker
	Elwood	b 4- 8-1836 d 14- 4-1878 m Elmira Moore
	William L	b 6- 1-1839 d 4- 7-1876 m Phebe M Barnard
	Mary E	b 22- 6-1840 m Thomas B Hambleton
	Sarah E	b 8-11-1842 m Jacob K Brown
	Priscilla S	b 19- 1-1845 d 27- 2-1847, bur Drumore
	Alice Anna	b 14- 4-1847 m William L Shoemaker
	Lucinda	b 22- 8-1849 m Benjamin F Tennis
	Lydia S	b 29-10-1851 m Amos G Smith
		Smedley Lamborn gct New Garden MM, (?) 16-8-1828; rocf New Garden MM 13-6-1829 (Note: Smedley Lamborn & Margaret Bolton were rptd m 15-1-1831 by Little Brittain MM, PA)
Susannah		b 8-10-1808 d 28- 1-1871 dt George & Mary (Smedley), rptd 16-5-1829 by Drumore PM to have been mou to David Frazier; disf same 15-8-1829

Thomas	b 13- 5-1793, s George & Martha (Marshall), dec, (she being his 1st w) of Little Brittain MM, PA, form of Kennett MM & London Grove MM, PA
Lydia Bradley	dt George & Mary of Little Brittain MM, PA, form of Bradford MM, PA
	rptd m 30-3-1822
	Thomas & Lydia (Bradley) Lamborn & minor s, Gilpin, gct New Garden MM, PA 19-4-1823
Townsend	w Ann, & s Aaron rocf Bradford MM, PA, 12-9-1807, dtd 7 mo-1807 (It was rptd that this fam & the fam of George Lamborn lived remote fr the mtg.) Townsend & Ann & their 3 ch, viz: Aaron, Israel & Clayton, gct Bradford MM, PA, 11-4-1809

LEA
Margaret	rec on req 17-5-1828

LEE
Rebecca	rec on req 16-6-1827

LEWIS
Minerva W	"presented" an ack for mou, 13-12-1834; ack acc 17-1-1835 (Note: she is not identified otherwise); gct White Water MM, IN 14-11-1835

LIVEZEY
Ezra	s of Jonathan, rem with father, gct Deerfield MM (?), 13-6-1829
Jonathan	s Daniel, dec, & Margery
Mary King	b 24- 7-1779 d 16- 3-1816
	dt Vincent, dec, & Mary (Brown) of Little Brittain Twp, Chester Co, PA
	m 1804
	Jonathan rptd rem & mcd 13-6-1829; disf same 17-4-1830 on rpt fr Deerfield MM, OH that he declined to make satisfaction

Ch:	Mary	b 27-11-1808
	Ezra	b 8-2-1812; gct Deerfield MM (?) 13-6-1829

LLOYD
Abel   req mbrp 6-10-1804; accepted 9-2-1805
On 7-9-1805, Eastland PM informed this Mtg that Abel Lloyd has been guilty of fornication with (Ann Reynolds) the woman he has since m through a Magistrate. Both dis 12-10-1805

LONG
Mary   late Reynolds, rptd guilty of fornication & mou since 6-10-1810; disf same 8-12-1810

LUKENS
Isaac   & w Hannah & their 5 minor ch, viz: John, Joseph, Marshall, Levi & Martha rocf New Garden MM, PA, 12-5-1810, dtd 5-4-1810; on various occasions Isaac Lukens has been dealt with for "taking too much strong drink"; after long care, with continued deviations by him, he was disf same 8-3-1817

John   s of Isaac, gct Wilmington MM, Del, 9-1-1819

Joseph   rptd by Drumore PM 2-6-1821 to have joined the M.E. Ch, dis 30-6-1821

Levi   s Isaac & Hannah, rem, gct Sadsbury MM, PA 13-6-1829

Mahlon   s Isaac & Hannah, rem, rpts he has joined the M.E. Ch, & wishes to be disunited fr us; granted 13-6-1829

Marshall   s Isaac & Hannah
"rptd by the comm, named to find the present addresses of Marshall, Levi & Mahlon Lukens, sons of

	Isaac & Hannah, to have found them all living within the verge of Sadsbury MM, PA & that Marshall had m a woman not in mbrp with us", 16-5-1829. On 13-6-1829 the comm rptd that Mahlon Lukens had j M.E.Ch; & wished to be disunited from this Mtg, which was acc; & they produced a cert Sadsbury MM, PA, for Levi Lukens, which is approved, signed & to be forwarded; Marshall dis for mou 17-10-1829 on rpt fr Sadsbury MM, PA
Martha (Lucans)	a minor, dt Isaac & Hannah Lukens, gct Wilmington MM, Del, 15-11-1824
Perry Mary	Both & ch, viz: Jane, Henry, Moore, Thomas, Richard, & Harriet, rocf Gwynedd MM, PA, 12-6-1813, dtd 1-4-1813; Perry & w Mary & their 6 minor ch, viz: Jane, Henry, Thomas, Richard, Harriet & Priscilla, gct Philadelphia MM, for N. Dist, 9-11-1816, as req by the father in 4mo last; it is rptd that another ch has since been born, whose name is unknown to the Mtg. On 10-5, it was rptd that Perry had ret the cert, with the information that he found he was living within the compass of Green St MM, Philadelphia, & had not deposited his cert with the Philadelphia MM, N.D. & wished another to Green St, in its place; it was also rptd that Perry had been keeping unprofitable company & had been taking strong drink to excess. Perry was dis on rpt fr Green St MM, Philadelphia; his w, Mary & their ch (listed above) gct Green St MM, Philadelphia, PA, 7-6-1817
McCLEARY Hannah	(late Reynolds) rptd 19-8-1826 by Eastland mou; dis 16-9-1826

McCULLOUGH
Susanna — (late Reynolds) rpts 7-10-1815 "guilty of fornication which is evident by her becoming a mother too early after marriage, which was accomplished by assistance of a Justice of the Peace, with a man not in mbrp with Friends"; disf same 9-12-1815; her ack acc & she rein 16-6-1827

McGINNIS
Mary — (form Reynolds) rptd 14-8-1824 as mou; her ack acc 18-6-1825, gct Short Creek MM, OH, 16-9-1826

McGOUGH
Ann — (late Atkinson) rptd 17-5-1834 by Women's Mtg as mou; disf same 19-7-1834

McMILLAN
Mahlon
Rachel (Richards) — Both & their s William, rocf Nottingham MM, 18-7-1829, dtd 16-5-1829;
Mahlon & Rachel & their minor ch, viz: William, Ruth, Hannah, & Thomas, gct Short Creek MM, OH, 13-8-1836

MARSHALL
Tabitha — (late Pickering) rptd 8-11-1817 by Eastland PM to Women's Mtg; disf same 10-1-1818

MARTIN
Edith — (late Penrose) rptd by Little Brittain PM 19-1-1833; disf same 16-3-1833

MASON
Benjamin — a minute issued for him to att next YM, Baltimore, 6-10-1804 (Note: he was a minister of importance)
Sarah Swayne — m at Kennett MM, PA

		(Note: Their 5 ch are listed in New Garden MM, & were as follows:
Ch:	George	b 17- 5-1783
	Benjamin Jr	b 19- 6-1785 m Sarah Stubbs, 1820
	Jane	b 3- 9-1788
	Mary	b 3- 1-1791 cert Kennett MM with parents 9-5-1812
	Sarah Jr	b 9- 3-1793 " " " " "

Note: This fam was trans fr Nottingham MM, MD to Little Brittain MM, Lancaster Co, PA, when the latter MM was set off fr Nottingham MM, 1804

Benjamin & Sarah (Swayne) & their s Benjamin Jr, gct Kennett MM, PA 9-5-1812; this cert also including John Griffith, a minor, at req of Benjamin Mason.

Note: The dts, Mary Sarah Jr, rec separate certs

George b 17- 5-1783   d 27- 7-1841, bur E Nottingham
s Benjamin & Sarah (Swayne), of Little Brittain Twp, Lancaster Co, PA
gct Nottingham MM, MD, 12-12-1807, clear to m

Tabitha Paxon m 21- 1-1808   bur 17-2-1856, E Nottingham Grvyd
dt Joseph & Mary (Kimble) of E Nottingham Twp, Chester Co, PA, the latter dec 29-11-1814, age about 56y, bur E Nottingham Grvyd
George gct Nottingham MM, MD, 9-7-1808; rocf Nottingham MM, MD 15-9-1827, dtd 17-8-1827

Benjamin Jr b 19- 6-1785, s Benjamin & Sarah (Swayne) (form of Little Brittain MM) of Kennett MM, PA
prcf Kennett MM, PA, 29-4-1820 to m

Sarah Stubbs rptd m 3-6-1820
Sarah (Stubbs) w of Benjamin Jr, gct Kennett MM, PA, 1-7-1820

Jane gct Kennett MM, PA 9-1-1813

MATTHEWS
John   b 22-2-1760   d 22-11-1835
                              s Thomas & Rachel (Price) of Gunpowder MM, MD,
                              form dec (m 1st Leah Price, m 2nd Martha Yarnall)
                              prcf Gunpowder MM, MD to m
3rd w Alice Kinsey   b 27-1-1775   d 20-9-1863, age 87y & ca 10m,
                              bur Salem, OH
                              dt John & Mary (Rice) of Little Brittain Twp,
                              Lancaster Co, PA & form of Buckingham MM,
                              Bucks Co, PA
                              m 7-9-1805, Little Brittain MH, at close of the Mtg
                              (Issue 6 ch; see Gunpowder MM, MD)
                              Alice (Kinsey) Matthews, w of John, gct Gunpowder
                              MM, MD, 7-12-1805 "to join husband"

William   prcf Gunpowder MM, MD, 14-2-1835 to m
Sarah Brown   rptd m 14-3-1835, at Little Brittain Mtg
                              Sarah (Brown) Matthews, w of Wm, gct Gunpowder
                              MM, MD, 18-4-1835 "to join husband" (Note: She
                              was 3rd w of Wm)

MAXWELL
Catharine   (late Jackson) rptd 18-10-1834 as mou; disf same 13-
                              12-1834

MAYBERRY
Esther   (late Allen) rptd 10-12-1814 by Eastland PM, as mou,
                              disf same 11-2-1815

MIFLIN
Joseph   gct Sadsbury MM, PA to m
Martha Huston   a mbr of that Mtg.
                              Martha (Huston) Miflin, w of Joseph, rocf Sadsbury
                              MM, PA, 9-5-1807, dtd 7-10-1806 "to join husband";
                              Joseph & Martha (Huston) & their s John, gct
                              Burlington MM, NJ, 12-9-1807; signed & sent

MILHOUSE
Margaret   d 27- 4-1809

MILLER
Thomas   s John & Sarah (Mitchell) of Bucks Co, PA
                             d bef 1827   prcf Falls MM, PA to m
Mary Ballance   rptd m 9-11-1811
                             dt Joseph & Anna (Pownall) of Little Brittain Twp, Lancaster Co, PA
                             Mary (Ballance) Miller, w of Thomas, gct Falls MM, PA, 11-1-1812 "to join husband"
                             Mary (Ballance) Miller, w of Thomas & their minor s, Thomas rocf Falls MM, PA 11-9-1813, dtd 11-6-1813
                             (Note: Mary, wid of Thomas Miller, m 2nd 1827 Benjamin Harlan as his 2nd w & had 2 more ch named Harlan)
Ch: Thomas   b 29-11-1812

MILNER
Cyrus   s Nathan & Mary of this Mtg
Sarah Carter   b 10-10-1785, dt Samuel & 2nd w Ruth (Taylor) of this Mtg rptd m 10-5-1806
                             (Nathan Milner, Sr, d 9-4-1808, age 66y, bur Eastland)
Ch: Ruth   b   9- 1-1807   mou rptd 19-6-1830 to ----- Pierce; dis
     Joseph   b 11- 3-1808
     Hester   b   3-10-1809   d   18- 2-1833, age 24y m ------ Peirce
     Samuel   b   2- 4-1811
     Jane   b 15- 3-1813
     Nathan   b 18- 1-1815
     Abner   b 19- 1-1817
     Cyrus Jr   b   2- 2-1819
     Emmor   b   8- 7-1822
                             Jehu Milner (not identified) d 27-5-1815, age 23y 10m 5d, bur Eastland

	Cyrus--Eastland PM rptd 8-10-1814 that Cyrus Milner, having been drafted for Militia service, hired his brother, Isaac, to go as substitute in his place; his ack acc 11-2-1815 (Note: Isaac had offered to go in his place & Cyrus acc & paid his brother to go.)
Elizabeth	gct Nottingham MM, MD, 10-9-1813
Isaac	s Nathan & Mary, rptd by Eastland PM 8-10-1814 to have offered to go as a substitute for his brother, Cyrus Milner (who had been drafted for military service) & on Cyrus having acc the offer & having paid Isaac a sum of money, Isaac had joined the army & had gone away; he was disf same 11-3-1815
Mary	(now Mary Sidwell Jr) rptd mou 11-1-1817 to Joseph Sidwell, (nm); her ack acc 12-4-1817; gct Nottingham MM, MD, 12-7-1817
Mary	& her son Daniel "rem some time past to the State of Illinois" gct White Water MM, IN, 15-7-1837 "White Water MM being the nearest MM to their new res."

MONTGOMERY

Ann	(late Wood) rptd 1-6-1822 by Eastland PM, as mou before a hireling minister (Note: A later entry gives the above date as 19-10-1822) dis 18-1-1823

MOORE

Elizabeth M	rocf Goshen MM, PA, 12-9-1818, dtd 7-7-1818
Hibberd	a minor, rocf New Garden MM, PA 13-3-1824, dtd 6-2-1824; gct New Garden MM, PA, 14-7-1827

Isaac		
Elizabeth, his w		Both now rec fr Cornwell MM (?) 6-8-1808, dtd 24-12-1807; but they having about a yr ago rem to within the compass of Rahway MM, NJ, their cert was end to that Mtg, 10-9-1808
Jacob		d 8- 3-1867, bur Eastland, Res Fulton, age 86y
Hannah		d 15- 8-1850, in 70th yr, bur Eastland; late res Fulton
Ch: Sarah		b 23- 5-1814 d 4- 4-1830, age 15y
Jacob Jr		b 21- 5-1822
		Jacob & w Hannah rocf Nottingham MM, MD, 11-7-1812, dtd 5-6-1812
Joshua		rptd 15-5-1825 by Sadsbury MM, PA, to have "been guilty of fornication with a woman whom he has since married"; Little Brittain is asked to treat with him; he ack the charge against him, but did not make ack; the comm is directed to so inform Sadsbury MM; further attention his case is referred to that mtg, he now res nearer to them than us.
Richard		rocf Muncy MM (called Fishing Creek MM after 1855) PA, 12-9-1812, dtd 20-5-1812; d 23-1-1829, bur Little Brittain, late res at Levan Jackson's
Sarah		a cert fr Buckingham MM, PA, dtd 7-1-1805, for her, directed to Sadsbury MM & end to this Mtg by that, was produced; but, being informed that she had settled within the compass of Indian Spring MM, MD, her cert is directed to be end to that Mtg, 12-4-1806

MORRIS

Samuel Dawes   gct Philadelphia MM for Southern Dist, 8-10-1808

MURRY

Absolom (nm)   of Little Brittain Twp, Lancaster Co, PA

Ann Reynolds	m 1817 ca 12mo, before a Justice of the Peace
	b 19- 7-1794 d 5- 4-1827, dt Manuel & Sarah (Sargeant) of same place
	(Note: Ann Reynolds was rptd mou to Absolom Murry 6-12-1817; disf same 7-2-1818; rein in mbrp on her ack being acc 4mo-1820
Ch: Mary	b 8- 4-1819 rec in mbrp 14-6-1828 on req of Sarah Brown, w of David Brown, who was dt Henry & Mary (Haines) Reynolds, & therefore the Aunt of the above named Mary Murry

NEAL
William — a minor, gct Concord MM, PA 9-11-1811, signed & forwarded

NORRIS
Eleanor — rec on req 15-12-1832

NORTON
Stephen — rocf Deer Creek MM, MD, 9-2-1811, dtd 27-9-1810 Eastland QM rptd 11-12-1813 that Stephen Norton had been guilty of fornication, which he does not deny. Disf same 7-5-1814

PARRY
David
1st w Elizabeth E   d 20- 1-1816, age 37y, bur Drumore
2nd w Lydia Richardson
                    rptd m 10- 1-1818   d 8- 6-1845, age 60y 23d
Ch: (by 1st w)
    Ely   b 11-10-1804   gct Buckingham MM, PA 14-7-1827
    Letitia   b 20- 9-1806
    Rachel   b 9- 1-1808
    James   b 31- 8-1809
    John   b 9- 5-1811

	Seneca	b 13-12-1813 d 23- 8-1848, age 34y 8m 10d, m Priscilla
	Thomas (by 2nd w)	b 9- 1-1816 d 25- 1-1816
	Samuel	b 17- 9-1818 d 3- 3-1879, age 60y 5m 16d, m Hannah
	Elizabeth	b 29- 1-1820
	Sarah	b 24-10-1821 d 25- 1-1840, age 18y 3m, bur Drumore
	David Jr	b 14- 1-1823 d 31- 5-1852, age 29y 4m 16d, bur Forest
	Joseph	b 29- 3-1825
	Ruthanna	b 18- 4-1827
John		gct York MM, PA 14-12-1833
John		rocf Buckingham MM, PA 10-12-1814, dtd 1-8-1814; gct Buckingham MM, PA 6-1-1816
Samuel		b 17- 9-1818 d 3- 3-1879, age 60y 5m 16d, bur Little Brittain s David & Lydia of Little Brittain; res Drumore
Hannah Ch:	Mary L	b 15- 4-1876 d 17- 7-1876, bur Little Brittain Grvyd
Seneca		b 13-12-1813 d 23- 8-1848, age 34y 8m 10d, bur Drumore Res Drumore, Lancaster Co, PA s David & 1st w Elizabeth E, dec, of Little Brittain, Lancaster Co, PA
Priscilla Ch:	John S	b 4- 1-1843
	Letitia	b 5-11-1844
	Mary Anna	b 5- 4-1846
Thomas		rocf Gwynedd MM, PA 12-2-1814, dtd 7 mo-1813; gct Buckingham MM, PA 8-11-1817

PASSMORE
Abijah   rocf Green St, Philadelphia MM, PA 29-4-1820, dtd
                        23-3-1820, gct Nottingham MM, MD, 13-7-1822
                        rocf Nottingham MM, MD, 18-2-1826, dtd 13-1-
                        1826
Naomi   rec on req 13-2-1830
                        Their ch Deborah Ann & Mary rec on req 19-2-1831
                        on req of parents
Ch: Hannah W   b   5- 7-1830
     Deborah Ann   b   rec on req 19-2-1831
     Mary   b   "   "   "   "
                        Abijah & w Naomi & ch, viz: Deborah Ann, Mary &
                        Hannah W, gct Cherry St MM, Philadelphia, PA, 16-
                        7-1831

Andrew M (Moore)
Judith Wilson   Both & their 4 minor ch, first listed below, excepting
                        Josiah Kirk who d in infancy, rocf Nottingham MM,
                        MD, 15-8-1835, dtd 17-7-1835
Ch: Phebe Pusey   b 30- 8-1821   m Enoch Mortimer Bye
     Samuel Wilson   b 18- 6-1824   m Emaline -----
     Ruth Moore   b   2- 4-1827
     Josiah Kirk   b 26- 5-1831   d 25- 3-1832
     George Birdsall b   4- 3-1833   m Elizabeth Passmore Broomall
     Lydia Emma   b 16- 4-1836
     Mary Elizabeth   b 19- 2-1839
     Hannah Ann   b   3-10-1842   d ca 30-6-1880,
                                      m Seneca P Broomall
     Ellis Andrew   b 17- 1-1847   d   5- 4-1848

John W   b   1-11-1802, s Ellis & Ruth (Moore) of Not-
                        tingham MM, MD
                        d 25- 6-1848, in 46th yr, bur Eastland, Chester Co,
                        PA
Deborah Brown   b 12- 1-1801, dt Samuel & Elizabeth of Little
                        Brittain MM (both mbrs of Society of Friends)

rptd 14-6-1823 by Eastland PM as mcd before Justice of the Peace; Deborah's ack acc 17-9-1823

Deborah (Brown) Passmore, w of John W, & her infant s, Ellis Pusey Passmore, gct Nottingham MM, MD 13-11-1824; John W & Deborah (Brown) & minor s Ellis P rocf Nottingham MM, MD, 13-1-1827, dtd 13-10-1826

Ch: Ellis Pusey   b   4- 8-1823
    Samuel B   b 13-12-1827
    Elizabeth R   b 12-11-1830
    John Andrew M   b 30- 6-1836

On 19- 3-1836 John W Passmore, having a dispute with a mbr of another Mtg, req permission of this Mtg to sue the other man at law; such action being contrary to rules of Discipline, the Mtg on 14-6-1836 refused permission.

PAXON
Elwood H
Elizabeth M White   rptd 19-10-1833 by Eastland PM as mcd, both being mbrs of the Society of Friends; ack acc fr each of them 16-11-1833; ret mbrs
dt Job & Phebe (Kinsey) White

Ch: Caroline   b 30- 5-1834
    Edith K   b 14- 1-1836
    Marian   b 14-11-1837
    Sarah J   b 26- 9-1839   d 31-11-1842, age 2y 10m 5d
    Hannah   b   7-11-1842   d   9-10-1845, age 2y 11m 2d
    Irene   b 22- 4-1845
    Leeta   b 15- 9-1851   d 15- 9-1863, age 12y
    Elwood Franklin   b   6-11-1853

Henry   b 12- 8-1804   d 12- 9-1865
s Joseph & Hannah (Harlan), dec, of Little Brittain MM, PA

Rachel B Job	d 15- 6-1851, dt Jacob & Letitia of same Mtg
	m 17-10-1827

2nd w Marib (Miller) Johnson, a widow, dt John & Hannah (Pillow) Miller
    m ca 1854

Ch: (by 1st w)

	Hannah Letitia	b 5- 8-1831	d 4-10-1836, bur Little Brittain
	Eliza Ann	b 15- 3-1834	m Isaac Massey
	Sarah Matilda	b 28- 4-1837	d 24- 5-1862
	Joseph Henry	b 4- 8-1839	d 9- 3-1855, bur Eastland
	Mary Louisa	b 16- 4-1842	d 1-11-1890 m George Pierce
	Martha Letitia	b 6-11-1844	M Wesley Young
	Alice	b 25- 2-1847	d 12- 2-1864
	Elwood	b 18- 6-1849	m Mary Jane Swisher, 14-3-1872
	(by 2nd w)		
	Orick	b 5- 9-1855	m Roberta Kennedy
	Howard L	b 13- 4-1860	m Elvisa Kirk (dt Theodore ?), 24-11-1886

John	b 21- 1-1786	d 29- 9-1820 in New Garden, bur New Garden
	s Henry & Matilda (Kimble) of New Garden, Chester Co, PA from Bucks Co, PA
Abigail Mercer	b 18- 3-1787	d 23- 2-1868, at Joseph Pyle's in E. Marlboro, bur Kennett Sq
	dt Solomon & Abigail (Sharpless) of E Marlboro
	m 16- 3-1809 at Kennett Mtg, PA
	John & Abigail (Mercer) & 3 minor ch, viz: Matilda H, Henry M & Abigail S, rocf New Garden MM, PA, 9-7-1814, dtd 9-6-1814
	(The ch's births listed below, are taken fr Sharpless Fam)

Ch:
	Matilda K	b 21-12-1809	d 19- 2-1879 m Nathan Brosius, s Henry & Mary (Roberts)
	Henry M	b 7- 9-1811	m Jane Pyle, dt Robert & Hannah (Clark)
	Abigail S	b 1-10-1813	d 22-10-1862 m William Young

Sarah L		b 11-10-1815 m Abram P Bennett, s Joseph & Lydia (Bailey)
Julianna		b 17- 9-1817 m Joseph Pyle, s John & Amy (Pennock)
Phebe W		b 4-11-1819 d 12- 8-1881, m Wm Gause, s Samuel & Mary (Beverly)
John S		b 27- 3-1821 m Lavina James, dt Thomas & Sarah (Richardson)

John & Abigail (Mercer) Paxon & minor ch, viz: Matilda K, Henry M & Abigail S gct New Garden MM, PA 10-6-1815; to be forwarded.

Joseph   b 15-12-1779 in Chester Co, PA
                       s Henry & Matilda (Kimble) of New Garden Twp, Chester Co, PA

Hannah Harlan 1st w   b 24-11-1780   d 24- 6-1806, dt James & Elizabeth (Swayne) of Little Brittain Twp, Chester Co, PA
                       m 2-11-1803

2nd w Sarah Dutton a widow of Kennett
                       m 16- 2-1809 at New Garden MH, PA

Ch: (by 1st w)

Henry   b 12- 8-1804   m (1) Rachel Job; (2) Marib Johnson (Miller)

Hannah   b 20- 6-1806   d 24- 6-1806

Joseph & s Henry gct New Garden MM, PA, 10-1-1807

Joseph & Sarah (Dutton) & s Henry rocf New Garden MM, PA, 10-6-1809, dtd 6-4-1809

Sarah   (late Harlan) dt James & Elizabeth (Swayne) of Little Brittain MM; rptd by Eastland PM mou before a Justice of the Peace; rptd mou 12-12-1818; her ack acc 10-4-1819; gct New Garden MM, PA 12-6-1819
(Note: She m Isaac Paxon, s Henry & Martha (Kimble); b 12-6-1798; d 25-1-1850 in Richmond, IN; Sarah (Harlan) Paxon was b 12-6-1798; d 12-8-1835, in

Richmond, IN; bur there; she d of typhus fever; she was a mbr of White Water MM, having been recd there on cert fr Little Brittain MM, PA, 27-5-1835, dtd 14-3-1835. Isaac Paxon was disf disunity by New Garden MM, PA 1817, & was never rein, as far as shown.) Sarah Paxon rocf New Garden MM, PA 17-5-1823, dtd 10-4-1823

Ch: (of Isaac & Sarah (Harlan) Paxon)
 Mary Swayne b 16-10-1819 d 17- 6-1882 m Marcutia C Lewis, 1841
 Henry James b 24- 4-1821 d 2 mo-1823
 Hannah Harlan b 8- 7-1823 d 19- 3-1864 m Edwin Parks, 1845
 John Milton b 7- 5-1825 m Nancy Warren & Elizabeth Battery
 Rebecca Jane b 6- 5-1827 d 7- 5-1844, unm
 Sarah M b 18- 3-1829 m Oliver P White, 1849
 Isaac Harlan b 15- 8-1834 m Ellen C Thomas, 1855

Sarah (Harlan) Paxon, w of Isaac, gct White Water MM, IN, 14-3-1835

PEIRCE

Ellis rec on req 7-8-1819
  d 27- 3-1830, age 33y

Phebe Furnis b 31- 7-1798 d 9- 6-1849, age 50y 10m 9d, bur Eastland
  dt Thomas & Mary of Little Brittain, form of Buckingham MM, Bucks Co, PA

Ch: Taylor b 10- 7-1822
 Mary b 4- 8-1824
 Rachel b 10- 5-1827

Esther (late Milner) rptd 19-5-1832 by Eastland PM, as mou; her ack acc 14-7-1832

Rachel rocf London Grove MM, PA 14-5-1825, dtd 5-4-1825
  d 7- 1-1862, age 87y

PENNOCK

Lea		rocf London Grove MM, PA 17-2-1827, dtd 4-10-1826 rem, gct New Garden MM, PA 16-5-1829
Simon		d 26-12-1868, age 87y 3m, bur Drumore; late res Drumore
Sarah		d 1- 8-1867, age 87y 3m, bur Drumore

Both with 4 minor ch, viz: Martha, Hadley, Robert L, & Joanna rocf Kennett MM, PA 6-7-1816, dtd 7-5-1816

Ch:	Martha	b (See Kennett MM)
	Hadley	b "
	Robert L	b "
	Joanna	b "
	Mary H	b 5-11-1818 at Little Brittain

PENROSE

Benjamin Res Drumore Twp, Lancaster Co, PA
rptd 18-4-1835 as mcd to a woman in mbrp; ack acc 16-5-1835

Hannah rptd mcd 18-4-1835
Hannah Penrose rocf Gwynedd MM, PA 13-8-1836, dtd 3- 6-1836

Ch:	Lukens	b 3- 3-1836 d 3- 1-1837, age 10m, bur Drumore
	Edith	b 3- 5-1837
	Everard	b 19- 8-1839
	Israel	b 9- 6-1841
	Lukens (2)	b 6- 9-1845
	Ann E	b 24- 1-1848
	Sarah S	b 10-10-1852
	Charles S	b 8- 1-1853 d 31- 7-1853, age 6m 24d, bur Drumore

Jane (sister of the above Benjamin Penrose) d 23-7-1870, age 69y 5m 25d, bur Drumore MH Grvyd

Jane F	rocf Buckingham MM, PA 16-6-1827, dtd 7-5-1827
Susanna	(wife of Israel) & her minor son, Joseph, rocf Buckingham MM, PA 16-6-1827, dtd 7-5-1827

PERRY

Abigail   (form Churchman), dt William & Abigail (Brown) Churchman of East Nottingham Twp, Chester Co, PA, both dec
     b 12-11-1755   d 28- 8-1829; in her 74th yr
     rptd mcd 6-6-1807 to Rowland Perry (nm)
     her ack acc 12-12-1807
     Abigail get New Garden MM, PA 6-2-1808
     rocf New Garden MM, PA 7-7-1810, dtd 10-5-1810

PICKERING

Anthony   b 29- 6-1792, s Jesse & Ann
     rptd mcd by the assistance of a Justice of the Peace by Eastland PM, 6-6-1818; his ack acc 12-9-1818

1st w Joanna Reynolds, dt Reuben & Margaret (King)
     b 22-11-1788   d 3- 9-1833, bur Eastland MH
     rptd mcd by Eastland PM 6-6-1818 by the assistance of a Justice of the Peace; her ack acc 12-9-1818
     was mcd (rptd by himself & Eastland PM 19-12-1835) to

Sarah Hambleton   both made voluntary ack; Sarah's ack acc 16-4-1836;
   2nd w   but Anthony was dis 13-2-1836
     d 29-12-1858, age 78y, bur Eastland MH

Ch: (by 1st w)
     Phineas   b 20- 5-1820   d 9-12-1829, age near 10y
     Jonathan   b 14- 8-1822
     Elias   b 4- 7-1825

Jesse   asks a re-hearing of an arbitration award, which is unsatisfactory to him 4-8-1821; at the next mtg, the comm approved the award as proper; but Jesse still

	refused it; it was rptd 1-6-1822 that he had settled the matter satisfactorily; the case was dropped.
John	b 11- 2-1788 d 29-12-1857, near Kirk's Mills s Jesse & Ann (Kemble) of Little Brittain MM rptd 9-1-1813 by Eastland PM as mcd before a Justice of the Peace (by whom he was m to a mbr of this mtg) as follows:
1st w Sidney Sharpless, mcd ca 12 mo-1812	
	b 2- 3-1789 d 17-12-1820, dt Joseph & Mary (Hibberd) neither denies their mcd; their ack's were acc 10-4-1813; ret mbrs
2nd w Mary Wilkinson (nm) (name of w fr Sharpless Fam Bk, p 377)	
	John Pickering (above) was rptd 16-7-1825 by Eastland PM as mou; he was disf same 15-10-1825 On 18-6-1836 he produced an ack as per the following minute: Quote in part: "John Pickering, dis some time since by this Mtg produced an ack for his transgression & req rein, which was acc & he rein" (Note: not being in mbrp, his 2nd w's death is not listed in B&D; nor are ch by this m listed if any were born.)
3rd w Phebe King	b 26- 5-1786 d 25- 8-1865, age 79y dt James & Phebe (Pyle) King m 25- 8-1836 (no ch)
Ch: (of 1st w)	
Mary Ann	b 26- 1-1815 m Samuel Overholt
Hannah	b 3- 8-1816 m Pearson Holcomb (no issue)
Mercy	b 10- 6-1818 d young (unm)
	Note: Little Brittain B&D, p 43, lists Phebe as John Pickering's 2nd w; but she was his 3rd w, as shown by the above records minutes. WWH
Sidney	gct Goshen MM, PA 7-3-1818

PIERCE

Hannah	rec on req 13-10-1832

Hannah	(late Kirk) rptd by Eastland PM 16-2-1828 as mou to Isaac Pierce (nm); disf same 14-6-1828; her ack recd & acc & she rein in mbrp 14-8-1853; on 14-9-1833 Isaac Pierce & their 2 minor ch, viz: Sarah & Henry were rec on req in mbrp; Isaac & Hannah (Kirk) Pierce gct Fallowfield MM, PA 19-3-1836 (Note: The name is written 3 ways: Pierce, Peirce, Pearse)
Ruth	(late Milner) dt Cyrus & Sarah (Carter) Milner rptd 17-7-1830 by the Women's Mtg as mou; disf same 14-8-1830

PIERSON

Mary	(late Wilson) rptd by Eastland PM 17-5-1828 as mou; disf same 16-8-1828

PRESTON

Isaac	of Octoraro Hundred, Cecil Co, MD s Jonas & Elizabeth (Brown) of same place
Mary B Stewart	dt Joseph, dec, & Rachel (Bradway) (now m to David Griscom) m 28-11-1833, auspices of Nottingham MM, MD (Issue 4 ch, the 1st 2 b at Little Brittain; the 2nd 2 b at Nottingham; for full history see Nottingham MM, MD
Ch: Edward Stewart	b 7-12-1834
Jonas B	b 12- 6-1837 Isaac & w Mary B (Stewart) & their minor s Edward Stewart Preston rocf Nottingham MM, MD, 13-8-1836, dtd 17-6-1836

PRICE

Elizabeth	(form Ring) rptd mou by Concord MM, PA, 9-9-1807 & disf same by that Mtg 4-11-1807 is rein in mbrp by Little Brittain MM, PA 19-2-1825 with

	consent of Concord MM & recd by Little Brittain MM as a mbr
PUSEY	
Samuel	s Joshua & Mary, dec, of Drumore, PA
	rocf London Grove MM, PA 15-4-1826, dtd 5-4-1826; gct New Garden MM, PA 19-8-1826 to m
Elizabeth Pyle	m 14- 9-1826 at W Grove MH, under auspices of New Garden MM, PA
	dt Job & Ruth of London Grove MM, PA
	Elizabeth (Pyle) Pusey, w of Samuel, rocf New Garden MM, PA 18-11-1826
	Mary, w of Samuel Pusey Sr, d 18-4-1824, bur Little Brittain
	Elizabeth, w of Samuel Jr, d 13-10-1839, bur Little Brittain
	Samuel d 25-11-1843, age 70y, bur Little Brittain; res Drumore
PYLE	
Amos	of Little Brittain Twp, Lancaster Co, PA
	s Moses & 2nd w Mary (Cook), both dec
	(Moses & Mary & ch were trans to Little Brittain MM fr Nottingham MM, MD, about 1779, where Moses d 1784)
Ruth Stubbs	b 3-11-1766, dt Daniel & Ruth (Gilpin) dec, of same place
	m 10- 1-1793, Little Brittain MH, auspices of Nottingham MM, MD
	This fam (Amos, Ruth & 6 ch) gct Deer Creek MM, MD 9-5-1807
Ch: Sarah	b 20-12-1794
Daniel	b 10- 9-1796
John	b 2- 8-1798
Phebe	b 24- 3-1801
Joseph	b 18- 8-1803

	Amos	b 27- 2-1806 Amos rocf London Grove MM, PA 16-6-1827, dtd 9-5-1827; gct Fallowfield MM, PA, 13-11-1830
John		of Little Brittain Twp, Lancaster Co, PA b 2- 8-1798 d 11-12-1839, bur Little Brittain Grvyd s Amos & Ruth (Stubbs) of Drumore, Lancaster Co, PA
	Abi Good	b 26- 1-1805 d 14- 8-1854, bur Little Brittain dt Joseph & Martha (Michener) of West Grove, PA m 17- 3-1825, at West Grove MH, PA John & Abi (Good) Pyle & 3 ch, 1st listed below, rocf Nottingham MM, MD, 17-4-1830, dtd 12-3-1830
Ch:	Francenia	b 23-11-1825 d 5- 6-1846, age 20y 4m 18d, bur Little Brittain
	Alfred	b 17- 7-1827 d 15-12-1854, bur Little Brittain
	Harriett	b 27- 5-1829
	Martha	b 25- 5-1832
	William	b 4- 6-1834
John		rocf London Grove MM, PA, 4-12-1819, dtd 3-11-1819 gct London Grove MM, PA 2-2-1822
Joseph		rocf Deer Creek MM, MD, 16-8-1823, dtd 15-5-1823; gct 17-1-1829
Nathan		
Grace Cope		m 30- 5-1804, Eastland MM, auspices Nottingham Nathan, Grace & 2 ch: David & Elizabeth, gct Deer Creek MM, MD, 11-4-1807
Ch:	David	b 17- 4-1805
	Elizabeth	b 1-12-1806
Phebe		rocf Deer Creek MM, MD, 13-12-1823, dtd 11-9-1823; gct London Grove MM, PA, 15-1-1825

QUARRELL
Hannah   rocf Sadsbury MM, PA, 14-12-1826; but she having settled within the verge of Nottingham MM, MD, it is decided to transfer her cert to that MM
(Nottingham MM refused to acc her as a mbr; the matter was again taken up by Little Brittain MM, and it was found that she was retailing spiritous liquors; she promised to stop, but did not; finally on 16-12-1837, when again visited, she said she belonged with the Friends who had separated; disf jas of that date.)

QUINBY
Aaron
Lydia
Ch: Rachel   b 20- 4-1783   d at 3d old
     Phebe   b 3- 3-1785
     Charlotte   b 24- 9-1786   d 10- 9-1840
     Mary   b 20- 3-1788
     Jesse B   b 25- 5-1789
     Miriam   b 22-12-1790   m Benjamin Cutler, Jr, 1811
     Ezra   b 27-11-1793
     Aaron B   b 19- 8-1795   disf striking a man in anger, 12-12-1818
     Isaiah   b 27- 1-1799   gct Little Falls MM, MD, 30-6-1821

Aaron   rptd 16-9-1826 by Little Brittain PM to have "been guilty of fornication with a woman (not in mbrp with us) whom he has since married & which is fully shown by his having a child by her before his marriage with her; & that he does not deny the charge." He is willing to make an ack but the mtg on consideration of the example resulting fr a person of his years concluded 14-10-1826 to dis him; dis 18-11-1826
(Note: it appears fr the above that this man is Aaron Quinby Sr, though it is not proven; there is no record of the d of his w Lydia)

Aaron Jr	(Aaron B) s Aaron & Lydia rptd 7-11-1818 by Little Brittain PM to have "given away to passion & struck a man in anger;" disf same 12-12-1818; ack acc
Ezra	rptd guilty of fornication by Little Brittain PM, 12-12-1812; does not deny it; disf same 8-5-1813
Jesse B	rptd rem without cert a "considerable time" 10-8-1816; our comm to write him that they found he had left without settling his debts rptd 11-1-1817 that they had rec a letter fr him ack that he owed some debts which are unpaid; and that he "declares he had never owned our religious principles, and disclaims having a right of mbrp with us;" disf same 8-2-1817
Mary	(now Allen) disf fornication & since being m to the man who is father of her ch, but who is not a mbr, 12-10-1811
Phebe	rptd 9-7-1814 by Little Brittain PM to have been guilty of fornication; disf same 8-10-1814; she having borne a ch in an unmarried state

REYNOLDS

Ann Mifflin	dt Stephen, dec, & Hannah (Kinsey) Reynolds, now w of Joshua Webster, gct Baltimore MM for W Dist, MD, 17-4-1824 on req of her mother Hannah (Kinsey-Reynolds) Webster
David Moore	b 14-12-1815 d 8-3-1867, Res Fulton Twp, Lancaster Co, PA (known as Peach Bottom) s Samuel & Mary of W Nottingham
Amanda Gregg	
Ch: Mary C	b 7-9-1860
Albert G	b 16-8-1862
Isaac G	b 7-9-1864 m Elizabeth W McFarland (West Chester, PA) 10-4-1895

Eli	s Samuel & Isabel (King) rptd 7-8-1813 by Eastland PM "has accomplished his m by a magistrate to a woman whom he ack has had a former husband, and there is no certainty whether he is dec, or not"; disf same 6-11-1813
Elisha Brown	rptd by Nottingham MM, MD, 19-9-1829 to have mcd; he res within the compass of this Mtg, we are asked to treat with him; on 17-10-1829 our comm rptd having visited him & that he did not appear to be willing to make an ack; this to be rptd to Nottingham MM
Elizabeth	dt Henry & Elizabeth (Sidwell) & gr-dt Henry & Mary (Haines) Reynolds & also gr-dt Hugh & Ann (Haines) Sidwell, rptd m 9-4-1808 to Jacob Gray (See Gray)
Elizabeth	(The Men's Minutes list her as Sarah) rocf Nottingham MM, MD 19-4-1828, dtd 14-3-1828
Elizabeth	(now Wickes or Weeks) rptd 13-6-1829 by Eastland as mou; disf same 15-8-1829 (Note: The name is written Wickes in Women's Min & as Weeks in Men's Min)
Elizabeth	d 25- 8-1840 (w of Henry Henry, husband of the above Elizabeth Reynolds, d 16-7-1845 (See Nottingham B&D)
Emily	(late Wilson) rptd 15-2-1823 by Eastland PM as "guilty of fornication with the man she hath since married"; dis 17-5-1823
Emmor	rptd 4-8-1821 by Eastland PM as "guilty of fornication with a young woman of training with the Militia;" "on the being with he ack to the latter;" but denied fornication, though he later admitted it; dis 1-12-1821

Hannah	(late Stubbs) rptd by Little Brittain PM 30-12-1820 as mou; her ack acc 31-3-1821
Henry Jr	b 1797 d 1878, age 81y, s Henry & Elizabeth (Sidwell) of Little Brittain Twp, Lancaster Co, PA
Mary Coppock	b 22-11-1792, dt Samuel & Ellen (Sidwell) of Little Brittain Twp, Lancaster Co, PA rptd m 11-4-1812

Ch: Elizabeth b 19- 6-1813
    Samuel   b 13- 1-1815
    Deborah   b 14-10-1817
    Ellen   b 9- 5-1818
    Mary Ann b 24-10-1819
    Henry   b 27- 2-1821   d 19-12-1822
    Rebecca   b 8- 3-1823
    Jacob   b 15-10-1824
    Henry (2) b 3- 2-1826
    Benjamin b 15-11-1827
    Josiah   b 22- 5-1829

Henry & w Mary (Coppock) & 11 minor ch, viz: Elizabeth, Samuel, Deborah, Ellen, Mary Ann, Rebecca, Jacob, Henry (2), Benjamin, Josiah & Sarah gct Nottingham MM, MD, 16-4-1831; to be forwarded

(Note: The youngest ch Sarah's birth not listed in B&D)

Henry	s Manuel & Sarah (Sergeant), the former dec, rptd 17-3-1827 by Eastland PM to have been "guilty of fornication with a woman to whom he is since married;" disf same 16-6-1827
Henry	d 7- 2-1809
Mary Haines, his w	d 27-12-1817 (See Nottingham B&D)

Isaac   rptd 17-9-1831 by Eastland PM to have been mou; res within the verge of Nottingham MM, MD, that Mtg is asked to treat within our behalf; on 17-3-1832, said Mtg rptd having visited him & that he proposed to relinquish his right of mbrp saying he attended military training & was not fit to hold a right & Friends need not take further trouble; disf mou 19-5-1832

Isaac G   of West Chester, PA
       b 7- 9-1864 at Peach Bottom, Lancaster Co, PA
       s David Moore & Amanda (Gregg) Reynolds, of Peach Bottom, Lancaster Co, PA
Elizabeth W McFarland, dt David M & Mary M (Rothrock) of West Chester, Chester Co, PA
       b 16- 5-1870
       m 10- 4-1895 at West Chester
Ch: (See W Chester)
  Mary   b 28- 1-1896
  Gregg David b 22- 5-1899

Isabella   (now Culberson) rptd 7-6-1833 by Women's Mtg as "guilty of fornication with a man not in mbrp, whom she has since married;" disf same 18-1-1834

Israel   b 3- 4-1782   d 6- 5-1869, age 87y, bur Eastland Res Little Brittan, s Joseph & Rachel
Hannah   Israel Reynolds, who was some time past dis by Nottingham MM, MD req rst 16-6-1829; rst 18-7-1829 by consent of Nottingham MM, MD; their 5 minor ch Vincent, Rachel B, Sarah S, Rebecca D & Priscilla rec on req 17-10-1829
Ch: Vincent   b 6- 4-1821
  Rachel B   b 20- 2-1823
  Sarah S   b 11-11-1824   d 16-10-1832, age 7y 11m 5d
  Rebecca D b 20-10-1826

Priscilla	b 3- 6-1828
Joseph	b 3-12-1830

Jacob   d 8- 4-1822 in his 71st yr

James, Abner & Lewis   minor sons of Levi & Jane (King) Reynolds, both dec, form of Nottingham MM, MD; on 12-8-1815, committees fr Nottingham MM & Little Brittain MM met & decided that the above named ch of Levi Reynolds, dec, should be considered mbrs of Nottingham MM, not of Little Brittain MM; but when this rpt was made to Nottingham MM, they objected to adopting the ch, since the ch themselves said they had always considered themselves mbrs of Little Brittain MM; thereupon, Little Brittain MM directed that certs be issued to Nottingham for them, & a cert was issued 9-12-1815 for Abner & Lewis Reynolds to that Mtg. At the same Mtg the same comm rptd that the above said James Reynolds had mou before a Justice of the Peace.

James   s Levi & Jane (King), both dec, rptd 9-12-1815 to have ack his mou before a Justice of the Peace; disf same 10-2-1816

Joanna   (now Pickering) w of Anthony; rptd 6-6-1818 by Eastland to have been mcd to a mbr of this mtg by the assistance of a Justice of the Peace; her ack acc 12-9-1818
(Note: Joanna Reynolds was dt Reuben & Margaret (King); b 22-11-1788 d 3-9-1833, bur Eastland MH. WWH)

Joshua   b 28- 2-1766 d 4- 1-1841, age 74y, bur Eastland
s Henry & Mary (Haines) of Little Brittain Twp, Lancaster Co, PA

Margaret Job		dt Archibald & Margaret (Rees), dec, of E Nottingham, Hundred, Cecil Co, MD m 7- 4-1791, at East Nottingham MH
Ch:	Morris	b 26- 1-1792 d 29- 4-1860, age 68y, bur Eastland m Lydia Reynolds
	Mary	b 26- 5-1793
	Lydia	b 28- 6-1795
	Elizabeth	b 20- 3-1797
Lydia		(now Chandlee) rptd by Eastland PM 9-5-1818 as mou; her ack acc 8-7-1818 Lydia (Reynolds) Chandlee (w of Evan Chandlee) gct Nottingham MM, MD, 7-11-1818 (See Chandlee)
Lydia		dt Samuel Jr & Ann (Reynolds) Reynolds, rptd by Eastland PM 19-6-1830 to have been "guilty of unchastity which is evidenced by her bearing a child in an unmarried state;" disf same 14-8-1830
Manuel		(originally Emmanuel) of Little Brittain Twp, Lancaster Co, PA, s Henry & Mary (Haines) of same place b 10-12-1762 d 12- 1-1825 in 63rd yr
Sarah Sergeant		dt Jeremiah & Ann (Sidwell) of W Nottingham Twp, Chester Co, PA m 8-5mo (May) 1788, at E Nottingham MH, auspices Nottingham MM, MD
Ch:	Elie	b 3- 5-1789 cert Nottingham MM, MD, 17-10-1829
	Nathan	b 18-12-1790
	Hannah	b 21- 8-1792 disf unchaste conduct 18-6-1825
	Ann	b 19- 7-1794 d 5- 4-1827 m Absalom Murry (nm)
	Mary	b 21- 1-1796 cert Nottingham MM, MD, 19-9-1829
	Jeremiah	b 1- 9-1797 d 13- 9-1799, age 2y 13d, bur Eastland

Henry	b 24- 7-1799
Sarah Jr	b 21- 4-1801 disf fornication 15-5-1824
Manuel Jr	b 22- 6-1804 cert Nottingham MM, MD, 19-9-1828
	Sarah gct Nottingham MM, MD, 19-9-1829; also her ch Manuel Jr & Mary, gct Nottingham MM, MD, same date; Elie cert same Mtg 17-10-1829
Margaret	(now Brown) rptd by Eastland PM 12-6-1819 as mou before a Justice of the Peace; disf same 4-12-1819
Michael	s Samuel & Isabel (King), gct Short Creek MM, OH, 9-4-1808
	Note: the above Michael Reynolds was b 21-5-1786 (See Nottingham B&D, p 111)
Michael	rocf New Garden MM, PA, 11-11-1809, dtd 14-9-1809
	(Note: This cert not found in New Garden certs or mins; it appears probable that the cert was directed to New Garden & end to Little Brittain MM by that MM; not proven)
Michael	gct London Grove MM, PA 12-5-1810
Morris	of Little Brittain Twp, Lancaster Co, PA
	b 26- 1-1792 d 29- 4-1860, age 68y
	s Joshua & Margaret (Job) of same place
Lydia Reynolds	b ca 1800 d 14- 7-1867, age 67y
	rptd mcd 15-8-1835
	ack of Morris & Lydia (Reynolds) Reynolds for their mcd acc 15-8-1835
Ch: Morris Jr	b 27- 2-1836
Joshua I	b 4- 1-1838
Reuben	b 27- 1-1839
Lydia K	b 21- 5-1843

Nathan		s Manuel & Sarah (Sargeant) rptd enlisting as a soldier 6-3-1813 by Eastland PM; fisf same 8-5-1813 "he being gone out of these parts with the army."
Phineas		s Richard & Mary (Harlan), gct New Garden MM, PA, 15-7-1826
Rachel		rocf Nottingham MM, MD, 18-11-1826, dtd 9-11-1826
Reuben		rptd 17-9-1831 by Eastland PM as mcd "with a woman in mbrp", disf same 17-11-1831
Richard		of Eastland Twp, Lancaster Co, PA b 20- 1-1784, s Reuben & Margaret (King) form of W Nottingham; later of Little Brittain; the former dec the 2nd (or 7th) of 8mo-1823; the latter dec 8-7-1847, age 86y, both bur Eastland
Mary Harlan		b 5- 4-1785 d 3- 9-1825, bur Eastland dt James & Elizabeth (Swayne) rptd mcd 10-1-1807 by Magistrate Ack acc 11-7-1807
Ch:	Hannah	b 25-10-1807 d 1838 m Thomas McClary
	Phineas	b 17- 1-1809 d 10- 1-1848 m Mary S Birchfield cert New Garden 15-7-1826
	Susanna	b 15- 5-1810 d 20- 7-1811
	Elizabeth	b 10- 7-1811 d 2- 9-1825
	Margaret	b 18- 3-1813 d 20- 5-1901, Oskaloosa, IA, m Wm Barrickman
	Mary Swane	b 13- 3-1815 d 29-11-1903, Ord, Neb, m Wm Gray
	Jane Mason	b 6- 5-1817 d 26- 1-1908, Jamaica, IA, m John S Birchfield
	Edith Webb	b 31-10-1818 d 1- 6-1820
	James Harlan	b 7-11-1820 d 28- 8-1825
	Sarah	b 12- 8-1823 d 24- 7-1906, OH, m Wm Clark

Richard	rptd by Eastland PM 15-3-1828 as complained of for not paying a just debt of frequenting taverns; disf same 19-7-1828, "after long care."
	(Note: he promised to settle the debt, but was dis for the other offense & for dallying over payment of the debt.)
Samuel	of Little Brittain Twp, Lancaster Co, PA
	b 11- 1-1782, s Samuel & Isabel (King), dec, of same place
Ann Reynolds	b 29- 3-1784 d 31-12-1850, bur Eastland Grvyd
	dt Henry & Elizabeth (Sidwell) Reynolds, of same place
	m 2- 5-1804 at Eastland MH, PA
Ch: Lydia	b 16- 2-1805
Josiah	b 9- 1-1807 rptd mou 19- 3-1831
Ira	b 6- 8-1808
Ahia	b 13-12-1810 rptd mou 18-11-1837; ack acc 17-2-1838
Isabel	b 3-10-1812
Leona	b 19-11-1815
Hyndford	b 12-10-1817
Henraetta	b 3-12-1820
Ortha	b 12-12-1822
Rebecca Jane	b 19- 2-1825
Samuel Jr	rptd by Eastland PM 18-3-1837 to "have ack threatening to shoot an officer of the law if he attempted or persisted in taking from him two oxen, which he, Samuel Reynolds, considered his own"; disf same 14-1-1837
Sarah Jr	rptd 14-2-1824 by Eastland PM to be "guilty of fornication"; dis 15-5-1824
Stephen	b 12- 9-1760 d 21- 4-1816, age 55y 7m
	s Jacob & Rebecca (Daye)
	prcf Nottingham MM, MD, clear to m

Hannah Kinsey	dt Isaac & Mary, both dec, late of Baltimore Co, MD & of Gunpowder MM rptd m 6 mo-1807 Hannah (Kinsey) Reynolds, w of Stephen, gct Nottingham MM, MD, to join husband 8-8-1807 (Note: Hannah (Kinsey) Reynolds, wid of Stephen, m 2nd, 5-7-1820, Joshua Webster, as his 2nd w)
Ch: Stephen Kinsey	b 24- 3-1808, gct Baltimore MM, W.D. 17-4-1824
Ann Mifflin	b 20- 2-1811 " " " " "
Mary Jane	b 14- 5-1813
Ruthanna	b Stephen Kinsey Reynolds, Ann Mifflin Reynolds, Mary Jane Reynolds & Ruthanna Reynolds, rocf Nottingham MM, MD, with their mother, Hannah (Kinsey-Reynolds) Webster, who is now w of Jushua Webster, 30-9-1820, dtd 29-9-1820
Stephen Kinsey	s Stephen, dec, & Hannah (Kinsey) Reynolds, now w of Joshua Webster, gct Baltimore MM for W D, MD, on req of his mother, Hannah (Kinsey-Reynolds) Webster, 17-4-1824
Thomas	s of Samuel, gct Nottingham MM, MD, 8-6-1805
Vincent	disf "dancing, fighting & using profane language" 7-8-1819

RICHARDS

Isaac	of Nottingham MM, MD b 8-1-1783, s Thomas & Hannah (Cox) of same place prcf Nottingham MM, MD, clear to m
Lydia Wood	b 5- 4-1775, dt Joseph & Katharine (Daye) of Chester Co, PA rptd m 6-2-1808 Lydia (Wood) Richards, w of Isaac, gct Nottingham MM, MD, 9-4-1808 to join husband

Thomas Jr	b 11-11-1787 d 15- 4-1864 s Thomas & Hannah (Cox) of E Nottingham prcf Nottingham MM, MD 9-4-1814, clear to m
Orpha Stubbs	b 8- 8-1791 d 16- 9-1853, age 62y dt Joseph & Ruth (Pyle) of Little Brittain Twp, Lancaster Co, PA rptd m 7-5-1814, at Little Brittain MH Orpha (Stubbs) Richards, gct Nottingham MM, MD, 11-3-1815, to join husband

RICHARDSON

Caleb	gct Philadelphia MM, PA, 8-10-1814 (Note: for further info see H-vol. 2, p 634)
Isaac	had taken of in 1822 by David Cope, Collector, "by unlocking a drawer 2 dollars for a demand of 2 dollars"; and in 1824 by order of N.W. Sample, Brigade Inspector, by Wm Ralston, Collector, "by unlocking a drawer, $2.25 for a demand of $2.00"; & in same year by order of said Sample, by Samuel Porter, Collector, "by opening a chest, $2.00 for a demand of $2.00"
Isaac Ann Carter	rptd m 14-5-1825; parents of both consenting Isaac & Ann (Carter) & their 2 minor ch, viz: Ruth & Hannah, gct Deerfield MM, OH, 15-3-1828
Ch: Ruth Hannah	b 6- 6-1826 b 13-10-1827
Joseph	b 3-10mo (Dec) 1743, OS d 10-1-1814 in Little Brittain Twp, Lancaster Co, PA
w Dinah	d 20- 3-1824, age about 76y 10m
Rebecca W, Margaret & Lydia	adult dts of Samuel & Rebecca (Webster) Richardson, gct Deerfield MM, OH, 19-4-1828

Samuel		Little Brittain Twp, Lancaster Co, PA
		s Joseph & Dinah
Rebecca Webster		b 21- 8-1775 "between the 12th & 1st hour"
		dt William & 2nd w Margaret (Coppock), both dec, of Little Brittain, Lancaster Co, PA
		m 6-11-1794, Little Brittain MH, PA, auspices of Nottingham MM, MD

Ch: Hannah   b 21- 6-1796   m Samuel Smith, 1816
    William   b 15- 2-1798
    Ruth   b 24-12-1799   m James Smith, 1818
    Rebecca W   b 9- 1-1802
    Margaret   b 29- 1-1804
    Lydia   b 30- 1-1806
    Mary   b 26- 5-1808
    Samuel   b 3- 8-1810
    Eliza   b 21- 8-1812
    Martha   b 14-10-1814
    Anne   b 6- 4-1817
    Joseph   b 25-11-1819

Samuel & Rebecca (Webster) & their 6 minor ch (last 6 named) gct Deerfield MM, OH, 19-4-1828; also separate certs for Rebecca, Margaret & Lydia to same Mtg, same date

William
Elizabeth Brown   rptd 19-3-1825, mcd, by Little Brittain PM, both mbrs of this Mtg; their joint ack acc 13-8-1825

Ch: Abner B   b 24-12-1825
    Samuel   b 18- 8-1829

RING
Rachel   rem some time past without a cert, gct Stillwater MM, OH 5-2-1820

ROBERTS
Ashton

Sarah	Both & their 2 minor ch, viz: Wilson & Anna, rocf Falls MM, PA (form of Makefield MM, PA) 13-5-1826, dtd 11-2-1826
Ch: Wilson	b See Makefield MM B&D
Anna	b "
Margaret	b 10- 9-1828 at Little Brittain MM

Nathan
Margaret, his w   Both rocf Middletown MM, Bucks Co, PA 16-9-1826, dtd 7-4-1826; also a cert fr same mtg, same date for Theophilas & Guy Roberts
(Note: Although the minute does not so state, the inference is that Theophilas & Guy Roberts are adult sons of Nathan and Margaret.)

ROGERS

Thomas   of E Nottingham, widower, s Wm & 1st w Grace, both dec prcf Nottingham MM, MD to m

Anna Brown   (widow of Jeremiah)* & dt Samuel & Catharine Wilson
rptd m 8-4-1809
d 25- 1-1820, age 70y (listed as 2nd w of Thomas Rogers in Nottingham B & D, p 131, Bk 1)
Anna Rogers, w of Thomas, gct Nottingham MM, MD 10-6-1809 to join husband
*(Jeremiah Brown was s Daniel & Elizabeth (Kirk) Brown)

RUSSELL
John (nm)
Ann Neal   mcd 4-4-1792
Ann, mbr of Concord MM, PA; disf mou 6-6-1792 by Concord MM, PA; she was rein in mbrp by Concord MM, 5-3-1806; & with their 3 ch, viz; Susannah, William & Ann Neal Russell, Ann Russell

was gct Little Brittain MM, by Concord MM, 9-4-1806 which certs (separate fr Ann & her ch) were rec & acc by Little Brittain MM, 10-5-1806

Ann, w of John d 10-10-1830, age in 61st yr, bur Little Brittain John, husband of Ann & Mary, d 21-9-1840, age 74y, bur Little Brittain, Res Drumore

Mary, wid of John, d 2-7-1860, age 75y, late res Fulton Town (Note: The above Shows that John Russell m Mary, as 2nd w)

John rec on req 14-7-1832, s Israel & Catharine Russell, & Mary Brown, dt Joshua & Deborah Brown, rptd m 17-11-1832. No issue listed.

SCOTTEN
Joshua

rptd 16-7-1825 by Little Brittain PM as mou; disf same 17-9-1825

William w Jane

Both & their minor s Joshua, rocf Deer Creek MM, MD, 2-10-1819, dtd 1-3-1819
(Note: This cert was presented in 6mo, but bearing no date, it was returned to be corrected); gct Deer Creek MM, MD, 4-8-1821 (no mention made of ch)

SHELTON
Euclidas P

rptd 13-8-1831 by Buckingham MM, PA, as "now res within the compass of Little Brittain MM" had been mcd asking us to treat with him on their behalf. His ack produced by him 15-10-1831 "appeared satisfactory;" Buckingham MM, PA to be so notified.

SHOEMAKER
Abram
Regina
Ch: Annie   b 28- 9-1859
     William G   b 25- 4-1862
     Mary A   b 24-12-1865

Isaac B	b 24- 9-1832, s Thomas & Abi of Little Brittain, Lancaster Co, PA	
Anna E	d 6- 5-1879, age 47y	
Ch: Walter	b 16- 9-1857	
Elwood	b "	
Irene	b 7- 3-1863	
Viola	b 26-11-1867	
Jacob	d 21- 6-1839	
Joyce	an Elder, of Dunmore PM	d 26- 3-1822
Ch: John	b 11- 1-1799	
Thomas	b 28- 1-1802	
Tacy	b 15- 5-1806	
George	b 6- 2-1810	d 24- 8-1815
Rachel	b "	
Jesse		
Sarah Lukens	of Drumore Mtg d 23- 8-1872	
	Jesse & Sarah (Lukens) & 2 minor ch: Hannah & Joseph, rocf Gwynedd MM, PA, 15-5-1830, dtd 1-4-1830 (H)	
Ch: Charles	b 17- 2-1840	d 17- 8-1851, age 11y 6m, bur Drumore
William L	b 20-12-1841	m Alice A Lamborn, 1870
Martha Ann	b	d 8- 7-1840, bur Drumore
Joseph L	b 9- 7-1829	d 4- 4-1899, bur Drumore, m Emeline Lamborn, 1854
John	d 16- 6-1843	
Sarah Bolton	d 18- 1-1838	
	rptd m 17-5-1834 by Little Brittain MM, PA	
Ch: Sarah E	b 12-11-1837	d 15- 4-1838
	Sufferings: John & Thomas Shoemaker "were each of them taken and imprisoned by Wm Ralston, Collector, in Lancaster Jail for a short time in the 3rd mo, 1826 for a demand each of $2.00."	

Joseph L		b 9- 7-1829 in Montgomery Co, PA d 4- 4-1899 at Fernglen, Lancaster Co, PA; a farmer s Jesse & Sarah (Lukens) of Bethesda, PA, both bur at Drumore
Emeline Lamborn		b 20- 9-1834 at Liberty Square d there 8-11-1880, age 46y bur Drumore dt Smedley & Margaret (Bolton) of Drumore, Lancaster Co, PA m 2- 3-1854 (by the mayor of Lancaster, PA)
Ch:	Cynthia	b 2- 2-1855 d 5-10-1876 unm
	Charles L	b 13- 3-1856 m M Ella Cutler
	Allison	b 3- 4-1858 living at Derandy, Wyo, unm 1900
	Leander	b 13- 2-1861 m Lenora S Kent, res Cochranville, PA
	Enos	b 2- 9-1865 d 16- 9-1865, age 14d
	Wm Lewis	b 8-11-1869 m Sarah Bradley, dt Amos K & Mary V (Hess) Bradley
	Edgar	b 13- 2-1872
Thomas		of Little Brittain, Lancaster Co, PA
Abi Bolton		dt Isaac & Elizabeth of Drumore, PA (form of Byberry MM, PA) rptd m 16-12-1826, the mc rptd handed to the Recorder
Ch:	Edwin	b 13- 1-1828
	Alfred	b 17- 4-1830
	Isaac B	b 24- 9-1832 m Anna E
	Anna	b 6- 6-1835
	Elizabeth	b 14- 2-1837
William L		b 20-12-1843, at Bethesda, Lancaster Co, PA s Jesse & Sarah (Lukens); farmer, school director; res near Liberty Square, Goshen, PA
Alice A Lamborn		b 14- 4-1847, Liberty Square, dt Smedley & Margaret (Bolton) of Drumore, Lancaster Co, PA m 20- 1-1870

Ch: Winona		b 7-12-1870 m Harry J Drennen, Fairmont, Lancaster Co, PA
Jesse		b 29-9-1880 d same day
Lula May		b 30-10-1888

SHORTLEDGE

Mary — rocf Wilmington MM, Del, 12-11-1808, dtd 6-10-1808
gct New Garden MM, PA 11-10-1817

SIDWELL

Ann — (now Brown) rptd 19-4-1828 by Eastland PM, as mou; her ack acc 19-7-1828 (See Brown)

Elizabeth — rec on req 11-1-1806 "after long care by the Women's Mtg.

Job — rptd 13-2-1830 as mou; his ack acc 17-7-1830

Joseph — rocf Nottingham MM, PA, 30-6-1821, dtd ?

Mary Jr — (late Milner) rptd mou to Joseph Sidwell (nm) 11-1-1817; her ack acc 12-4-1817; gct Nottingham MM, MD 12-7-1817

Mary — (NI) rocf Nottingham MM, MD, 3-9-1820, dtd 30-6-1820

Mary — (NI) gct Nottingham MM, MD, 1-6-1822

Mary — w of Levi, rocf Nottingham MM, MD, 7-1-1809; gct Nottingham MM, MD, 7-2-1818

Rebecca (Wilson) — widow of Job, dec, & 3 minor ch, viz: Rebecca, Ann & Lavina, rocf Nottingham MM, MD, 18-11-1826, dtd 13-10-1826; her two sons, viz: Job & Wilson, rocf Nottingham MM, MD, 19-5-1827, dtd 13-4-1827

(For full list of ch of Job & Rebecca (Wilson) Sidwell, see Nottingham MM)

Rebecca Sidwell & her 3 dts, viz: Ann, Levina, & Rebecca Jr, gct Nottingham MM, MD, 16-8-1834

SMEDLEY

Eli		b 4-12-1785 (at Willistown) d 7-5-1865, Fulton Twp, Lancaster Co, PA
		s Joseph & Rebecca (Lewis) of Little Brittain Mtg, PA
Elizabeth Hambleton		b 14- 5-1786, Solebury, Bucks Co, PA, m 16-12-1813 at Penn Hill
		d 24- 3-1858 in 72nd yr, Fulton, PA, bur Little Brittain
		dt James & Elizabeth Lupton (Paxon) Hambleton of Lancaster Co, PA, both bur at Penn Hill
Ch:	Lydia	b 5-12-1814 d 6- 9-1851, m Andrew B Magough, 2nd w
	Mary	b 3- 4-1816 d 21- 9-1879, m Nathan Smith
	Emmor	b 27- 7-1817 d 15-12-1888, m Elizabeth Adams
	James	b 27- 2-1819 d 4- 9-1888, m Adaline B Ambler
	Eli Jr	b 5-10-1820 d 4-10-1825, age 4y 11m 29d
	Rebecca	b 13-12-1822 m Amos C Paxon
	Elizabeth	b 29- 9-1824 d 10- 4-1900, m J Penrose Ambler
	Sarah	b " d 1-11-1853, m Joshua Eckman
Emmor		b 27- 7-1817 d 15-12-1888
		s Eli & Elizabeth (Hambleton) & gr-s Joseph & Rebecca (Lewis) Smedley; all of Little Brittain, Lancaster Co, PA
Elizabeth Adams		of Philadelphia, PA, dt John & Sarah
		b 29- 5-1818 d 9- 8-1896
		m 11- 2-1841

Ch:	Abel Kinsey	b 5- 3-1842 d 3- 3-1861, age 18y 11m 28d, bur Little Brittain
	Enoch Beal	b 17- 9-1843 d 21-11-1843, bur Little Brittain
	Mary Edith	b 6-10-1844 d 8 mo-1884, Goshen, m Enos W Marsh, at Philadelphia
	Carsildia	b 4-10-1853 m Joseph S Townsend; res Wilmington, Del

James		b 27- 9-1819 d 9- 4-1888 bur Little Brittain s Eli & Elizabeth (Hambleton) of Little Brittain, Lancaster Co, PA
Adaline B Ambler		b 27- 7-1818 in Montgomery Co, PA, dt William & Elizabeth (Penrose)Ambler, of Martic Twp, same Co & State m 21-10-1846
		(Note: He settled on the old homestead, in Fulton Twp, Lancaster Co, PA; owned 100 acres of land & was a farmer; was a school director and a Friend; also a debater; an expert rifle shot when young. See Smedley Fam Book, p 438)
Ch:	Clarinda	b 12- 8-1847 m Vincent Richards, s Stephen & Rebecca (Stubbs)
	Owen A	b 25- 4-1852 d 9- 9-1853, bur Little Brittain Grvyd
	Louisa	b 13- 9-1856 m Henry Pownall, s Henry & Deborah (Walker)
	Lizzie Penrose	b 5- 5-1858 m Samuel Preston Paxon, s John S & Mary L (Moore)

Joel	b 4-11-1799 d 31- 5-1872 in Fulton Twp, Lancaster Co, PA
	s Joseph & Rebecca (Lewis) of Little Brittain, Lancaster Co, PA
	gct Byberry MM, PA 15-8-1835 to m
Martha Wildman	b 11- 8-1805 d 5-11-1863, Fulton, PA
	dt John & Mary (Knight) of Byberry, PA, both bur Fulton Twp, at Penn Hill Grvyd;

		m 29-10-1835
		"Joel was a millwright by trade, & purchased a farm & mill on Big Conowingo Creek"
		Martha (Wildman) Smedley rocf Byberry MM, PA 14-5-1836, dtd 24-4-1836 to join husband
Ch:	Charles	b 1-11-1836 d 16-11-1864, age 28y 5d, bur Little Brittain (Rebel Prison)
	Mary W	b 18-12-1837 d 17- 7-1880 m Benjamin C Reynolds (2nd w)
	John Wildman	b 13- 7-1839 m Lucretia Wood
	Lewis	b 20- 8-1840 d 29-10-1863 unm
	Anne	b 27- 1-1842 m Benjamin C Reynolds (3rd w)
	Elwood	b 9-11-1843 m Hannah K Russell

Joseph		s Thomas & Lydia (James)
		b 8- 7-1757, Willistown d 24-12-1811 at Little Brittain Twp, Lancaster Co, PA; bur Little Brittain (Note: Joseph Smedley of the above death record m
Rebecca Lewis		b 28-10-1759 d 1847, dt Samuel & Margaret (Trotter) of Whiteland
		m 28- 4-1784 at Goshen Mtg
		& had issue as per the list below, which is taken fr The Smedley Family Book by Gilbert Cope, p 150)
Ch:	Lewis	b 14- 3-1785 d 8- 1-1841 m Mary Harlan & Tacy Heston
	Eli	b 4-12-1785 d 7- 5-1865 m Elizabeth Hambleton
	Joseph	b 27- 3-1788 d 19- 3-1866 m Rachel Ballance
	Lydia	b 11- 7-1790 d 14- 3-1816 unm bur Penn Hill
	Sarah	b 31- 8-1792 d 14- 8-1878 m James Meloney
	Rebekah	b 6- 9-1794 d 8- 4-1850 m James King
	Thomas	b 13-12-1797 d 14-10-1855 m Hannah Knight & Mary Wildman
	Joel	b 4-11-1799 d 31- 5-1872 m Martha Wildman

Joseph	b 27- 3-1788 d 19- 3-1866 s Joseph, dec, & Rebecca (Lewis) of Little Brittain, Lancaster Co, PA
Rachel Ballance	b 4- 2-1787, Bucks Co, PA d 12- 4-1858 Fulton Twp, Lancaster Co, PA
	dt Joseph & Anna (Pownall) of Lancaster Co, PA (both bur at Little Brittain)
	m 16-11-1814 at Eastland MH, PA
	"Joseph Smedley was a farmer & blacksmith, ingenius in his craft; kind and gentle; a good neighbor & respected by all"
Ch: Anna	b 4- 9-1818 d 13- 1-1876 m Walker Moore
Joseph	b 13- 4-1823 m Ann H Buckman
	Joseph disf joining the Separatists (Orth) 14-3-1829 Rachel, w of Joseph, j Orth; dis 13-6-1829
Lewis	b 14- 3-1785 d 8- 1-1841
	s Joseph & Rebecca (Lewis) of Little Brittain Twp, Lancaster Co, PA
Mary Harlan	of Bucks Co, PA, dt Joseph & Hannah (Webster)
	b 30-11-1779 d 4- 9-1813
	m 17- 3-1808, at Little Brittain MH
	Lewis gct Middletown MM, PA, 10-6-1815
2nd w Tacy Heston	b 18-12-1776 d 21- 5-1839, dt David & Rachel
	m 3mo-1815; issue: 1 ch, d in infancy
	"He res some time in Bucks Co, PA; but ret to his mother's (in Little Brittain) before his death"
	(Note: The 2nd m, above, is fr Smedley Fam., p 260)
Samuel	Made a voluntary ack of having been guilty of fornication 16-10-1824; his ack was acc 13-11-1824, he having settled the matter to the satisfaction of the woman (He m her 16-10-1824); gct Byberry MM, PA, 17-11-1827
Thomas	b 13-12-1797 d 14-10-1855 in Fulton Twp, Lancaster Co, PA

Hannah Knight	s Joseph & Rebecca (Lewis) of Little Brittain, Lancaster Co, PA gct Byberry MM, PA, 14-4-1832 to m b 5- 1-1798 d 23- 2-1850, dt Jonathan & Elizabeth (Thomas) m 3- 5-1832 Hannah (Knight) Smedley rocf Byberry MM, 15-9-1832
2nd w Mary Wildman	b 2- 2-1815 d 3-11-1876 dt John & Mary (Knight) m 2-10-1851

Ch: (by 1st w)
    Thomas   b 19- 8-1836 d 1- 4-1890 m Sophia C Stubbs
    Jonathan   b 30-12-1839 d 8- 6-1866, age 26y 5m 8d, unm
(by 2nd w)
    Hannah   b 19-10-1852 d 20-12-1859

Thomas	b 19- 8-1836 d 1- 4-1890, Fulton Twp, Lancaster Co, PA s Thomas & 1st w Hannah (Knight) of Little Brittain, Lancaster Co, PA, & gr-s of Joseph & Rebecca (Lewis) Smedley, of same place
1st w Sophia C Stubbs,	dt Vincent & Mary E (Haines) of Little Brittain, Lancaster Co, PA & gr-dt Vincent & Priscilla Stubbs of same place b 21- 4-1836 in Fulton Twp, Lancaster Co, PA d there 3-8-1885 m 22-10-1857 at Ashland House, Philadelphia

2nd w Isabella Brown, widow by whom there was no issue
Ch: (by 1st w)
    Eva   b 17-10-1858 m Moses Pownall, s Ambrose & Joanna (Denny)
    Hannah   b 29- 6-1863 m James M Paxon, in Philadelphia, s James S & Mary L (Moore)
    Jonathan   b 22- 9-1866 d 17- 3-1880
    T Jules   b 17- 8-1871 m Jennie V Jones, dt Matthew G & Joel (Gilbert) Jones

SMITH

David   rocf London Grove MM, PA, 12-7-1806, dtd 4-6-1806; on 9-1-1813, Little Brittain PM rptd that David Smith had rem to within the compass of Fallowfield MM, PA without a cert; gct Fallowfield MM, PA, 6-2-1813

David
Hannah   Both & dt Asenath, rocf Fallowfield MM, PA, 9-1-1819, dtd 12-10-1818 (B&D p 74: Hannah d 26-9-1842)

Ch: Asenath   b   d   18- 8-1843 rocf with parents
      Hannah W   b 29- 5-1819
      David M   b 29- 8-1822   d   8- 6-1843
      Elizabeth   b 25-10-1824

Mary Smith d 4mo-1818 (prob an earlier ch b & d at Fallowfield MM, PA)

Isaac   rocf Philadelphia MM, PA, 7-6-1806, dtd 28-2-1806; lives remote fr our Mtg; on 6-1-1810 he was cof fornication by Little Brittain PM "which he did not deny"; disf same 10-3-1810; ack acc & he rst 12-1-1811; gct Gunpowder MM, MD, 6-7-1811

Margaret   Both & ch, viz: Mary Ann & Samuel Cole, rocf Nottingham MM, MD, 11-5-1816, dtd 10-5-1816

Ch: Samuel   b 19-12-1812   d   20-12-1812
      Mary Ann   b 30-10-1813
      Samuel Cole   b 3- 6-1815
      Comly   b 2- 7-1817
      Edwin   b 28- 2-1819
      Philina   b 27- 4-1821

Isaac & Margaret Smith & ch, Mary Ann, Samuel Cole, Comley, Edwin & Philina, gct Goshen MM, PA, 1-9-1821 (which had been requested a year previously but had been held back until Isaac could settle certain debts to make him eligible)

On 1-12-1821 this cert was ret by Goshen MM, PA, as "they were not free to acc it for want of being mentioned in it that his outward were settled to satisfaction"; after many months of care, Isaac's outward affairs were settled, and a new certificate to Goshen MM, PA, was issued to him & family, 1-6-1822 & directed to be forwarded.

James	s Joseph & Eleanor, form of London Grove MM, PA, now of this Mtg
	prcf London Grove MM, PA 11-4-1818, dtd 8-4-1818, showing him clear to m
Ruth Richardson	b 24-12-1799, dt Samuel & Rebecca (Webster) of Little Brittain MM
	rptd m 9-5-1818
Ch: Rebecca R	b 13-10-1819
Kersey	b 6- 4-1821
Mary	b 27- 4-1823
Joseph	b 14-12-1825
	James & Ruth (Richardson) & 4 minor ch, viz: Rebecca R, Kersey, Mary & Joseph, gct Deerfield MM, OH, 19-4-1828

Joseph Jr	b 1801, Goshen MM, PA d 19-7-1878, age 77y bur Drumore
	s Joseph & Eleanor (form of Goshen MM, PA; now of Little Brittain MM)
Tacy Shoemaker	b 15- 5-1806, dt Jacob & Joyce of Little Brittain MM (form of Gwynedd MM, PA; but m ca 1798 at Horsham MM, PA)
	rptd m 18-10-1823
Ch: Rachel	b 24- 6-1825
George	b 19- 5-1827
Amos	b " d 6-11-1847, age 20y 5m 17d, bur Drumore
Levi	b 6- 3-1829 d 24-10-1834

Mary	b 7- 8-1831	d 20- 7-1848, age 16y 10m 13d, bur Drumore
Albert	b 10-12-1833	d 22- 6-1836
Ellen W	b 2-12-1840	

Joseph Smith Sr (father of Joseph Jr of this record)
d 11- 9-1825, bur Drumore

Joseph   & w Eleanor, & their ch, viz: Joseph Jr (minor), 2 dts Ann & Eleanor, & their s James, rocf London Grove MM, PA, 11-4-1818, dtd 8-4-1818; the dts Ann & Eleanor & s James rec on separate certs; and the said James Smith rpcf sd meeting of sd date of his clearness to m Ruth Richardson; they are altm.

Samuel   of London Grove, PA, s Joseph & Eleanor
d 9- 5-1823
prcf London Grove MM, PA 9-12-1815, clear to m

Hannah Richardson   b 21- 6-1796, dt Samuel & Rebecca (Webster) of Little Brittain MM, PA
rptd m 6-1-1816
Samuel rocf London Grove MM, PA, 11-5-1816, dtd 3-4-1816

Ch: Preston   b 27-12-1816
     Howard   b 21- 2-1818
     Maria   b 29-12-1819
     Elizabeth W   b 4- 4-1821
     Samuel R   b 4-10-1823

Hannah (wid of Samuel) & her dt Maria gct York MM, PA, 15-6-1833; Hannah & dt Maria rocf York MM, PA, 17-10-1835, dtd 9-7-1835

STEADY

William   & w Jane rocf London Grove MM, PA, 6-9-1806, dtd 9-7-1806, Little Brittain PM rptd 6-11-1813 that Wm Steady had refused to carry out the terms of a written contract which he had signed. On 12-2-1814, our committee to investigate the matter and try to settle it rptd that they had found that the issue concerned the sale of a parcel of land by Wm Steady to James & Eli Thompson, who are the complainants; he ack that he drew the Instrument in writing; but the title was in the name of a 3rd person; & that Wm Steady, being in possession of the land refuses to give it up. Arbitration was agreed to by all parties; but later Wm Steady refused to abide by the agreement unless compelled to do so by Law. There being no prospect of further labour being useful, he was dis 12-3-1814. On 10-5-1817, Wm Steady produced a paper ack his error & asking for rein, which was acc & he rein; he was gct Sadsbury MM, PA, 19-7-1823

STREEPER
Richard

rptd by Eastland PM 17-4-1830 as mcd & that he res within the compass of Gwynedd MM, PA; that Mtg to be asked to treat with him. His ack acc 19-2-1831 on report fr Gwynedd MM; gct Gwynedd MM, PA 19-3-1831

William
Martha

Both with their 3 youngest ch viz: Hannah, Richard & Mary, rec on req 10-2-1816

STUBBS
Amor (or Amos)

s Isaac & Hannah (Brown) rocf Deer Creek MM, MD, 18-11-1826 dtd 12-10-1826. On 19-6-1830 Amor Stubbs was rpts by Little Brittian PM to be "in the practice of selling spirituous liquors as an agent for other persons"; disf same 19-3-1831 "after long care."

Anna

rocf Warrington MM, PA, 12-8-1815
(Note: not clearly identified in these records; but thought to be w of John Stubbs)

Cooper   of Fulton Twp, Lancaster Co, PA; farmer & friend
                        b 25- 4-1833 at Peters Creek, Lancaster Co, PA
                        s Thomas (farmer) b 3-9-1804 in Lancaster Co, PA,
                        by his 1st w Elizabeth (called Betty) (Trego) Stubbs,
                        b 13-3-1801 in Chester Co, PA

Anna Mariah Carter   b 3- 5-1833, dt Henry, a farmer, b 18-4-1804 in
                        Harford Co, MD, d 1-4-1896 in Fulton Twp,
                        Lancaster Co, PA & his w Mary Ann (Jackson)
                        Carter, b 8-9-1803 in London Grove Twp, Chester
                        Co, PA; d 11-5-1894; bur beside her husband in
                        Fulton Twp, Lancaster Co, PA; dt Joel & Alice
                        (Morris) Jackson
                        m 1-5mo (May) 1856, at Philadelphia, PA

Ch: Lizzie Estelle   b 12- 8-1857   m Charles Gatchell, 7-10-1880
     Mary Ann   b 4-12-1859
     Alice Anna   b 25- 5-1862   m Barclay Hollingsworth, 10-1-1883
     Edith Rebecca   b 28- 1-1865   m Charles Swisher, 30-1-1890
     Harriett Tenel   b 12- 1-1868
     Harlan C   b 30- 5-1870   d 14- 8-1874, age 2y 2m 14, bur
                        Little Brittain
     Kate Amelia   b 1- 2-1874

Daniel   of Fulton Twp, Lancaster Co, PA
                        d 3-11-1848, age 56y, bur Little Brittain Grvyd
Jane   d 23-10-1860, age 65y 1m 27d, bur Little Brittain
                        Jane, w of Daniel, rein 30-10 (or 11)-1819 by per-
                        mission of Nottingham MM, MD, which had pre-
                        viously dis her Elwood, their s, rec on req 7 mo-1820

Ch: Elwood M   b 9-12-1818
     Joseph C   b 10- 2-1820
     Ruthanna   b 2- 8-1822
     Sarah   b 25-12-1823   d 28- 6-1824, age 6m 3d
     Mercy M   b 8- 3-1826
     Priscilla   b 17- 3-1828
     William P   b 6-10-1830   d 30- 6-1834, age 3y 8m 24d

Daniel & Vincent Jr rec on req 12-12-1818

Daniel Sr	(form of Bradford MM, PA; later of Little Brittain Twp, Lancaster Co, PA)
	b ca 1724/5 ? d 6- 5-1808, age 86y
	s Thomas & ----- of Chester Co, PA
Ruth Gilpin	b ca 1731 d 27- 7-1781, bur Little Brittain, PA
	dt Joseph & Mary (Cordwell) of Chester Co, PA
	m 20-1mo (Mar) 1751/2 OS (Issue 12 children)
	For Ch, see Nottingham B&D, p 103.
Hannah	(now Reynolds) rptd by Little Brittain PM, 31-12-1820 as mou; ack acc 31-3-1820
Hannah & Sarah	dts of Vincent (& Priscilla) Stubbs, rec on req 10-8-1816
Isaac	b 21- 6-1774 d 15- 2-1840, age 65y 7m 24d
	s Daniel & Ruth (Gilpin), dec, of Little Brittain Twp, Lancaster Co, PA
1st w Hannah Brown	b 15-10-1778 d ca 1824 (?)
	dt Jeremiah & Hannah (England) of Little Brittain Twp
	m 11- 6-1801, Little Brittain MH
	Isaac & Hannah & ch rocf Nottingham MM, MD, 10-1-1807, dtd "yesterday"; Isaac & Hannah & 3 minor ch, viz: Amor (or Amos), Jeremiah B & Daniel, gct Deer Creek MM, MD, 12-9-1807 "they having already rem", cert to be forwarded; Isaac & Hannah & 7 minor ch viz: Jeremiah B, Hannah B, Sarah Ann, Daniel, Joseph I, Slater & Deborah K, rocf Deer Creek MM, MD, 18-12-1824, dtd 12-10-1826; their eldest s, Amor, adult, rocf Deer Creek MM, MD, 18-11-1826, dtd 12-10-1826; their sons Daniel (1) & Isaac having d at Deer Creek

2nd w Sarah (Askew) Dunn, a widow of E Nottingham Twp, Cecil Co, MD
dt Parker & Hannah Askew of Brandywine Hundred, New Castle Co, Del
m 1-10-1829 at East Nottingham MH
Sarah (Askew-Dunn) Stubbs, rocf Nottingham MM, 14-8-1830, dtd 18-6-1830
Isaac & Sarah (Askew-Dunn) & their 2 minor ch, viz: Joseph I & Slater, gct New Garden MM, PA, 13-7-1833

Ch: (by 1st w)
    Amor (Amos?)   b 18-12-1801
    Jeremiah B   b 13- 4-1804   gct Nottingham MM, MD, 13-6-1829
    Daniel (1)   b   2- 4-1806   d young at Deer Creek, MD
    Hannah Brown   b 27- 5-1808
    Sarah Ann   b 31- 8-1810
    Daniel (2)   b 17- 7-1812   d 29- 4-1869   m Rachel N Kirk (Nottingham)
    Isaac Jr   b   9- 4-1815   d   5-11-1823
    Joseph I   b   2- 1-1818   d 25-12-1884   m Martha P Pierson (Nottingham)
    Slater   b
    Deborah K   b   5-10-1823

Jeremiah B   s Isaac & 1st w Hannah (Brown), dec, gct Nottingham MM, MD, 13-6-1829

John   of Fulton Twp, Lancaster Co, PA
    d 23-12-1856, bur Little Brittain Grvyd
Anna   b   1784   d   3-10-1863, age 79y 9m 9d
John Stubbs & 3 minor ch: Priscilla, Benjamin & Gilpin, rec on req of himself & wife (already a mbr) 3-6-1820

Ch: Priscilla   b 25- 4-1815
    Benjamin   b   8- 9-1816   d   4-10-1831, age 15y 26d
    Gilpin   b 26-10-1818

John D	b 22-12-1821 d 23-12-1851, age 30y 1d, bur Little Brittain Grvyd
Susannah	b 3- 4-1824
Sarah Ann	b 18- 9-1826
Rachel	b 20- 9-1828 d 12- 9-1860, age 31y 11m 22d, bur Little Brittain

Joseph	b 27- 5-1761 d 4- 8-1856 in 96th yr
	s Daniel & Ruth (Gilpin), dec, of Little Brittain Twp, Lancaster Co, PA
Ruth Pyle	dt Moses & 2nd w Mary (Cook), both dec, of same place
	d 14- 3-1837, bur Little Brittain Grvyd
	m 4- 5-1786, Little Brittain NH, PA, auspices Nottingham MM, MD
Ch: Mary	b 7- 6-1788 m Jesse Cutler
Orphah	b 8- 8-1791 d 16- 9-1853
	m Thomas Richards, Jr (See Nottingham)

Joseph	
Rachel Ann	of Fulton Twp, Lancaster Co, PA
Ch: Mary A	b 6- 8-1855 d 20- 9-1855, age 1m 14d, bur Little Brittain
Jennie	b 13- 5-1857
Mary B	b 21- 8-1858
Hannah	b 31- 1-1860
Ruthanna	b 26-10-1861

Martha	(late Furniss) rptd 14-4-1832 as mou; disf same 16-6-1832

Ruth	dt Vincent, dec, rec on req 17-1-1824

Ruth	dt Vincent, dec, & Priscilla, rptd m 19-6-1824 to William Barnard, s Richard & Sarah, of Sadsbury MM, PA (See Barnard)

Thomas   of Fulton Twp, Lancaster Co, PA
1st w Isabella R   d   12- 1-1856, age 23y, bur Little Brittain Grvyd
2nd w Mary Ann
Ch: (by 2nd w)
    Lewis Kirk   b 28- 6-1862
    Slater Russell   b   "

Thomas   of Little Brittain Twp, Lancaster Co, PA, res Drumore
                             b 3- 9-1804   d   29- 4-1842, age 37y 7m 26d, bur Little Brittain Grvyd
1st w Elizabeth (Betty) Trego   b 13- 3-1801
2nd w Martha L
Ch: (by 1st w)
    Cooper   b 25- 4-1833
    Edwin   b 12-11-1834
    John Trego   b   7- 6-1837
  (by 2nd w)
    Priscilla Thomas   b 25- 8-1842   d   26-12-1844, age 2y 4m 1d, bur Little Brittain

Vincent   of Little Brittain Twp, Lancaster Co, PA
                             s Vincent & Priscilla of same place   d 8-4-1875
                             gct Nottingham MM, MD, 4-12-1819 to m
Mary E Haines   b 14- 7-1802   d   21- 4-1874
                             dt Joseph & Rebecca (Reynolds), both dec, of W Nottingham Hundred, Cecil Co, MD
                             m 5-1mo (Jan) 1820 at W Nottingham MM, MD
                             Mary E (Haines) Stubbs, rocf Nottingham MM, MD 2-9-1820, dtd 4-8-1820, to join husband
Ch: Joseph   b 18- 3-1821   d   6- 9-1839, age 18y 5m 18d
    Rebecca   b 25- 1-1824
    Thomas   b 14- 7-1826
    Elizabeth   b 10- 2-1829
    Verlinda   b 19- 4-1831   d   8- 4-1875
    Hannah   b 13-12-1833

Sophia	b 21- 4-1836
Priscilla	b 21-11-1839
Mary Haines	b 8- 5-1843

SWAYNE
Mary   gct Kennett MM, PA, 6-6-1812
rocf Kennett MM, PA, 1-6-1822 dtd 7-5-1822
"recommending her a minister"
d 30- 5-1829 in her 92nd yr
(Note: She was a minister in Eastland PM)

TAYLOR
Susannah   (form Neal) rptd mou 9-8-1806; dis 6-9-1806 rein 10-9-1808; gct London Grove MM, PA 12-11-1808

TEMPLE
Sarah   rocf Kennett MM, PA, 1-7-1820, dtd 6-6-1820; gct Kennett MM, PA, 15-5-1824

TENNIS
Benjamin F   b 26- 3-1845 in Drumore Twp, Lancaster Co, PA
Res Fernglen, Lancaster Co, PA
s Israel & Elizabeth (Lukens) of Drumore; farmer; soldier Civil War (11th Penna Cavalry) 11-8-1864/5-6-1865 hon discharge

Lucinda Lamborn   (usually called Lucy) dt Smedley & Margaret (Bolton) of Liberty Square, Lancaster Co, PA
b 22- 8-1850 at Liberty Square, Lancaster Co, PA
m 24-12-1869

Ch: Cynthia L   b 3- 2-1872   m Oliver F Carter, res Liberty Square, Lancaster Co, PA

     Elizabeth M   b 9-12-1876   m Walter Earnhart of Liberty Square

Israel
Elizabeth Lukens   Both & 2 minor ch, viz: Elamine & Sarah Ann roof Gwynedd MM, PA, 15-5-1830, dtd 1-4-1830

Ch:	Emaline	b 23- 9-1827		
	Sarah Ann	b 22- 1-1829		
	Enos L	b 26-10-1830	d	11- 3-1831
	Mary Jane	b 7- 4-1832		
	Lukens	b 7-12-1833	d	14- 6-1834
	Samuel	b 7- 5-1835	m	Mary R
	Hannah Margaret	b 5- 1-1837		
	Enos L (2)	b 23- 9-1838		
	Anna Maria	b 10 - 1-1840		
	William	b 30-10-1842, bur Drumore	d	22- 2-1868, age 25y 3m 22d,
	Benjamin F	b 26- 3-1845	m	Lucinda Lamborn, 1869

Samuel of Drumore Twp, Lancaster Co, PA
b 7- 5-1835, s Israel & Elizabeth (Lukens) of same place

Mary R d 30-12-1873, age 38y 2m 13d, bur Drumore

Ch:	James R	b 11- 2-1862		
	Charles L	b 15- 6-1863		
	William H	b 16- 7-1865		
	Thomas B	b 13- 9-1867	d	19- 6-1874, bur Drumore
	Benjamin F	b 1- 8-1869		
	Clinton E	b 2- 1-1872		

THOMAS

Caleb d 5- 5-1872 in 76th yr
Rebecca Webster d 15- 3-1830, bur Little Brittain Grvyd
Caleb & Rebecca altm 7-11-1818
(Caleb prcf ? MM showing his clearness; also consent of his parents; Rebecca Webster produced consent of her guardian)

2nd w Mary Hewes rptd m 15-1-1831

Ch:	(of 1st w)			
	Pamela W	b 16- 8-1820		
	Mary	b 20- 9-1822	d	3- 7-1825
	Rachel	b 15- 6-1827	d	6- 7-1827

Ruth Anna	b 17-12-1824 d 7- 4-1833
Nathan W	b 4-11-1828
(by 2nd w)	
Lydia	b 28- 2-1833
Rebecca	b 22- 8-1837
William	b 10- 9-1840

Thomas Thomas, father of Caleb Thomas (above) d 27-2-1828, bur Little Brittain Grvyd

Mary Thomas, wid of Thomas Thomas, of this record, d 31-5-1837

Joseph — s Joseph & Elizabeth of Wilmington, Del
b 27-12-1802 d 7- 1-1875, age 72y 10d

Adrianna Moore — b 28-12-1807, dt Joseph & Mercy (Cutler) dec, of Cecil Co, MD
m 22- 3-1826 at W Nottingham MM, MD
Joseph & Adrianna (Moore) Thomas rocf Wilmington MM, Del, 18-8-1827, dtd 29-6-1827

Thomas — (d 27-2-1828, bur Little Brittain) & w Mary & 3 minor ch, viz: Agness, Sarah & Caleb, rocf Goshen MM, PA, 7-6-1806, dtd 9-5-1806
(Note: Goshen MM, PA shows: Thomas Thomas, s Jacob, gct Chester MM, PA, 11-3-1791 to m Mary Minshall; fr Men's Min.; Women's Min: Mary Thomas, w of Thomas Thomas, rocf Chester MM, PA, 10-6-1791; Goshen B&D Records, show Agness Thomas, dt Thomas & Mary, was b 17-4-1792)
Thomas, father of Caleb, d 27-2-1828, bur Little Brittain Mary, widow of Thomas, b 31-5-1837
Caleb, s of Thomas & Mary, d 5-5-1872 in 76th yr
(This establishes his birth in 1797)
Agness, dt of Thomas & Mary, b 17-4-1792 (Goshen B&D vl, p 51.)

THOMPSON
John
Elizabeth | Both rocf New Garden MM, PA, 6-1-1810, dtd 4-12-1809
John & Elizabeth & their 4 minor ch, viz: Ruthanna, Sarah, Caleb & Rebecca gct New Garden MM, PA 7-6-1817

TOMLINSON
Elizabeth | (late Sidwell) rptd by the Wom's Mtg as guilty of fornication with the man whom she has since married, 9-5-1812, disf same 11-7-1812. Her ack acc 6-6-1818; rein; gct Short Creek MM, OH 2-10-1819

TREGO (TRAGO ?)
Thomas — of Drumore Twp, Lancaster Co, PA
Phebe — d 6-12-1875, age 64y 2m 18d, bur Little Brittain
Res Drumore Twp
On 17-3-1838 Phebe Trago offered ack (she having been dis by London Grove MM "some yrs past"; acc 14-7-1838 with permission of London Grove MM, rein in mbrp

Ch: Emily — b 16- 6-1829 d 19- 3-1873, age 43y 9m 3d, m ------ Pyle
Orpah — b 24-11-1831 d 10-11-1847, age 15y 11m 16d, bur Little Brittain
Phebe Ann — b 4-11-1833 d 6-12-1849, age 16y 1m 2d, bur Little Brittain
Vincent — b 10- 7-1836 d 1- 7-1838, age 2y 9d
John Pyle — b 28- 8-1840 d 25- 4-1846, age 5y 7m 27d

WALTON
Amos Jr | disf joining in military exercises 16-10-1824

Amos | dis 2-3-1822 for refusing to withdraw a suit at law & pay the costs and settle the matter among Friends.

	On 4-5-1822 Amos Walton gave notice of his appeal to the QM; did not appeal
Elizabeth	(w of Amos) & their 9 ch, viz Emily, Hiram, Mary, Amos, Jesse, Eliza, Holcomb, Joseph & Elijah, rec on req 11-10-1817 (all minors except Emily, the eldest ch); Elizabeth & 2 of her ch: Jesse & Mary, rel fr mbrp on their req 17-6-1826

Ch: (of Amos & Elizabeth)

Emily	b 24-10-1798	
Hiram	b 4- 4-1800	disf joining the Militia 19-10-1822
Mary	b 25- 2-1802	rel on req 17-6-1826
Amos	b 9-12-1803	
Jesse	b 8- 2-1806	rel on req 17-6-1826
Eliza	b 24-12-1808	d 29- 6-1811, bur Little Brittain
Holcomb	b 23- 7-1811	
Joseph	b 12- 4-1813	
Elijah	b 8-11-1815	
John C	b 15-12-1819	

Jacob
Hannah

Ch:		
Evelina	b 10- 1-1803	
Eliza	b 22-12-1804	
John	b 21- 3-1807	
James	b	
Martha	b	

Jacob & Hannah & 5 minor ch named above, gct Buckingham MM, Bucks Co, PA, 6-4-1816; to be forwarded

WATSON

William	s Joseph & Sarah, late of Cumberland Co, Old England, both dec)
Martha Jay	dt Stephen & Hannah, late of Harford Co, MD, both dec

Ch:	Sarah W	m 5-3-1801, Deer Creek MM, MD b bef coming to Little Brittain
	Joseph D*	b 5-5-1804
	William	b 5-8-1806
	Hannah	b 27-7-1808

William & w Martha & 4 minor ch named above, gct Deer Creek MM, MD, 9-12-1809

*In the B&D records, p 12, he is listed as James D; but as Joseph D in the Minutes of both M & W, granting the above cert Deer Creek

WAY

Thomas

Lydia — Both & 1st e ch listed below rocf Kennett MM, PA, 30-6-1821, dtd 5-6-1821

Thomas & w Lydia & 6 minor ch (listed below) gct Kennett MM, PA, 13-5-1826

Ch:	Chandler	b
	David	b 11-6-1818
	Ziba	b
	Martha	b 20-10-1821 (at Little Britain)
	William	b 7-8-1823 " " "
	Paskill (Pascal)	b

WEBSTER

Isaac S — rptd 13-10-1827 by Little Brittain PM as mou; for which he made a voluntary ack; his ack acc 15-12-1827

Isaac — of Fulton Twp, Lancaster Co, PA
d 13-4-1858, bur Little Brittain Grvyd

Ann Hewes — d 21-3-1877
dt Joseph Hewes & Ann (King) (who d 24-2-1850, age 67y 2m 21d) (Joseph Hewes, father of Ann, d 28-9-1841, age 70y 23d)
m

Pamela	(now Rea or Ray) rptd 19-5-1832 as mcd to her 1st cousin; disf same 14-7-1832
Samuel	rptd 19-12-1829 by Little Brittain PM as mcd to Deborah Kirk, both mbrs; both made ack which ere acc 13-3-1830

WENTZ

Sarah	w of Joseph b 9-11-1778 d 17- 2-1843, rocf London Grove MM, PA, 8-6-1816, dtd 3-4-1816

WHITE

Job	s Benjamin & Martha, dec, of Little Brittain MM
Phebe Kinsey	b 18- 6-1782, dt John & Mary (Rice) of Little Brittain rptd m 8-6-1811 Job & Phebe (Kinsey) gct Baltimore MM for Eastern Dist, 9-1-1813; Job & Phebe (Kinsey) & 2 ch, viz: John Kinsey & Elizabeth Moore, rocf Baltimore MM, E D, 10-6-1816, dtd 13-6-1816
Ch:John Kinsey	b (See Baltimore MM for E D)
Elizabeth Moore	b "
Oliver	b 14- 1-1818
Martha	b 11-12-1819
Benjamin Clayton	23-12-1822
Mary Hannah	b 14-12-1825

WHITSON

Hannah	(w of Henry) rocf New Garden MM, PA, 12-9-1818, dtd 9-7-1818; gct London Grove MM, PA, 17-7-1824

WICKERSHAM

Hannah	(late Gray) rptd 16-10-1837 as "guilty of unchastity with a man whom she has since married"; disf same 16-12-1837

Isaac	rocf Bradford MM, PA, 9-2-1805, dtd 5-12-1804; at the mtg held 9-4-1808, it was rptd that he had remained here only a short time & had then gone away; investigation discovered that he had returned to the vicinity of Bradford MM & on 11-6-1808, his cert was end back to Bradford MM
WICKES (WEEKS ?)	
Elizabeth	(late Reynolds) rptd 13-6-1829 by Eastland PM as mou; disf same 15-8-1829 (Note: The name is written Wickes in Wom's Min & as Weeks in Men's Min)
WILEY	
Hannah	(late Kinsey) rptd by Eastland PM 19-3-1825 as mou; disf same 14-5-1825; her ack acc 18-3-1826; gct Goshen MM, PA 13-5-1826 (removed)
Margaret	rocf Nottingham MM, MD, 2-9-1820, dtd 30-6-1820
WILKINSON	
Thomas	rocf New Garden MM, PA, 9-7-1814, dtd 9-6-1814; on 9-12-1815 he req cert Little Falls MM, MD; but on 6-1-1816 the comm rptd that he had been mcd before a Justice of the Peace; disf same 6-7-1816
WILLIAMS	
Charity	rocf Burlington MM, NJ, 11-1-1806, dtd 2-12-1805 (Note: She had been recd by Burlington MM on cf Gwynedd MM, PA, 7-12-1801, dtd 24-11-1801)
Isaac	(a minor) rocf Sadsbury MM, PA, 4-12-1819, dtd 2-11-1819; gct Sadsbury MM, PA, 15-2-1823
WILSON	
Amelia	rocf Nottingham MM, MD, 7-2-1818, dtd 5-9-1817

Anna		w of Benjamin, & their 5 minor ch, listed below, rocf Nottingham MM, MD, 6-9-1817, dtd 5-9-1817 (Note: Anna Wilson, w of Benjamin was dt Hugh & Anna (Haines) Sidwell, of Nottingham MM, MD; & Benjamin Wilson was son of Benjamin & Lydia (Job) Wilson, of E Nottingham Twp, Chester Co, PA) Anna Wilson, w of Benjamin, d 22-11-1843, bur Eastland Grvyd
Ch:	(of Benjamin & Anna (Sidwell) Wilson)	
	Isaac	b
	Sarah	b
	Mary	b
	Deborah Ann	b d 27- 2-1843 m ----- Reah; bur Eastland
	Susan Jane	b 2-10-1814 d 3- 3-1838, age 23y 5m 1d; bur Eastland
Emily		(now Reynolds) rptd 15-2-1823 by Eastland PM, as "guilty of fornication with the man she hath since married"; dis 17-5-1823
Isaac		Eastland PM rpts 1-7-1820 that he has been training in Military exercise, which he does not deny; dis 3-2-1821
John		
Catharine		Both with the 4 ch (1st listed below) rocf London Grove MM, PA 6-7-1805, dtd 5-6-1805; with their 5 minor ch, viz: Elizabeth, Nathan, Janes, Joseph Milner & Catharine, they were gct Nottingham MM, MD, 11-9-1813
Ch:	Elizabeth	b (See London Grove)
	Nathan	b "
	James	b "
	Joseph Milner	b "

Mary S	b 19- 3-1807	d 1- 5-1807, age 1m & some days old
Stephen	b 21- 6-1808	d 4- 3-1811
Catharine	b 15- 3-1812	
Esther	b 3- 4-1817	

Mary   (now Pierson or Pearson ?) rptd by Eastland PM, 17-5-1828 as mou; disf same 16-8-1828 (See Pierson)

Needham   rocf Nottingham MM, MD, 8-8-1818, dtd 8-5-1818; at the Mtg held 11-9-1819 Eastland PM rptd that "A young woman charged him with being the father of her bastard ch; which he denies; but on being brought face to face with his accuser he appeared unable to clear himself"; out comm apptd to investigate the matter rptd 1-1-1820 that "they had a full opportunity with him & his accuser & in their opinion there is not sufficient ground to proceed against him"; case dismissed.
Eastland PM rptd 5-8-1820 that Needham Wilson has been training in the militia, which he ack; dis 31-3-1821

Sarah   (now Cox) dt Benjamin & Anna (Sidwell) produced an ack for her mou to ----- Cox, 18-11-1826; ack acc 14-12-1826 (See Cox)

WOOD

Alfred	b 3-12-1845, s James & Mercy Moore (Carter) surveyor, of Lyles, Fulton Twp, Lancaster Co, PA
Elmira King	b 26- 8-1849, dt Thomas P & Phebe Moore (Preston) of Lancaster Co, PA
	m 31- 1-1878
Ch: Cora	b 27- 2-1879
Walter	b 25-10-1880
Galen	b 27-12-1887

	Helen	b 27-12-1887
	Norman	b 24- 1-1891
David		b 21-11-1779 d 4-10-1854, age 74y, bur Eastland
		s Joseph & Katharine (Daye) of W Nottingham Twp, Chester Co, PA & of Nottingham MM, MD
Hannah Carter		b 20- 3-1784 d 31- 7-1850, age 66, bur Eastland
		dt Samuel & 2nd w Ruth (Taylor) of Little Brittain Twp, Lancaster Co, PA
		m 9-2mo (Feb) 1803, Little Brittain MH, auspices Nottingham MM, MD
		David & Hannah (Carter) & dt Elizabeth rocf Gunpowder MM, 6-7-1805
Ch:	Elizabeth	b 27- 3-1804
	Samuel C	b 26- 1-1807
	Abner	b 4-10-1809
		At the Mtg held 7-11-1807, David Wood appeared with a paper ack "drinking strong liquors to excess & quarrelling & fighting." Ack acc 6-2-1808
Day		b 7- 8-1812 d 19-10-1865, age 53y 2m 12d, bur Eastland
		s Jesse & 1st w Rachel (Carter) of Little Brittain, PA; & gr-s Joseph & Katharine (Daye) Wood of W Nottingham Twp, Chester Co, PA
Eliza Jackson		b 13- 3-1813, dt Joel & Alice
		rptd m 15-3-1834
Ch:	John J	b 7- 5-1835 d 13-11-1836, age 1y 6m 6d, bur Joel Jackson place
	Rachel	b 29-11-1838
	Henry	b 24- 7-1841 d 2- 8-1844, age 3y 8d, bur Joel Jackson place
	Edward	b 11- 9-1846
	Day	b 25-12-1849 m Ann Elizabeth

Day   b 25-12-1849   res Fulton Twp, Lancaster Co, PA
                        s Day & Eliza (jackson); gr-s Jesse & Rachel (Carter)
                        Wood & grt-gr-s Joseph & Katharine (Daye) Wood
Ann Elizabeth
Ch: Harriet R   b 25- 8-1875
      Granville E   b 13- 8-1881

Henry C   b 31- 8-1829   s John & Ruth of Little Brittain,
                        Lancaster Co, PA; gr-s Joseph & Katharine (Daye)
                        Wood of W Nottingham Twp, Chester Co, PA

Hannah
Ch: William C   b 5- 5-1857

James   b 17- 7-1821   d 9- 8-1894, s Jesse & 2nd w
                        Sidney, of Little Brittain, Lancaster Co, PA; gr-s
                        Joseph & Katharine (Daye) Wood
Mercy Moore Carter   b 29-11-1822, dt Jeremiah & Susan (Moore)
                        m 26- 2-1845
Ch: (All b in Little Brittain)
      Alfred   b 3-12-1845   m Elmira King
      Susan   b 5-10-1847   m Ellwood H Townsend
      Jesse Jr   b 26- 2-1849   m Margaret Killough
      Mary   b 12- 9-1850   d 22-12-1877, age 27y 3m 10d; m
                        Davis E Allen
      Lucretia   b 2- 3-1852   m John W Smedley
      Lewis   b 27- 1-1854   m Luella King
      Ida   b 25-12-1855   d 19-10-1890
      James   b 17- 9-1860

Jesse   b 21- 7-1773   d 8- 1-1852, in 79th yr, bur
                        Eastland Res Little Brittain Twp, Lancaster Co, PA
                        s Joseph & Katharine (Day), the form dec, of W
                        Nottingham Twp, Chester Co, PA
1st w Rachel Carter   b 12- 5-1789   d 18-12-1817, age 29y
                        dt Samuel & 2nd w Ruth (Taylor), (dt Enoch Taylor)
                        of East Bradford, Chester Co, PA

		rptd m 7-10-1809
		Jesse gct Chester MM, PA 29-4-1820 to m
2nd w Sidney Yarnall		b ca 1785 d 27-10-1857, in her 67th yr, bur Eastland
		m 1820
		Sidney (Yarnall) Wood rocf Chester MM, PA, 30-9-1820, dtd 28-8-1820
Ch:	(by 1st w)	
	Mary	b 15- 7-1810 d 26- 2-1829 in 19th yr, bur Eastland
	Day	b 7- 8-1812 d 19-10-1865, age 53y 2m 12d, bur Eastland, m Eliza Jackson
	Henry	b 29-10-1814 d 14- 6-1817, in 3rd yr
	John	b 6- 3-1817 d 7- 3-1817, age 36hrs
	(by 2nd w)	
	James	b 17- 7-1821
		Note: Jesse Wood was appt Clerk of Little Brittain MM, 1826
John		b 11 mo-1781 d 1 mo-1839, bur Eastland
		Res, Little Brittain
		s Joseph & Katharine (Day) of W Nottingham Twp, Chester Co, PA
		produced an ack for mcd 14-4-1827 to Ruth Cutler, who also ack her mcd at same time; both acks acc 16-6-1827
Ruth Cutler		mcd 1827
		b 25-12-1791 d 13-8-1857, age 65y 7m 8d, bur Little Brittain
		dt Benjamin & Susannah (Dunn)
		John Wood, cof paying a muster fine 6 mo-1808; his ack acc 10-9-1808
Ch:	William	b 17-12-1827
	Henry C	b 31- 8-1829; m Hannah ------
	Catharine	b 4-12-1830
	Isaac	b 23- 9-1833

Joseph	cof "taking strong drink to excess" by Eastland PM, 9-2-1805; a comm visited him again & again trying to reform him, but he fell every time; on 11-1-1806 he offered a paper condemning his conduct & confessing having been many times intoxicated, which paper was acc; but on 12-9-1807 Eastland PM rptd that he had again been "drinking to excess"; after long care, & after his many promises to stop drinking entirely, he was again found deviating, for which he was dis 12-3-1808
Joseph Jr	disf joining the Militia 15-1-1825 "after long care."
Lewis	b 27- 1-1854 s James & Mercy Moore (Carter) of Little Brittain, Lancaster Co, PA Res Little Brittain; mbr Eastland Mtg (H) Lancaster Co, PA
Luella King	b 22- 7-1857, dt Thomas P & Phebe Moore (Preston) of Wakefield, PA; res Little Brittain m 25- 1-1893
Ch: Ida	b 12- 5-1894
Edith A	b 19-12-1896
Lydia	rptd 30-3-1822 by Eastland PM to have "been guilty of fornication"; disf same 1-6-1822
Margaret	gct Nottingham MM, MD, 19-9-1829
Samuel C	b 26- 1-1807 res Little Brittain s David & Hannah (Carter) of Little Brittain Twp, Lancaster Co, PA; gr-s Joseph & Katharine (Daye) Wood
1st w Hannah B Brown, dt Levi & Harriett, of same place	
	b 23- 2-1806 d 24- 9-1841, age 35y 7m 1d, bur Little Brittain rptd m 16-4-1831

2nd w Hannah		
Ch: (by 1st w)		
Granville Brown	b 19-10-1834	d 6- 3-1879, age 44y 4m 17d, bur Little Brittain
Harriet Mary	b 3- 1-1838	
(by 2nd w)		
Ann Elizabeth	b 6- 8-1844	
Hannah C	b 15- 1-1846	d 31- 7-1851, age 5y 6m 16d, bur Little Brittain
Samuel D	b 10- 6-1850	

Thomas   b 30- 9-1769   d 25-12-1812 in 44th yr, bur Eastland, PA
                s Joseph & Katharine (Daye) Wood of W Nottingham Twp, Chester Co, PA; res Eastland, Lancaster Co, PA

Elizabeth Gray b ca 14- 7-1776 d 2- 8-1850, age 74y 18d, bur Eastland
                dt Joseph & Ann, of Little Brittain Twp, Lancaster Co, PA
                m 8-11-1797 at Eastland MH, auspices Nottingham MM, MD

Ch: Joseph Gray	b 3- 8-1798	
Lydia Day	b 9- 3-1800	
Ann	b 25- 9-1802	
Thomas Jr	b 20- 9-1805	d 7- 1-1877, age 71y 3m 17d
Hannah R	b 11-12-1807	d 7- 3-1841, age 33y 6m 22d, bur Eastland
Margaret	b 10- 2-1810	
Sarah	b 6-12-1811	

Thomas   gct Nottingham MM, MD, 19-9-1829

WOODROW

James   rocf Kennett MM, PA, 16-8-1834, dtd 3-5-1834

Levi   rptd by London Grove MM, PA (he being a mbr of that Mtg) 14-2-1835 as mcd; as he res within our verge, we are asked to treat with him; on 19-12-1835 the comm rptd that after many months of effort to gain an interview with him, further effort was abandoned & so rptd to London Grove MM. On 19-3-1836 this Mtg recd a paper dis Levi Woodrow with req to inform him of same, which was done.

WOODWARD

Levi	s Samuel & Sarah of London Grove, PA
Phebe Hutton	m 11- 1-1816 at New Garden MH, PA
	dt Joseph & Sarah of New Garden
	Both with their infant dt, Sarah, rocf New Garden MM, PA, 12-7-1817, dtd 10-4-1817
Ch: Sarah	b 16- 2-1817
Isaac I	b 10- 8-1818
Sibillah	b 1- 4-1820
Samuel	b 16-12-1821
Joseph	b 17- 5-1823
Cassandra	b 1- 7-1825
Hadassah	b 16- 9-1827
Ann Eliza	b 16- 6-1832

WORRELL

Joseph	offered a voluntary ack that he had been guilty of drinking to excess, in that state joined with others in pitching cents and quoits for drinks at a public house 11-9-1819; his ack acc 2-10-1819
Joseph	
Elizabeth	Both & their minor dt Jemima, rec on req 7-2-1818
	Res Drumore Twp
	Joseph had trouble with 4 of his neighbors, which was finally settled satisfactorily when Joseph made an ack which was acc, 1821
Ch: Jemima E	b 3- 9-1807; gct Fallowfield MM, PA, 17-3-1827

CENTRE MONTHLY MEETING
CENTRE COUNTY, PA

ALLEN
Sarah   d   bur Center

ANTIS
Esther   (form Iddings) mou by a magistrate; 10-18-1806; dis 12-13-1806

BAILEY
Caleb   & w Elizabeth & 8 minor ch: Eliza, Margaret, Ann, Daniel, Calib, Charlotte, Elizabeth & Titus pcf Munsy, 10-18-1806

Eliza   7-15-1809, hath renounced our profession & joined the Methodists; dis 11-18-1809

BANE
Mary   3-15-1806 pcf Guined MM

BARRT
Elizabeth   (form Underwood) mou by magistrate 1-17-1818

BEHRES
David W   & Eva J (request) Center
                 Ira   1-12-1891
                 Esther   5-14-1897
                 David   4-12-1902

David   d 11- 3-1917

BLACKBURN
John M   d   8-30-1887, age 69y 5m 4d, bur Centre
Ruth S   d   3-11-1891, age 68y 7m 12d, Center

BOY
Charrity   See Packer

BOYD
Elizabeth   (form Levingston) mou by magistrate 10-19-1811 Notice sent to Muncy

BROKS
William   & w Sarah & s Thomas, pcf London Grove, 1-19-1805

BROOKES
Starr   d   6-13-1812, age 4y bur Bald Eagle, res Center Co
Sarah   d   4-13-1822,   "   "   "

William
Sarah   Centre Co
Ch: William   b   2- 4-1804
       Mary   b   2-21-1805
       Starr   b   9- 9-1808
       Sarah   b   8-22-1810
       Jerushah (Green?)   5-11-1813
       Wm Chandler   b   3-23-1816
       Thomas   b   2- 4-1804 ? 1817 ?
       Richardson   b   2-26-1819

BYE
Sarah   6-19-1813 req cert to Middleton MM, OH; approved 7-17-1813

CADWALADER
See Crafford, Grace
See Kincade

CADWALLADER

Elizabeth	d	5- 3-1809, age 70y 5m, bur Center
Phoebe Jane	d	4-30-1899, age 63y 1m 10d, bur Bald Eagle
William S	d	9-16-1900, age 77y 11m 27d, bur Bald Eagle

CARR

Elizabeth   (form Thomson) 9-14-1816 mou by magistrate
12-14-1816 testimony against signed

CLEAVER

Hannah   4-14-1810, mou by a Magistrate, rptd fr Muncy, wishes to retain mbrp

Hannah   6-15-1811, pcf Muncy MM

Hannah   3-15-1817, with husband & 5 minor ch Nathan, William, Elizabeth, Martha, Andrew rct Dunnons Creek
9-13-1817 approved & signed

Jesse   d   1898

Kezia   d   5-14-1846, Bald Eagle

Wm Clever
Ann   Center Co
Ch: Thomas   b 10-13-1834

Wm Clever
Kezia   Bald Eagle, Center Co
Ch: Charles   b 11-22-1841
      Jesse   b 2- 5-1844

CRAFFORD

Grace   (form Cadwalader) 4-14-1804 mou by hireling teacher with a man not in mbrp

DAVIS

Joseph		of Pike Twp, Clearfield Co, s Elisha & Alice of Warrior mach Twp
Rebecca Moore		dt James & Lydia of Pike Twp
		m 16-10-1823
Ch:	Lydia	b 6-13-1824 (West Branch)
	Rachel	b 10-29-1825
	Esther	b 6-30-1827
	John	b 7-24-1829

DEAL

Ann   8-19-1809 pcf Munsy MM

DOUGHMAN

Gulielma   d 3-12-1842, age 27y 11m 27d, bur Center

DOWNING

Bulah   pcf Sadsbury 5-18-1811

Bulah   & husband & 2 minor ch Daniel & Rebecca, req cert Middleton, OH 8-19-1815; approved 9-16-1815

Elizabeth   d 10-12-1886, age abt 73y, bur Center, res Center

Jacob
Jane W   Bald Eagle, Center Co

Ch:	Hannah Margaret	b 8-14-1839
	Rebecca	b 1-26-1842
	Alvina	b 4- 1-1844
	Rebecca Star	b 5-16-1846
	Mariah ?	b 10-15-1848
	Matilda Jane	b 4-10-1851
	(faded)	b 6-20-1855 or 1854
	Jeremiah	b 8-31-1856
	Joseph Jeremiah	b 10-20-1858

Jane   d 9-18-1849, age 68y 10m 4d, bur Half Moon

Rebecca	d 7-15-1819, age 58y, bur Center, res Center
Samuel	s Thomas & Rebeckah, dec
Jane Wilson	dt George & Esther, all of Half Moon Twp
	m 22- 3-1821 at Center
	George & Esther Willson, Thomas Downing, Rebecca Downing
Thomas	s William & Ellen, Bart-- Twp, Lancaster Co
Elizabeth Kirk	Lawrence Twp, Clearfield Co
	dt Wm Garison & Lydia, Newberry Twp, York Co
	m 23-11-1820 at Center
	John Kirk, Lydia Kirk, Jason Kirk, Samuel Downing, Thomas & Jacob Downing
Thomas	bur Center

ELDER

Esther	(form Wilson) 5-19-1810 mou by a magistrate; dis 9-15-1810

ENGLAND

Isaac	of Half Moon, s Nun & w Margaret of Chinclecommoore Twp, Clearfield Co
Dinah Moore	dt Isaac & Lydia of Half Moon
	m 21-12-1809 at Center
	Abraham Moore, Nun England, Margaret England; Moore's in attendance: Isaac, Lydia, Amy, Sarah, Eleanor, Isaac Jr, James & Samuel
Ch: Lydia	b 11-22-1810
Isaac	b 9-24-1812
Sarah	b 7-15-1814
Elizabeth	b 2- 8-1817
Stephen N	b 5-16-1822
Margaret	d 8-26-1824
Susannah	b 12-17-1826

Wm Thomas   d 10-14-1829

ERWIN
Sarah   d   6- 8-1811, bur Bald Eagle, res Bald Eagle

ERVAN
John Jr   & w Mary & dt Hannah, pcf Monsy MM, 5-19-1804

ERVIN
John   & w Sarah & 2 ch Isabella & Martha pcf Monsy 8-18-1804

EVANS
Jonithan   & w Priscilla & 5 minor ch pcf Muncy MM, 4-16-1814

EVES
Hannah Margaret   d 7-29-1886, bur Center

Joseph   d 12-30-1903

Mary P   d 11-18-1917

EWIN
John
Sarah   Chester Co
Ch: Isabel   b 12- 1-1779
     Martha   b   1- 4-1789 or 1780

FAGON
Lydia   & husband req cert Middleton MM, OH 9-18-1813; approved 10-16-1813

Uphemy   2-13-1813 req mbrp; received 3-13-1813
                            9-18-1813 rct Middleton MM, OH (Euphemia)

FARQUHAR
Caleb[5]   (Phebe[4]) ?
                            b 3-26-1776

208

Sarah Poultney	dt Anthony & Susanna of Frederick Co, MD
	m 4-23-1807 at Bush Creek
	They died early, leaving one child
Ch: James P	b 6-26-1808 m Sarah Warner d at Quincy, IL

FENTON

Esther*	7-18-1818 guilty of fornication with 1st cousin, to whom she is married by magistrate
	4-11-1819, Esther Finton, test against;
	5-15-1819, test against approved
	*See Esther Moore

FISHER

Deaths recorded 1942, dates lacking
Ira
Rebecca
Hannah Fisher Wiser
Mary Jane
George W
Sarah R Fisher Everett   d   6-22-1942 Los Angeles
Samuel D
Malissa Bing
Ulysses Grant

Living 11-29-1937
Sarah Fisher
Samuel Fisher
Nancy Fisher

Beulah	4-15-1809, guilty of adultery; dis 9-16-1809
Esther W	d 12- 4-1886, age 63y 2m 21d, bur Bald Eagle
Ezra	d 1917
Hannah	d 2-26-1814, age 55y, bur Bald Eagle, res Bald Eagle

Ira	s Buela
Rebecca Wilson	dt Thomas & Hannah Downing
	m 5-13-1846
	She was birthright; he joined in 1846
Ch:Hannah Mariah	b 8- 5-1848
Mary Jane	b 10- 8-1837 ?
George Wilson	b 9-15-1853
Sarah Rebecca	b 10-19-1835 ?
Samuel Downing	b 3- 9-1858 ? 38?
Nancy Margaret	b 10- 7-1861
Malissa Bing	b 8-29-1864
Ulysses S Grant	b 9-13-1867
	Above dates inserted in 11-29-1837 (?) by Nancy Margaret Fisher Williams, Recorder, who stated they were all birthright.
John I	d 3- 3-1843, age 13y 9m 2d, bur Bald Eagle
Lilian	d 5-28-1904
Lydia	See Kirk
Rebecca	6-14-1806, a minor, pcf Bradford MM
	(Rebekah) 3-18-1809 cpt Bradford
T. W.	d 8-13-1906
Ira	d 12-24-1892
William	3-17-1804 pcf Monsy, also for w Hannah & ch Lydia, Hannah, Elizabeth & William, Bulah, Sarah & Thomas
William P	
Esther	Bald Eagle
Ch: Lucretia M	b 11-17-1848
Thomas W	b 2-23-1851
Elwood	b 7-16-1856

Sarah J (?)	b	10-23-1858
Wm Penn	b	4-25-1862
Mary	b	9-26-1864
Hanna C	b	6- 6-1867

William
Rachel   Center Co
Ch: Hannah	b	7-18-1812
Rachel	b	2-20-1814
Elijah	b	3-20-1816
William	b	5-15-1818
Beulah	b	7-16-1820

William
Rachel   Bald Eagle
Ch: Mary J	b	7-17-1823
John J	b	6- 1-1829
Ezra	b	7-30-1831

William P	d	8-26-1903
Rebecca	d	1-14-1903
Elwood	d	11- 2-1903
Mary J	d	1- 8-1905

William   of Boggs Twp, Center Co, s Thomas & Elizabeth of Chester Co
Sarah Moore   dt Joshua Hains & Hannah of Lancaster Co
m 18- 1-1816
Samuel Moore, Thomas Moore, Robert W Moore, Wm Fisher, Rachel Fisher, Beulah Fisher

FLETCHER
Sarah   5-19-1804 pcf Warrington

GEARY
Mary J (Fisher)   d 2-20-1862, age 38y 7m 3d, bur Bald Eagle

GILPIN
Mary & husband & 5 minor ch: Sarah, John, Rebecca, Thomas, Hennery rct Cesor Creek, OH, 2-18-1809 3-18-1809, approved

GREENLIEF
Hanna A (Underwood) d 2- 7-1890, dt Wm & Alvina

GRIEST
Budd d a few yrs previous to 1940
Martha Russell his wife, d 1940; d at their Florida home
former residents of Unionville, PA
bur Oak Ridge Cem

Nathan 8-29-1885
Marry Ann 4- 9-1890
Martha 4- 5-1874
Charles 3-26-1884

GROSS
Frank
Lilian
Ch: Wm Orlando b 6- 7-1911

HASTINGS
Mary d 2-20-1805, age 72y, bur Center

HATTEN
Rachel 2-15-1817 rct Miami MM, OH; 3-15-1817 approved, signed

HICK
Hannah (Hanah Hik's case) 12-19-1807
5-1-1808 produced ack for outgoing in mar
7-16-1808 retained in mbrp

HICKLEN
Albina d 11-28-1893

Rachel Ann	d 10-28-1899, age 59y 5m, bur Bald Eagle, res Philadelphia
Phebe Jane	See Cadwallader
Thomas	d 6-18-1862
Isaac	d 1-15-1859
E. J.	d 3-24-1904

HOLLINGSWORTH

Israel	req cert for himself & 5 minor ch: Samuel, Lydia, Asapt, Gared, Ann, to Centre MM, OH; 6-17-1815; Approved 9-16-1815
Sarah	9-18-1813, req cert Centre MM, OH; 10-16-1813 approved & signed

HUCKER

Mary	2-15-1812 pcf Muncy

IDDINGS

Elizabeth	d 7-15-1798, age 1y
Henry	d 9-20-1889
Elizabeth	d 4-14-1894
John	
Ann	Chester Co
Ch: Esther	b 1-18-1788
Joseph	b 12-17-1789
James	b 2-12-1792
Elizabeth	b 6- 8-1797 Center Co
William	b 5-14-1795
Lewis	b 12-16-1805
Hannah	b 3-23-1808
John	2-16-1805, & w Ann & 4 minor ch Esther, Joseph, James, William, pcf Munsey MM. See Antis

Joseph
Margaret   Clearfield Co
Ch: Ann   b   2- 2-1826
    Elis   b   11-22-1828
    Lydia   b   9-22-1832, Bald Eagle, Centre Co
    Mary   b   5-10-1834
    Margaret   b   6-24-1836

Martha   d   2-14-1832, 15y 9m 13d, Bald Eagle
Elis   d   1-15-1833, 4y 1m 23d,   "   "

William   d   6-16-1912

IRWIN
Ellis   s John & Mary of Boggs Co
Hannah Iddings   dt John & Ann of same place
                        m   1-10-1827

John   d   3-28-1829, age 79y, bur Bald Eagle

JOHN
Martha   & husband req cert New Garden, OH, 11-18-1815;
                        approved 12-16-1815; signed 3-16-1816

Hannah (Johns)   See McMullen

JOHNSON
Samuel
Hannah Fisher   ami 5-15-1819
                        mtg to be held at Milsburgh to acc marriage
                        m rptd acc 4-11-1804
Ch: James   b   7-10-1806 (Clearfield Co)
    Thirza   b   2-11-1809
    Elah   b   6-24-1811
    John Simpson   b   10-28-1813
    Wm Fisher   b   11- 8-1815
    Nancy   b   2- 6-1818

214

Garretson	b 9-17-1820
Hannah	b 1-29-1823

JONSTON
See Levingston

Samuel	s James, dec, & Elizabeth, Half Moon Twp
Hannah Fisher	dt Wm & Hannah, Spring Twp.
	m 20- 3-1804 at Milesborough, Spring Twp.
	Wm Fisher, Hannah Fisher, Elizabeth Fisher

KINCADE

Deborah	(form Cadwaleder, mou by a hireling teacher 7-13-1805
	8-17-1805 testimony against produced

KIRK

Hannah Jr	8-15-1812 req cert Centre MM, OH, approved 9-19-1812
Hannah	& husband & 4 minor ch req cert Centre MM, OH, 8-15-1812, approved 9-24-1812
Jason	s Thomas & Hannah, dec, Elk Twp, Clearfield Co
Mary Spencer	dt John & Susanna, Half Moon Twp
	m 30- 5-1805 at Center
	Hannah Kirk, Jr, Thomas Spencer, John Kirk, Lidia Kirk, Thomas Jr, John Spencer, Susanna Spencer, Hannah, Samuel, Susanna, Mary

John		
Lydia	Center Co	
Ch:	Hannah	b 5- 6-1804
	Joseph	b 1-14-1806
	Elizabeth	b 2-27-1808
	William	b 1- 3-1810
	Thomas	b 9-15-1811

Lydia	b 8- 3-1813
John Jr	b 11- 3-1815
Mary Ann	b 9-27-1817
Sarah F	b 11-15-1819

Lydia   (form Fisher, guilty fornication with man in mbrp, m by Magistrate 6-16-1804
8-18-1804 Lydia & John Kirk appeared with ack, acc

Sarah   & husband & 3 minor ch: Israel, Hannah & Elizabeth req cert Centre MM, OH, 7-17-1816
Cert signed 9-14-1816

Thomas   s Thomas & Hannah, dec, of Chinclamoose Twp, Clearfield Co

Sarah Taylor   dt Jacob & Hannah of Half Moon
m 23-11-1809 at Center
Jacob Taylor, Hannah Taylor, Israel Taylor, Susannah Taylor, Thomas Kirk, Elizabeth Kirk

LAMBORN

Levi   of Half Moon, s Thomas & Dinah, dec, of New Garden Twp, Chester Co

Mary Wall   dt Absalom & Margaret, Half Moon Twp
m 24- 3-1808 at Half Moon
Sarah Lamborn, Absalom Wall, Margaret Wall, William, Azariah, Sarah Wall

Mary   & husband & 3 minor ch: William, Margaret & Dinah req cert Dunens Creek, 2-19-1814

Sarah   5-18-185(?) req cert to Concord MM, Chester Co

Sarah Jr   rct Concord MM, in Chester Co; 5-13-1805; granted 6-15-1805

Wm Wall   b 3- 3-1809, s Levi & Mary, Center Co

LEVINGSTON
Ann   pcf Monsy MM 10-24-1804 (1-18-1806)
             4-19-1806 Ann Jonston, form Levingston, mou by Magistrate
             6-14-1806 dis (See Boyd)

LINGERFELTER
Sarah   (form Wall) 7-19-1817, mou, does not wish to retain mbrp 10-18-1817 testimony against approved

McDOWEL
Sarah   form Moore, 7-19-1817 mou by magistrate
             11-15-1817 testimony against approved

McMILDON
Jane   12-19-1807 req cert

McMILLEN
Jane   10-13-1810, p--also for family

McMULLEN
Hannah   form Johns, mou by a priest, 7-13-1805
             10-19-1805 testimony against produced & signed

McNOLL
Hannah   10-17-1818, guilty fornication--mou by hireling teacher
             3-13-1819, testimony against approved
             3-15-1819, dis

MILLER
Eliza   See Thomas

Elizabeth   m Ellis Cleaver on 4-7-1791, see Ellis Cleaver

Hannah   9-18-1813 pcf Warrington MM
             1-18-1817 rct Dunnons Creek
             2-15-1817 approved & signed

Lydia	m Josiah Jordan on 6-17-1789, see Josiah Jordan
Mordecai	& Eliza pcf Bradford, 12-14-1816
Priscilla	(form Whitson) mou by Magistrate (11-18-1815, 9-16-1815) 1-17-1816 testimony against approved
Sarah (Miler)	& husband & 7 minor ch: Robert, Hannah, Eli, Sarah, Martha, Mary, Thomas req cert 2-19-1814; approved
Tamson	12-14-1816 pcf herself & 3 minor ch: Isaac, Jane, Mordecai
Tamson	late Whitson, mou by hireling teacher, 4-15-1815, dis 6-17-1815, dis
Thomas	& w Sarah & 4 minor ch: Robert, Hannah, Eli, Sarah pcf Warrington, 5-16-1807

MILLS

Susanna	m Harman Updegraff on 1-14-1801; See Harman Updegraff

MOORE

Abraham	s John, Sadsbury Twp, Chester Co
Susanna Taylor	dt Jacob, Half Moon Twp m 20- 6-1811 at Half Moon Sarah Moore, Mary Moore, Jacob Taylor, Hannah Taylor, Israel Taylor, Jesse, Mary, Elizabeth

Allen
Mary
Ch: Caleb W   b   4-11-1826
     Ezra A   b   8-27-1827
     Thomas O (?)   b   9-10-1829

David	b 12-29-1830
Elijah	b 8-31-1832
Sarah	b 12-24-1834

Amey (Moor)   See Way

Andrew
Elizabeth   Clearfield Co
Ch: Alice   b 10-15-1823
    James   b 3-24-1824
    Elisha   b   "
    Nathan   b 4-16-1826

Andrew   s James & Lidya of Pike Twp
Elizabeth Davies   dt Elisha & Alice (?) sp Alice, of Warrior Mark
    m 17- 9-1822 at Center
    Elisha Davis, Joseph Davis, Margaret Davis, Alice Davis, ? Davis, Samuel & Ann Moore, Thomas, James Moore, Hannah Moore, Hannah Moore, Jr, Rebecca

Dinah   d 11-11-1822, age 55y, bur Center

Elijah
Sarah   Center Co
Ch: Elizabeth   b 2-13-1800
    Thomas   b 4-22-1802
    Allen   b 11-28-1804
    Anna   b 7- 6-1805
    Sarah   b 11-22-1807
    Elijah Jr   b 3- 9-1809

Elijah   d 5mo-1809, age 33y 9m, bur Center
Rebekah   d 2-26-1808, age 72y, bur Center

Esther[5]   (Lydia[4])?
    b 7-18-1788   d 10-?-1843
    m 1st cousin Thomas Fenton, b 8-2-1798

	d 7-27-1853
	s Benjamin & Rebecca Moore Fenton; both bur West Branch
	They settled on a farm adjoining her father's
Ch: Anna	b 10-10-1817 d 7-29-1854, m Thomas Blackburn
Mary A	b d 11-18-1867, m Benjamin F Taylor

Isaac
Lydia   Centre Co
Ch: Ellen   b   3-13-1801
     Isaac Jr   b   2-16-1804

Isaac   d   3- 5-1835, bur Center

Jeremiah   s James & Lydia, Pike Twp, Clearfield Co
Susannah Shivery   dt Andrew & Sarah, Patton Twp, Center Co
                          m 12- 5-1819 at Center
                          Hannah Moore, Samuel Moore, Rebecca Moore

Lydia Jr   (Moor) 5-18-1811 att marriage consummated contrary to Rules of our Discipline, also attended place of diversion, has been guilty of dancing
                          7-13-1811, dis

James & Lydia   See Sharples, page 225

Phebe   (Moor) req mbrp, received 5-6-1804

Lydia   d   3-24-1839, bur Center

Mary   d   8-24-1898, age 35y 3m, bur Center, res Center

Phebe   (Moor) 3-17-1804, req mbrp; 5-19-1804, rec into mbrp

Phebe   req cert with husband & 2 ch: Mary & Jeremiah to Sadsbury 5-1-1808

	cert p for Jeremiah Moore & fam to Sadsbury 8-13-1808
Samuel Hannah Shivery	s Isaac, Half Moon Twp dt Andrew, Patton Twp m 22-10-1818 at Center Susanna Shivery, Isaac More, Lidy More, Andrew Shivery, Sarah Shivery (not present)
Samuel Hannah Ch: Andrew Lydia	Center Co b 8-29-1819 b 10-11-1821
Sarah	See McDowel
Sarah	See Thomson
Sarah	d 9- 3-1819, age 11y 9m 11d, bur Center
Susanna	8-17-1811 req cert to Sadsbury granted 9-14-1811
Thomas Dinah Ch: Hannah	Center Co b 4- 5-1803

Thomas
Sarah
Ch: John
     Caleb
     Thomas
     Robert
     Isaac
	Center Co
	b 1-31-1798
	b 9-27-1800
	b 8- 7-1803
	b 5- 7-1806
	b 10- 2-1808

Thomas Sarah	Half Moon, Center Co

Ch:Lydia Ann	b	1- 3-1832
David Richards	b	3- 9-1833
Milton Young	b	3- 6-1835
Samuel Spencer	b	5-27-1837
Edward Thomas	b	4- 5-1839
Sarah Elizabeth	b	3-31-1841
Elmira	b	12- 2-1843

Thomas   d 12-28-1851, age 85y 7m 19d, bur Half Moon

Thomas Jr   d 7- 4-1808, age 41y 8m, bur Center

PACKER
Charrity   (form Boy) 6-16-1804, m by Magistrate to man in mbrp 11-17-1804, produced condemnation paper, she is retained in mbrp

July   See Wilson

Rose   6-15-1805, pcf Uchland MM to Monsy MM, to Center

William L   & w Anna & 3 minor ch: Lewis, Lamborn & Elizabeth pcf Kennet MM, 11-18-1809

PENNINGTON
Eliza   2-15-1817 req cert to Miami MM, OH, also for husband & ch
3-15-1817 approved & signed

John
Eliza Hatton   8-18-1804, ami
10-13-1804, rptd acc

John   s Daniel & Martha, Warrior Mark Twp, Huntingdon Co

Eliza Hatton   dt Robert & Ann, Half Moon Twp

	m 20- 9-1804 at Center
	Robert Hatton, Ann Hatton, Rachel, Jervis, George, Edward, Daniel Pennington, Martha Penington, Paul, Jane, Josiah, Ruth, Levi Penington
Levi	s Daniel & Martha, Warrior Mark Twp, Huntingdon Co
Mary Bye	dt Hezekiah & Sarah, Half Moon Twp
	m 25- 6-1807 at Center
	Ludia Bye, Hezekiah Bye, Sarah Bye, Samuel Bye, Samuel Penington, Martha Pennington, Paul Pennington, Ruth Pennington
Mary	& husband & 3 minor ch: Sarah, Martha, Meriah, req cert New Garden MM, OH, 7-17-1813
	8-14-1813 approved

PROSSER
Elizabeth	10-18-1806 Antiant friend, Elizabeth Prosser, pcf Gunpowder MM 12-14-1805

RANDEL
Jennet	3-13-1813 pcf Warrington
	9-19-1818 req cert New Garden MM, OH
	(Cert approved 10-17-1818, spelled Jennet Rennalds)

RANDOLPH
Margaret	(form Davis) 8-13-1808, m by Magistrate 10-15-1808, she desires to retain mbrp
	2-18-1809 testimony against approved, dis

RICH
Benjamin	
Jane	Bald Eagle
Ch: John G	b 3-25-1862
Lydia L	b 12-29-1865
Margaret M	b 8- 4-1867

Anna	b 9- 7-1870
Mary J (?)	b 9- 7-1873
Martha J	d 7- 3-1901
Benjamin	d 11-17-1885

RICHARDS

Lydia	d 6-26-1836, age 64y 9m 4d, bur Center, res Center
Naomy Richard	req cert Centre MM, OH, 12-14-1805
Neomei	(form Way) guilty forn, mou by a Magistrate 12-14-1805 2-15-1806 testimony against & approved 3-15-1806
Neomia	6-15-1816 req mbrp 7-17-1816, rec in mbrp

RIGLEY

Ann	(form Dale) mou by a Magistrate, 3-16-1811 11-16-1811, dis

ROWAN

Hanna (Thompson)	d 12-30-1889
Sara	d 1908
George	d 1919

RUSSELL

Abel	
Amanda	Bald Eagle
Ch: Edward A	b 4-18-1837
A.N.	d 1- 1-1892
Amanda	d 10-12-1889
E A	
Louisa A W	Bald Eagle

Ch: Edward Wright   b 10-29-1875

E W
Marian
Ch: Agnes Louise   b 4- 2-1908

Hyram
Alice Wright   of Menallen MM
Ch: Louisa A Wright b 9-17-1850

Louisa A W   d 4-19-1921
E A, M.D.   d 6- 1-1922

SHARPLES
Lydia[4]   Abraham[3]
                     b 8-18-1760 d 4-24-1828 at West Branch, Clearfield Co
                     m 4- 6-1785 at Sadsbury Mtg, Lancaster Co
                     James Moore   b 1- 8-1760 d 9-17-1834 at his son Jeremiah's at Pennsville, PA
                     s Andrew & Rebecca Starr of Sadsbury
                     They moved to York Co, near Susquehanna in 1796, they moved to Half Moon Valley. In 1810 they settled in Clearfiled Co, then an almost unbroken forest.
                     West Branch Mtg was held first at their house in 1813. Both buried at that meeting.

Ch: (of James & Lydia Moore)
     Abraham   b 8- 1-1786 d 1808, unm, bur Centre Mtg.
     Esther   b 7-18-1788 d 10 mo-1843, m Thomas Fenton
     Lydia   b 1-22-1790 d 1-15-1873,   m Joseph Spencer
     Anna   b 3- 6-1792 d 5- 9-1872,   m Jesse Spencer
     Jeremiah   b 8-14-1794 d 7-26-1873,   m Susanna Shivery

Andrew	b 10-20-1796 d 2-26-1881, m Elizabeth Davis
Rebecca	b 12- 5-1798 d 2-23-1871, m Joseph Davis
James	b 10-27-1801 d 7- 4-1847, m Jane W Shivery

SHIVERY
Andrew
Sarah Center Co
Ch: Mary b 3-31-1804

Eleanor d 3-12-1840, bur Center
Sarah d 3-11-1825, " "

Mary d 8-31-1819, age 15y, bur Center

Sarah 8-17-1811, req mbrp; 9-14-1811, rec into mbrp

Sarah 11-16-1811, req mbrp for 6 minor ch: Hannah, Susanna, Rachel, Mary Jane, Sarah; 12-23-1811, received

SHUGART
Hannah 10-18-1817, pcf Muncy

Hannah Jr 9-19-1818, pcf

Mary 11-16-1811, pcf Moncey at Fishing Creek

SIGEL
Elizabeth d 11-24-1912, Center Co

SPENCER
Anna (form Moore) 7-18-1818 guilty fornication, mou by magistrate; testimony against approved 5-15-1819

David
Rachel Half Moon
Ch: Sarah Jane b 12- 6-1828

Aquilla	b 7-19-1831
Mary Ann	b 6-25-1836
Hannah	b 10-18-1838
Susannah	b 4-17-1841

John   & w Susanna req mbrp for 4 minor ch: Samuel, Sarah, Susanna & William, 3-16-1805; req granted

John
Susanna   Center Co
Ch: David   b 10-20-1802
       Aquilla   b 2- 8-1808

John   d 1-31-1829, age 75y 8d, bur Center
Susanna   d 8-22-1834, age 67y 7d, " "

John   & w Susanna req mbrp for 4 minor ch: Samuel, Sarah, Sisana, William, 4-13-1805; req granted 6-15-1805

Mary   dt of John, req mbrp, received 3-17-1804

Mary   the Elder, req mbrp 6-16-1804
             8-18-1804, rec into mbrp

Sarah   6-16-1810, mou
             9-15-1810 ? Sarah Penson dis

STAGE
Margaret   (form Bailey) 7-13-1811, joined Meth & mou, dis

TAYLOR
Hannah   & husband & 4 minor ch: Elizabeth, Jesse, Neomy, Hannah, req cert Centre MM, OH 9-18-1813
             10-16-1813 approved & signed

THILER (?)
Zilla   pcf Monsy MM 9-14-1805

THOMAS

Eliza	11-14-1818 (form Miller) m by a magistrate to man in mbrp
	12-19-1818, she produced ack & is retained
Richard Logan	d 10-17-1822, 2y, bur Bald Eagle, res Center Co
William A	
E M	Center Co
Ch:Jacob Valentine	b 5- 9-1819
Richard Logan	b 1-26-1820
Samuel Valentine	b 8-31-1822

THOMPSON

Almeda (Russell)	
Andrew H	d 4-13-1904
Andrew Sr	d 4-26-1865
Sara	d 11-18-1837
Eleanor	d 12-13-1822, bur Center
Elizabeth	1-17-1818, rct Stilwater MM, OH
	approved & signed 2-1818
Elizabeth Thomson	See Carr
Mary	2-15-1817, rct Miami MM, OH
	3-15-1817 approved, signed
Sarah Thomson	(form Moore) 11-14-1812, guilty of fornication, mou by magistrate
	1-16-1812, dis
	5-13-1815 Sarah Thompson dis (2nd time ?)

TRESTLER

Mamie	d 12- 1-1902

UNDERWOOD
Anna M   1-19-1849 came in by request

Owen
Anna M   Bald Eagle
Ch: Myra H   b   7- 7-1876
    Gilbert O   b   9-14-1879
    Susan R   b   3-29-1884
    Chapman E   b   11- 1-1885

Anna M   d   9-18-1916
Owen   d   2-28-1925
Martha   d   11- ? -1924
Charles L   d   1- ? -1918

Chapman
Miriam
Ch: Clyde   b   7- 7-1914
    Charles L   b   "
    Annis (?)   b   4-28-1916
    Helen   b   9-16-1917 State College

Charles
Jane   Bald Eagle, Centre Co
Ch: David W   b   9-12-1841
    Ruben L   b   10-28-1842
    Elizabeth A   b   8-29-1849

David W
Caroline   Bald Eagle, 5-10-1843 came in by request
Ch: George T   b   9-30-1865
    Alice W   b   8-31-1867
    Hanna M   b   10-22-1868
    John G   b   10- 4-1869
    Charles O   b   8-17-1873
    Joner M   b   3-17-1875
    Walter B   b   6- 6-1878

Elizabeth	See Barrt
Hanna M	d 12- 6-1868, age 2m, Bald Eagle
Jesse Susanna Ch: William Alice	Center Co b 12-25-1840 b 9- 4-1842
Jesse Susannah Ch: Isaac Jason Owen Warner Mary A Zephaniah William I	Bald Eagle b 4- 4-1844 b 3- 3-1846 b 12-19-1847 b 5- 9-1851 b 3- 7-1853 b 1-28-1856 b 3-24-1860
Jesse	d 9- 3-1876, Bald Eagle
John Matilda Ch: Jesse W	Bald Eagle, Center Co b 4- 6-1845
Martha	came in by request
Isaac Martha Ch: J Irwin Hannah Mary Anna Blanch	Bald Eagle b b 9-21-1876 b
Rebeckah	& dt Mary req cert to join Middleton MM, OH, 12-13-1817 1-17-1818 approved & signed

Reuben L
Emeline G   Bald Eagle
Ch: William A   b   4-11-1870
      Ida J   b   1- 5-1869
      Miles W   b   6- 7-1871
      Eli G   b   6- 7-1873
      Eva T   b   5-25-1875
      Jesse H   b   1-24-1877

Susan   d   1-17-1909, age 87y

Warner
Eliza   Bald Eagle
Ch: James Harris   b   9-27-1876

William   d   9- 5-1842, age 1y 8m 11d, Bald Eagle
Alice   d   5- 2-1844, age 1y 7m 29d, "   "

William
Alvina   Centre Co
Ch: Eliza   b   10-29-1838
      Joseph   b   3-22-1841
      Phebe Jane   b   2- 8-1836   Bald Eagle

William   10-18-1817, req for Wm's 4 minor ch: Ezekial,
                         Rebeckah, Hannah, Deborah, to Centre, OH
                         11-15-1817 approved & signed

WAITE
Dorothy   d   11- 2-1917

William W
Della Seigel   mbrs by req
Ch: G Ralph   b   12- 1-1892   resigned
      Darius A   b   4- 9-1895
      Elizabeth   b   11- 4-1897
      Paul   b   1- 9-1902

Ruth	b 6-15-1904	
Dorothy	b 4-30-1909	Center MM

WAKEFIELD
Eli   s George & Rebecca of Wane Twp, Mifflin Co
Elizabeth Way   dt Caleb & Jane of Half Moon
m 19- 9-1822 at Center
Ageston Wakefield, William Wakefield, Rebecca Wakefield, Jr, The following Ways: Caleb, Jane, Sarah, John, Matilda, Robert, William, Jesse, Lidia, Mary, Caleb Jr, Job

WALL
David   s Absolom & Margaret of Half Moon Twp
Elizabeth Fisher   dt William & Hannah, Spring Twp
m 19- 4-1806 at Center
Wm Fisher, Beula Fisher, Absalom Wall, Azariah Wall, Rebecca Wall, Sarah Wall

Jonathan   & w Jane & 4 minor ch: Sarah, Isaiah, Sidney, Eliza pc 4-11-1819
11-18-1818, received

Margaret   & husband req cert to Dunens Creek MM, 2-19-1814 approved, 9-17-1814, signed

Mary   5-16-1807, pcf Warrington

Rebecca   & husband & 5 minor ch: Pheby, John, Thomas, Absolam, Rebecca rct Cesor Creek, OH 2-18-1809
3-18-1809 approved

Sarah   See Lingerfelter

WAY
Amey   (form Moor) mou by a magistrate 3-16-1811
8-17-1811 ack acc

Andrew   d 12-30-1840, age 1y 5m 13d, bur Half Moon
Susannah C   d   5-21-1843, age 8m 23d, bur Half Moon

Caleb   d 12- 5-1842

Caleb
Jane   Center Co
Ch: Matilda   b   3-25-1813

Caleb Jr
Lydia   Center Co
Ch: Allen   b   6- 3-1832

Caleb
Sara   Bald Eagle
Ch: Irwin   b   1-18-1868

D H
Ina   Center
Ch: Morris Borton   b   1-19-1916
     Roger Darlington 11- 7-1918
     Elwood Archie   b   3-11-1920
     Rebecca Jane   b 11-27-1921
     Joseph H   b   5-29-1923
     Robert L   b   6- 2-1925
     Ralph Walter   b   3- 4-1934

Edwin B (Blackburn) d 11- 9-1911
Martha Ann   d 11-24-1912   Center Co

Edwin B
Martha   Center near Stormstown
Ch: Sara H   b   6- 4-1897
     L Lucretia   b 10-21-1898
     E Pauline   b   2- 2-1902
     David Caleb   b   8-24-1903
     Elenor Lorain b   1- 8-1905

Edwin Elsworth	b	9-6-1906
Isabel Marie	b	7-9-1909

Esther C   d 10-3-1891, age 13y 9m 11d, bur Center

Ezra   d 10-19-1884, age 34y 1m 14d, Bald Eagle

Hannah   10-17-1812 req mbrp; 11-14-1812 rec in mbrp

Hannah I   d 6-15-1830, age 26y 10m, bur Bald Eagle, res Bald Eagle

Hanna (Fisher   d 8-31-1892, age 80y 1m 12d, Bald Eagle

Harris   d 4-9-1890

Jane   d 5-22-1827, bur Center
Amy   d   "   "

Jane   6-13-1812, with husband req mbrp of minor ch: William, Elizabeth, Jesse, Lyia, Mary, Caleb, Job, Jane, Ann
                         8-15-1812 rec into mbrp, husband's name Caleb

Jane   d 5-22-1827, age 59y, bur Center, res Center

Jesse   d 9-20-1836, age 11m 2d, bur Center, res Center

Job
Jane
Ch: Thomas B   b 10-18-1834 Center Co
     David   b 1-12-1837
     Mary Jane   b 6-12-1839

John
Mary   Half Moon, Center Co
Ch: Malinda   b 8-11-1827
     Jeremiah   b 3-23-1829

Phebe Jane	b	4-16-1831
Ann	b	9-29-1833
Mary	b	3-29-1836
Andrew	b	10-12-1838
Sarah	b	4-25-1841
William B	b	

Lydia   d   6-17-1823, bur Center

Malissa   d   4-25-1918, Bald Eagle
William F   d   11-13-1918,   "   "
Robert A   d   1916

Margaret (Wilson) d   4-19-1889, bur Center
Robert   d   "   "
Martha   d   "   "

Mary E   d   2-19-1898, bur Center, late res Center
Mary Ann (Beans)   d   2- 8-1913
Margaret   d   4-19-1889
Jeremia   d   4-28-1917, age 88y 1m 5d
C E   d   10- 6-1876
Sara R   d   1906

Meredith   d   12-24-1853, age 7m, bur Bald Eagle

Neomei   See Richards

R Orlando   d   5-23-1918

Robert D P   d   4-19-1819, bur Center

Robert
Hannah   Center MM
Ch: Thomas ? M   b   4-21-1826
      Jane   b   11-27-1828
      Caleb M   b   3- 9-1832   (or 3-2-1832)
      Jesse   b   10-18-1835

Robert A
Lucretia   Center
Ch: Hanna M   b   3-12-1874
     Darlington H   b   10-11-1875
     Esther C   b   12-22-1877
     William F   b   9-18-1880
     Verna M   b   10-25-1887
     S Margaretta   b   10- 2-1890

Robert
Martha   Center Co
Ch: Hannah M   b   7-13-1841
     Susanna C   b   8-28-1842

Robert
Martha   Half Moon, Center Co
Ch: Hannah M   b   7-13-1841
     Susannah B   b   8-26-1842
     Robert   b   5-14-1844

Susanna C   d   5-21-1843, age 8m 23d, bur Centre

T M   d   3-19-1912

William   d   11-11-1875, age 79y 9m 3d, Bald Eagle

William B   d   8-12-1908
Sarah   d   6-26-1917

William
Hannah   Bald Eagle
Ch: Harris F   b   11- 2-1832
     Rachel Jane   b   8-21-1834

William
Hannah   Bald Eagle, Center Co
Ch: Bulah   b

236

Caleb	b	6- 4-1839
William F	b	6-12-1842

William
Hannah   Bald Eagle
Ch: Rachel Jane   b
    Cecelia M   b   8-27-1845
    Malissa T   b   3-26-1848
    Ezra   b   9- 5-1850
    Meredith   b   5-24-1853

WEAKFIELD
George   & w Rebecca pcf Nottingham MM, end by Warrington, 11-16-1805; rec 8-9-1804

WHITSON
Priscilla   See Miller

WIDEMERE
Hannah   6-16-1810 req mbrp
9-15-1810 req left under care
6-15-1811 rec into mbrp

WILSON
Ester Jr   req a right in mbrp, granted 9-15-1804

Esther   d 2- 3-1837, age 82y 11m 18d, bur Center, res Center

George   d 8-26-1832, age 78y 11m 2d, bur Center, res Center

George   bur Center

July   (form Packer) 10-17-1818 mou by Magistrate, fr Muncy MM

Lydia   11-15-1807 pcf Moncy

Mary I	d	8-15-1900
Robert	d	10- 9-1856 73y Half Moon
Mary Ann	d	9-15-1856 18y 7m 6d, Half Moon
Rebecca	d	7-19-1855, 38y 10m 15d " "

Sarah   3-13-1813, pcf Warrington

Thomas   s George & Esther, Half Moon Twp
Hannah Downing   dt Thomas & Rebecka, dec, Half Moon Twp
                  m 18- 1-1821 at Center
                  Thomas Downing, Rebecca Downing, Margret Downing, George & Esther Willson, Jane Willson

Thomas
Hannah   Center Co
Ch: Rebecca   b   2-22-1821
    Ester   b   9-13-1823
    Meriah   b   5- 8-1825
    Margaret   b   6-17-1826
    Jane E   b   2-10-1828
    George D   b   10-18-1830
    Sarah   b   5-12-1833
    Mary   b   6-10-1836

Thomas   d   12-16-1879
Hanna   d   12-12-1879

WEST BRANCH MARRIAGES

Near Grampian, PA, original records in Friends Historical Library, Swarthmore, PA
West Branch fire 5 mo-1847, part of records destroyed. Bk 702-pp87

BLACKBURN
Robert   s John A & Sarah, Napier Twp, Bedford Co
Susanna S Clever   dt Andrew, dec, & Hannah, Penn Twp, Clearfield Co
m 12-29-1843

Thomas   of Penn Twp, Clearfield Co
Anna Fenton   dt Thomas & Esther of same place
m 7- 5-1838
Signed: Thomas Fenton, Esther Fenton

CLEAVER
Thomas   s Andrew, dec, & Hannah, form Pike Twp, Clearfield Co
Eliza Davis   dt Joseph & Rebecca, Penn Twp
m 6-26-1851
Signed: Joseph Davis, Rebecca Davis, Hannah Cleaver

William   s Andrew, dec, & Hannah, Half Moon Twp, Centre Co
Hannah Kirk   dt Jason & Mary, dec, Penn Twp, Clearfield Co
m 5-10-1849
Signed: Jason Kirk, Hannah Cleaver

DAVIS
Washington   s Thomas & Rachel, Fall Creek Twp, Madison Co, IN

Mary E Garretson	dt Isaac, dec, & Louisa, Clearfield Co, Lumber City (borough) m 3-21-1861

DOWNING

Joseph	s Jacob & Jane W, form of Centre Co, of Miami MM, Warren, OH
Almira J Spencer	dt Joseph & Lydia Ann m 5-10-1883

FOX

William S	s Charles J & Esther C, Short Creek, Harrison Co, OH
Esther J Moore	dt Jeremiah & Sarah, Grampian Hills, Clearfield Co m 10- 6-1876

JOHNSON

Garretson	s Samuel & Hannah, dec, Penn Twp, Clearfield Co
Lydia Davis	dt Joseph & Rebecca, of same place m 2-10-1842 Signed: Samuel Johnson, Joseph Davis, Rebecca Davis
William F	s Samuel & Hannah, Penn Twp, Clearfield Co
Louisa W Porter	dt Asabel & Mary Walker, Adams Co m 1-25-1877

KESTER

Samuel L	s Isaac & Mary, Penn Twp, Clearfield Co
Alice Wall	dt Reuben & Sidney, of same place m 10-20-1865 Signed: Reuben Wall, Sidney Wall, Isaac Kester, Mary Kester

KIRK

Asaph	s Jason & Mary, Pike Twp, Clearwater Twp
Eliza Waln	dt Jonathan & Jane, of same place

	m 12- 4-1834
	Signed: Jason Kirk, Jonathan Waln, Jane Waln
Samuel	s Jason & Mary, Penn Twp, Clearfield Co
Alice Moore	dt Andrew & Elizabeth, of same place
	m 2- 5-1846
	Signed: Jason Kirk, Andrew Moore, Elizabeth Moore

MOORE
Caleb W	s Allen & Mary, of Half Moon, Centre Co, of Pike Twp, Clearfield
Eliza Spencer	dt Joseph & Lydia, Penn Twp, Clearfield Co
	m 10-10-1850
	Signed: Joseph Spencer, Lydia Spencer

PARKER
John K	of Columbia Co, PA
Susan E Kester	Clearfield Co
	m 10-13-1872 at house of Isaac M Kester in Bell Twp, Clearfield Co
	Signed: Isaac M Kester, Mary W Kester
	(Recorded under the new order of Discipline)

SMITH
Samuel	s Thomas & Phebe, of Bedford Co
Eluzai A Clever	dt Andrew & Hannah, Clearfield Co
	m 5- 4-1847
	Signed: Hannah Clever

SPENCER
Harrison W	s Joseph & Lydia, Penn Twp, Clearfield Co
Amanda M Garretson	dt Isaac, dec, & Louisa
	m 4- 6-1855
	Signed: Joseph Spencer, Lydia Spencer

UNDERWOOD
Charles	s Zephaniah & Hannah, Boggs Twp, Centre Co

Jane H Waln   dt David & Elizabeth, dec, Penn Twp
                     m 10- 2-1840
                     Signed: Zephaniah Underwood, David Waln

WALL
Reuben   s David & Elizabeth, Penn Twp, Clearfield Co
Sidney Waln   dt Jonathan & Jane, of same place
                     m 2- 8-1844
                     Signed: Jonathan Waln, Jane Waln

Miles   s Reuben & Sidney, Penn Twp, Clearfield Co
Elizabeth Cleaver   m 10-20-1871, dt Charles & Mary
                     Signed: Charles Cleaver, Reuben Wall, Sidney Wall

DUNNINGS CREEK HISTORY

8-13-1806	$8.41 collected to assist in relieving Indians
1-14-1807	William Kenworthy Jr appt recorder
1807	William Kenworthy Jr appt clerk
6-10-1806	Mary Witchel, Abington; Rachel Price, Concord; & Samuel Schofield, their companion, att mtg, whose company & Gospel labours have been satisfactory, they being on their way in the course of a religious visit to the Southward and Westward & to the mtgs of Friends generally in the state of OH.
"	William Kenworthy Jr has recorded minutes as far as they have been corrected and proposed charging seven pence half-penny by the page for recording them. Approved.
12-16-1807	Thomas Penrose chosen as clerk
"	Jesse Kenworthy appt recorder
8-12-1807	Sufferings--4 mbrs "are appt a committee to collect an account of the sufferings of our mbrs on account of military services, arrange them in suitable order & if they find their way clear, sign a transcript of such accounts on behalf of the mtg & forward it by representatives to QM & rpt to next mtg of procedure
8-14-1811	We the comm appt to discourage the common use of spirituous liquors having several times met agree to rpt that we believe there appears but little encouragement of its declining since last year, though a number of our mbrs have declined the frequent use of this article, yet some continue to make use thereof particularly in harvest
1-11-1809	Jesse Kenworthy appt clerk

12-13-1809	John Heald, Middleton MM, Salem QM (minister) & Wm Heald, companion (elder) religious visit to Eastern PA, NJ, Del, MD & VA
2-14-1810	Mtg now appts a 3rd Overseer
4-11-1810	Dispute over the line above the MH. Finally referred to QM to assist with problem
	When someone applied for mbrp, a comm was always appt to inquire into his "motives" for wanting to join. The comm usually rptd they "saw nothing to hinder the req"
2-12-1812	John Bateman appt clerk
6-10-1812	Memorial for John Thomas, elder
9-16-1812	Thomas Bowen req rel as overserr
10-14-1812	Thomas Blackburn suggested, Morgan Jones appt
4-14-1813	Jesse Kenworthy appt clerk
4-14-1813	Burying ground needs enlarging & new fence
7-14-1813	Ann Ferris & companion pcf Wilmington gospel labours edifying & comfortable
3-?-1815	Discussed minute relative to education of our youth together with state of schools
4-?-1815	Subject of educating our children together with the state of schools is concluded in considering the situation of our mbrs that there can be no school had among us at this time
6-15-1814	Nathan Williams appt clerk
7-12-1815	Advices on war
11-15-1815	Beloved Friend William Williams pcf Whitewater MM on his ret fr Eastern states, whose company & labours are very acceptable
11-15-1815	Thomas Jennings appt to have care of old books of minutes after recording
1-10-1815	Thomas Penrose Jr clerk
1-10-1815	Huldah Sears pcf Upper MM, Prince George Co, VA, love & gospel labours were edifying. James Stanton & Sarah Soars also acceptable

11-13-1816   Ann Edwards fr Chester MM, NJ, pc, favored in
                    gospel labour

CLERKS: Thomas Penrose
           William Kenworthy Jr

EARLY MBRS:
  Morgan Jones   Ruth Fisher
  Nathan Hammond   William Blackburn
  Isabel Calahan, late Bowen   Joshua Pickering
  Mary Griffith   Thomas Penrose
  Mary Neill   John Bateman
  Eve Vore, late Blackburn   Hannah Thomas
  Jonah Thomas   Thomas Griffith
  William Willis   Samuel Way
  John Neill & ch Rachel,   Thomas Bowen
      Ruth & John   Jonathan Bowen
  Margaret Neill   Jesse Vore
  Edward Thomas   James Hancock
  John Fisher   Abigail Penrose
  Lydia Kenworthy   Elizabeth Fisher
  Margaret Sink   William Kenworthy
  Patience McGrew & 4 ch, Peter,   Jonathan Potts
      Finley, Margaret & Rebekah   John Thomas, Jr
  Ann McGrew   Jesse Kenworthy
  Mary McGrew   John Hancock
  Joseph Vore   Anthony Blackburn
  Rebekah Vore   Thomas Oldham
  Sarah Blackburn   James Smith Jr
  Susanah Griffith   Alice Bowen
  Elizabeth Hiner Garretson   Thomas Jennings
  Aaron Garretson, s of John   Mary Smith, Jr
  Mary Smith (McGrew)   Jesse Griffith
  John Bateman, w Hannah & ch   John Thomas
      Lydia, Maryan, & Joel   William Oldham
  Joseph Hewit   Mary Hammond

Robert McCreery
James Smith, Jr
Nathan Williams
William Penrose
Phebe Smith
Rebekah Thomas
Mary Wherry (Neill)
John Davis
Joseph Sopher
David Way
Elizabeth Blackburn
Mary Blackburn
William Neal & 6 ch Margaret,
    Samuel, John, William,
    Mary & Richard
Susannah Neil
Morgan Jones
Hugh McCoy
Ruth Miller
Isaac Kenworthy
Amos Kenworthy
Joshua Davis, Jr
James Garretson
Alice Oldham
Jesse Blackburn
Thomas Sheperd
Jonathan Potts
Peter Vore
William Kenworthy
Rebecca Kenworthy
James Brown & Thomas, Benjamin,
    James, David, Jesse, John & William

Nathan Williams
Silas Hibberd
William Blackburn
Hannah Penrose
Bettee Vore, Joseph, Benjamin,
    Abner, Sarah, Peter, Bettee,
    Rachel & Hannah
Ruth Fisher
Benjamin Bowen
Mary Fisher
William Garretson, s of John
Thomas Blackburn
Mary Brown
Elizabeth Fisher
John Everitt
Sarah Hancock
James Brown
John Smith
Thomas Smith
Moses Blackburn
Joseph Blackburn

BATEMAN

5-11-1803	John Bateman & Hannah Thomas altm
	(Jonathan Bowen & Jesse Vore, comm in charge of m)
8-10-1803	Hannah gct Monallen MM
11-16-1803	Cert ret as not satisfactory, altered & signed
5-16-1810	John, w Hannah & 3 ch Lydia, Maryann & Joel pc, acc
7-13-1814	John, w Hannah rct Miami MM, OH, also 5 minor ch Lydia, Mary Ann, Joel, Mahlon & Rachel

BLACKBURN

6-15-1808	Jesse att muster
9-14-1808	Jesse dis
12-11-1805	Joseph is guilty of dancing
2-12-1806	Testimony produced against Joseph
2-12-1806	Jesse charged with dancing
4-16-1806	" ack accepted
12-11-1805	Moses, guilty of fighting & dancing
4-16-1806	" dis
7-13-1808	Sarah submits her case to mtg
9-14-1808	" dis
9-11-1816	Thomas, s of John, mou
10-16-1816	" ack acc
4-10-1815	William & w Amy gct Westland MM

BOWEN

2-13-1805	Benjamin & Mary Fisher, altm

BROWN

9-11-1816	Benjamin & Rebeccah Blackburn, altm
2-12-1805	James & ch Thomas, Benjamin, James, David, Jesse, John & William, rec in mbrp
8-14-1805	Mary rec in mbrp
3-16-1814	Thomas dis, fighting & attending muster

CALAHAN

10-15-1806	Isabel, late Bowen, mou by justice, had birth & education among Friends

11-12-1806   Isabel ack acc

DAVIS
1-10-1810   Hannah, form Vore, p ack acc
12-11-1811   John rec in mbrp
6-14-1815   "   mou by magistrate
7-12-1815   "   dis
12-11-1805   Joshua Jr res within our midst. Redstone MM rpts he has mou
1-15-1805   "   not in condition to condemn conduct, does not att mtgs, "has not had the appearance of a Friend amongst us", has attended muster

EVERITT
10-16-1805   John & Sarah Hancock, altm
6-14-1815   John & w Sarah req ct to Short Creek MM

FISHER
1-11-1815   Elizabeth gct to Redstone MM
12-13-1815   "   "   " Short Creek
6-12-1805   "   pcf Warrington
3-16-1808   John & Lydia Kenworthy, altm
1-11-1815   John & w Lydia & 2 minor ch Mary & Rebecka, gct Westland MM
12-15-1812   Ruth, cert approved
12-12-1804   Ruth, pcf Westland MM

GARRETSON
3-13-1815   Aaron Jr, att 2 marriages out of unity, one of each couple a Friend
4-10-1815   Ack accepted
12-14-1808   Aaron, s of John, na & mou
1-11-1809   "   dis
9-15-1813   Benjamin, dis for fighting & attending the muster
7-10-1816   Hannah, dis, mou
3-12-1806   James & Alice Oldham altm
                James pcf Warrington MM, clear

4-16-1806	Alice, form Oldham, gct Warrington MM
8-13-1806	John ack acc
9-13-1815	Samuel, minor, under age to chose a guardian himself. Mtg appts Joseph Hewitt "to go forward to the court to be appt to that station."
12-14-1814	Sarah pcf Monallen MM, dtd 11-23-1814
9-14-1808	William & John, dis, att muster & na
1-16-1805	William, s of John, guilty of unchastity with woman, not a mbr, has since married her
4-10-1805	William, testimony p against

GRIFFITH

6-11-1806	Abner gct Monallen MM to m Mary Owen
1-11-1804	Jesse mou by a magistrate to a woman not a mbr
3-14-1804	" ack acc
3-12-1806	" charged with fighting
5-14-1806	" ack acc
1-16-1805	" strikes man, sends paper of ack, very interesting ack
12-10-1806	Mary pcf Monallen, 10-23 recd
9-14-1808	Susannah, dis, does not wish Friends to trouble with her

HAMMOND

9-14-1808	Nathan Jr, dis for attended muster & na
8-13-1806	Nathan Jr, mou by Justice
10-15-1806	" " ack acc
9-14-1808	Samuel, dis for att muster & na

HANCOCK

6-15-1805	James pcf Warrington MM, 11-13

HARBAUGH

7-16-1806	Rachel, late Hammond, mou by Justice of Peace
8-13-1806	" ack acc

HINER

12-14-1808	Elizabeth, form Garretson, mou, dis

HIBBERD
7-10-1805	Silas gct Pipe Creek

HORN
6-15-1808	Sarah, form Garretson, mou by Methodist preacher
8-10-1808	Testimony against produced

JONES
5-10-1815	Isaac E req cert to Miami MM, OH

KENWORTHY
6-15-1814	Isaac & w Hannah req cert to join Westland MM
"	Jesse & w Hannah req cert to Westland MM
"	Amos req cert to Westland MM
3-10-1813	Isaac gct Warrington to m Hannah Cleaver
6-16-1813	Hannah pcf Warrington, dtd 5-20
1-16-1805	Jesse & Hannah Penrose altm
7-13-1814	Ruth gct Westland MM
3-12-1806	William & w Rebecca pcf Alexandria MM, 1-23 accepted
7-13-1814	William req cert to Westland MM
11-11-1807	William Jr expects to remove from these parts, would like to be rel as clerk
12-16-1807	William & w Rebecca gct Baltimore MM, W.D.

LAMBORN
5-11-1814	Levi, & w Mary & 3 minor ch, William Wall, Margaret & Dinah rocf Center MM

McCOY
6-10-1812	Hugh rec in mbrp
11-11-1812	Hugh & Ruth Miller altm

McCREARY
8-10-1814	Mary, form Shepherd, guilty of unchastity with man she has since married
1-11-1815	Mary, ack acc
1-10-1813	Hannah rec in mbrp

11-14-1810	Robert rocf Monallen
12-12-1810	Robert & Rebecca Sheperd, altm

McGRAIL
8-15-1804	Elizabeth pcf Nonallen MM 6-21

McGREW
5-11-1808	Patience & 4 ch Peter, Finley, Margaret & Rebekah pcf Monallen MM 3-23
"	Ann pcf Monallen 3-23
"	Mary pcf Monallen 3-23
3-16-1814	Peter Jr dis, att muster
3-10-1813	Nathan, s of Peter, Monallen MM req treat with for fighting

McGRAGER (4-14-1813 - not of mind to condemn fighting)
6-12-1816	Sarah, form Blackburn, mou by Meth preacher
7-10-1816	" ack acc

MILLER
5-11-1814	Thomas, w Sarah & 7 minor ch, Robert, Hannah, Eli, Sarah, Martha, Mary & Thomas rocf Center MM

NEILL
7-13-1808	John & 3 youngest ch Rachel, Ruth & John rec in mbrp
"	Margaret rec in mbrp
4-13-1807	Mary rec in mbrp
1-12-1814	Rachel guilty of unchastity
7-15-1812	Susannah req care of mtg, believe she was dis from Redstone
11-11-1812	Susannah rec, no objection fr Redstone

NEAL
5-13-1812	William & 6 ch, Margaret, Samuel, John, William, Mary & Richard rec in mbrp

OWEN
7-13-1814	Mary, form Garretson, mou by a Magistrate
10-12-1814	" testimony produced against

OLDHAM
7-13-1814	Hannah & dt Rebecca req mbrp
10-13-1813	Thomas mou by Magistrate
11-10-1813	" ack acc
6-13-1804	William & Mary, form Hammond, m by a Magistrate, dis

PENROSE
4-10-1815	Josiah & w Racheal gct Monallen MM
4-12-1815	Josiah req cert to Monallen to m Rebecca Garretson
9-13-1815	Rachel G Penrose rocf Monallen 7-20-1815
9-11-1811	William, dis, unchastity, att m contrary to Friends, giving off in a disorderly manner

PICKERING
12-15-1812	Joshua pcf Hopewell, does not res amongst us
6-14-1815	" Hopewell req mtg to treat with him for serving Militia & mou

POTTS
7-13-1814	John, dis dancing
8-10-1814	Joseph, dis, att shooting match, shooting for a prize, making a ball, mou by a hireling minister with a young woman not of our Society

ROSS
6-12-1815	Ann, form McGrew, dis, mou by Magistrate

SHEPHERD
9-14-1814	Joshua & David, minors, have with consent of their mother settled within limits of Pipe Creek. Cert is granted
2-12-1806	Thomas charged with dancing
3-12-1806	" ack acc
11-14-1810	Thomas has come out of Gaol by taking benefit of Insolvent Act, defrauded a creditor
11-16-1810	Thomas, by adjournment, mtg thinks case should be dropped

SINK
9-14-1808	Margaret, form Blackburn, mou, dis

SMITH
2-15-1804	James Jr & Alice Bowen, altm
7-12-1809	Mary, form McGrew, mou, dis
2-15-1804	Mary Jr, rec in mbrp
2-13-1811	Thomas gct Hopewell MM to m Phebe White
8-14-1811	Phebe pcf Hopewell, acc
1-11-1804	Thomas rec in mbrp

SOPHER
5-13-1812	Joseph rec in mbrp
6-16-1813	Joseph & Phebe Kenworthy, altm
7-13-1814	Joseph & Phebe req cert to Westland MM

SYLER
1-12-1814	Elizabeth, form Vore, mou, dis

THOMAS
2-10-1808	Edward mou by Magistrate
4-13-1808	" ack acc
12-15-1813	John, guilty of unchastity with woman he has since married
10-?-1808	Jonah gct Monallen MM
5-13-1807	Jonah rptd guilty of fornication, now lives at Monallen
9-16-1807	" ack acc
10-16-1811	Rebekah, dis, unchastity, having ch in unmarried state

VORE
12-12-1804	Bettee & 8 ch, Joseph, Benjamin, Abner, Sarah, Peter, Bettee, Rachel & Hannah, pcf Warrington
12-11-1805	Benjamin rptd guilty of fighting & dancing
1-15-1805	" testimony to be prepared against
5-13-1807	Eve, late Blackburn, mou by Magistrate
1-13-1808	" ack acc
12-14-1808	Joseph, dis, att muster, mou by Meth preacher, na

11-16-1808	Abner, dis, att muster, accompanied his bro to his marriage
8-14-1805	Joseph, Benjamin & Abner, guilty of dancing
10-16-1805	Joseph & Abner, ack acc
3-12-1806	Benjamin, dis, fighting & dancing
3-12-1806	Joseph is charged with fighting
7-16-1806	" is charged marching in rank with militia
8-13-1806	" is " in improving situation of mind, offers paper, mtg continues case
4-15-1812	Peter & w Bettee, dis, quarreling, "such violence was used between them that blood was drawn from both of them"
3-12-1806	Peter pcf Warrington MM 9-7-1805
12-12-1816	Peter dis, takes strong drink, att muster
2-11-1807	Peter's ack read & acc (very interesting)
7-13-1808	Rebekah, testimony against (form Blackburn)
8-10-1808	" " " produced
11-15-1815	Thomas & Rachel Blackburn altm

WALL
5-10-1815	Absolom & w Margaret pcf Center MM

WAY
5-13-1812	David & Elizabeth Blackburn, altm
6-11-1806	Mary pcf Pipe Creek 4-19
6-15-1814	Robert req cert to Center MM, OH
5-16-1804	Samuel writes a paper ack he was drunk, asks to be continued, acc (an interesting ack)
11-15-1815	Samuel Jr & James att 2 mou, one of each couple were mbrs
1-10-1815	" " offered ack, acc
11-13-1816	Samuel, ack acc for taking strong drink & using bad language
12-11-1816	Thomas, dis, mou by hireling teacher

WILLIS
12-16-1807	William rec in mbrp

WHERRY
11-13-1811	Mary, form Neill, mou, dis

DUNNINGS CREEK
WOMEN'S MEETING 1803-1887

Meeting for worship & prep. mtg settled at Dunning's Creek in 1795, a branch of Monallen Mtg, but "being situated about one hundred miles therefrom the great difficulty of attending that Mtg occasioned D.C. Prep. Mtg. in the second month one thousand eight hundred & two, to forward a request to Monallen MM to have a MM settled at Dunnings Dreek."

Monallen Mtg sent comm to visit & in 8th mo laid before Warrington QM, request granted in second mo following.

First Mtg held 1st fourth day after the second second day in each mo, and Prep Mtg to be held the fourth day in the week preceeding.

4th mo-13-1803, MM of Women Friends of Dunnings Creek - p 1-2.

BATEMAN
4-11-1810	Hannah pcf Monallen 3-21 with husband & 3 ch, Lydia, Mary Ann, Joel
7-13-1814	Hannah req cert to Miami MM with husband & 5 minor ch Lydia, Mary Ann, Joel, Malon, Rachel; cert granted 8-10-1814
4-13-1803	John & Hannah Thomas ami
6-15-1803	" " " mra
7-13-1803	Hannah Bateman req cert Monallen Mtg to which she has rem with her husband; cert produced 8-10-1803

BLACKBURN
1-10-1816	Amy req cert Westland with her husband, Samuel Jesse, William, Ruth, Amy; granted 5-15-1816
6-15-1808	Sarah, form Vore, att her brother's marriage & likewise acc her mar by a Magistrate with a man not in mbrp Submitted to men Friends; 8-10-1808 dis.

BOWEN

8-14-1816	Benjamin Bowen & Rebecca Blackburn ami; rptd acc 10-16-1816
1-16-1805	Benjamin Bowen & Mary Fisher ami; rptd acc 3-13-1805

BROWN

7-10-1805	Mary Brown, rec into mbrp (8-14-1805)

CALAHAN

10-15-1806	Isabel, form Bowen, m by a magistrate with a man not in mbrp Ack acc 11-12-1806

DAVIS

4-10-1811	Hannah, form Vore, mou; ack rec 5-15-1811

EVERITT

9-11-1805	John Everitt & Sarah Hancock, ami; mar rptd acc 11-13-1805
6-14-1815	Sarah req cert (also husband) Short Creek MM, OH Cert granted 7-12-1815

FISHER

7-10-1805	Elizabeth pcf Warrington MM, 5-11-1805
2-15-1815	Elizabeth Jr req cert Redstone MM; granted 3-15-1815
11-15-1815	Elizabeth req cert Short Creek MM, OH, granted
2-10-1808	John Fisher & Lydia Kenworthy ami; rptd acc 4-13-1808
2-15-1815	Lydia req cert Westland MM with husband & 2 dts Mary & Rebecca; granted 3-15-1815
12-12-1804	Ruth pcf Westland MM
11-11-1812	Ruth req cert Redstone; granted

GARRETSON

5-15-1816	Hannah, form Way, mou by a hireling minister; dis 7-10-1816
2-12-1806	James Garretson & Alice Oldham ami; rptd acc 4-16-1806
5-14-1806	Alice req cert to Warrington MM, where she has gone with her husband to reside, cert granted
12-14-1814	Sarah pcf Monallen 11-23-1814

GREEN
7-12-1812	Roland Green, Joseph Medcalf (beloved frds on religious visit fr Wilmington
7-14-1813	Ann Ferris, Sarah Ferris (beloved frds on religious visit fr Wilmington

GRIFFITH
6-15-1808	Susanna, form Blackburn, m by magistrate by a man not in mbrp "does not wish Frds to put themselves to any more trouble with her"; dis 8-10-1808
12-10-1806	Mary pcf Monallen; received 10-23-1806

HARBAUGH
7-16-1806	Rachel, form Hammond, m by magistrate "with man not in mbrp with us"; ack acc 8-13-1806

HINER
10-12-1808	Elizabeth, late Garretson, m by Methodist preacher to a man not in mbrp; dis 12-14-1808

HORN
5-18-1808	Sarah, form Garretson, m by Methodist preacher, to man not in mbrp; 6-15-1808, case submitted to Men Frds; 8-10-1808, dis

KENWORTHY
6-16-1813	Hannah pcf Warrington 5-20-1813
6-15-1814	Hannah, w of Jesse, req cert Westland MM, with husband; granted 7-13-1814
12-12-1804	Jesse Kenworthy & Hannah Penrose, ami; 2-13-1805, rptd acc
8-11-1813	Mary, an elder, d 3mo-27-1813
3-12-1806	Rebecca, with husband, pcf Alexandria MM, 1-23-1806
11-11-1807	Rebecca req cert Baltimore W.D. with her husband; granted 12-16-1807
6-15-1814	Ruth rct Westland MM; cert granted 7-13-1814

LAMBURN
4-13-1814   Mary & husband & w minor ch, William Wall, Margaret & Dinah, fr Center MM

McCOY
11-11-1812   Hugh McCoy & Ruth Miller ami; m acc 12-16-1812

McCRERY
2-10-1813   Hannah req mbrp; granted 3-10-1813
7-13-1814   Mary McCreary, form Shepherd, mou by a magistrate; also guilty unchastity; ack acc 1-11-1815
10-10-1810   Robert McCrery & Rebeccah Sheperd ami; ami 2nd 12-12-1810

McGRAIL
8-15-1804   Elizabeth pcf Monallen MM; 6-21; rec

McGREW
5-11-1808   Ann pcf Monallen
5-11-1808   Patience pcf Monallen 3-23-1808, & 4 minor ch Peter, Finley, Margaret & Rebecca
5-11-1808   Mary pcf Monallen MM

McGRIGOR
5-15-1816   Sarah McGrigor (or McGregor), form Blackburn, mou by Methodist teacher; p ack 6-12-1816

MILLER
4-13-1814   Sarah & husband & 7 minor ch, Robert, Hannah, Eli, Sarah, Martha, Mary, Thomas fr Center MM, dtd 3-19-1814

NEILL
3-11-1807   Mary, having been under care, rec into mbrp 4-15-1806
1-13-1808   Margaret, w of John, req mbrp; rec 7-13-1808 & her three minor ch, Rachel, Ruth & John
9-15-1813   Rachel guilty unchastity; 3-16-1813 dis

5-13-1812	Susanna req to be again united with Friends & req with her husband for 6 ch Margaret, Samuel, John, William, Mary & Morton; letter fr Redstone where she was dis does not object

OLDHAM
7-13-1814	Hannah req to come under care of mtg, also for dt Rebecca; rec in mbrp 11-16-1814
5-16-1804	Mary, form Hammond, m by a Magistrate with a man friend

OWEN(S)
7-13-1814	Mary, form Garretson, mou by a magistrate; 9-14-1814, dis

PENROSE
9-13-1815	Rachel G, pcf Monallen, 7-20-1815
3-13-1816	Rachel G req cert Monallen MM with husband; 4-10-1816, approved

ROSS
4-10-1816	Ann, form McGrew, mou by a magistrate; 6-12-1816, dis

SEARS
1-10-1816	Huldah Sears pcf Prince George Co, VA, 4-15 on "gospel labours"; also Sarah Sears - companion; 11-13 Ann Edwards & Rebecca Roberts pcf Chester MM, NJ on "gospel labours"

SINK
4-13-1808	Margaret, form Blackburn, acc m by a Magistrate with non-Friend; case submitted to Men Friends, 5-18-1808; 8-10-1808, dis

SILER
9-15-1813	Elizabeth, form Vore, mou by a Magistrate; dis 1-12-1814

SMITH
1-11-1804	James Jr & Alice Bowen ami; m rept acc 3-14-1804
4-12-1809	Mary, form McGrew, m by a Methodist to a man not in mbrp; 7-12-1809, dis

1-11-1804	Mary, dt James & Mary, req to come under care of Friends; 2-15-1804, rec in mbrp
8-11-1811	Phebe pcf Hopewell MM

SOPHER
4-14-1813	Joseph Sopher & Phebe Kenworthy ami; 7-14-1813 m rptd acc
8-10-1814	Phebe req cert Westland MM with husband; cert granted Joseph & Phebe Sopher 9-14-1814

THOMAS
4-10-1811	Rebecca guilty unchastity, dis 11-13-1811

VORE
12-12-1804	Bette, w of Peter, pcf Warrington MM, 11-12-1803; also for her eight children: Joseph, Benjamin, Abner, Sarah, Peter, Bettee, Rachel, Hannah; rec
4-15-1812	Bettee guilty of quarrelling with husband; dis 7-15-1812
4-15-1807	Eve, form Blackburn, m by a Magistrate to man not in mbrp; 6-10-1807 sends ack which is under consideration
6-15-1808	Rebecca, form Blackburn, m by a Methodist preacher to a man in mbrp; case submitted to Men Friends; 8-10-1808 dis
10-11-1815	Thomas Vore & Rachel Blackburn ami; 12-13-1815, rptd acc

WAY
3-11-1812	David Way & Elizabeth Blackburn ami; 6-10-1812, rptd acc
6-11-1806	Mary pcf Pipe Creek Mtg, 4th mo-10

WALL
4-12-1815	Margaret with husband pcf Center MM 9-17-1814

WHERRY
7-10-1811	Mary, form Neill, mou; 9-11-1811 John Niel wrote that his dt, Mary, had been precautioned by three mbrs of Westland MM & by himself; 11-13-1811 dis

www.ingramcontent.com/pod-product-compliance
Lightning Source LLC
Chambersburg PA
CBHW020418010526
44118CB00010B/318